The Forgotten Emancipator

Congressman James M. Ashley was a member of the House of Representatives from 1858 to 1868, and was the main sponsor of the Thirteenth Amendment to the American Constitution, which declared the institution of slavery unconstitutional. Rebecca E. Zietlow uses Ashley's life as a unique lens through which to explore the ideological origins of Reconstruction and the constitutional changes of this era. Zietlow recounts how Ashley and his antislavery allies shared an egalitarian free labor ideology that was influenced by the political antislavery movement and the nascent labor movement – a vision that conflicted directly with the institution of slavery. Ashley's story sheds important light on the meaning and power of popular constitutionalism: how the Constitution is interpreted outside of the courts and the power that citizens and their elected officials can have in enacting legal change. The book shows how Reconstruction not only expanded racial equality but also transformed the rights of workers throughout America.

REBECCA E. ZIETLOW is Charles W. Fornoff Professor of Law and Values at the University of Toledo, College of Law. She is a recipient of the University of Toledo Outstanding Faculty Research award and a leader of the Thirteenth Amendment Project. She is the author of *Enforcing Equality: Congress, the Constitution, and the Protection of Individual Rights*, and her work has been published in the *Columbia Law Review*, *Boston University Law Review*, *Ohio State Law Journal*, *Florida Law Review*, and the *Wake Forest Law Journal*.

Cambridge Historical Studies in American Law and Society

Recognizing legal history's growing importance and influence, the goal of this series is to chart legal history's continuing development by publishing innovative scholarship across the discipline's broadening range of perspectives and subjects. It encourages empirically creative works that take legal history into unexplored subject areas, or that fundamentally revise our thinking about familiar topics; it also encourages methodologically innovative works that bring new disciplinary perspectives and techniques to the historical analysis of legal subjects.

Series Editor

Christopher Tomlins, *University of California, Berkeley*

Previously Published in the Series

Andrew Wender Cohen, *The Racketeer's Progress: Chicago and the Struggle for the Modern American Economy, 1900–1940*

Michael Willrich, *City of Courts: Socializing Justice in Progressive Era Chicago*

Barbara Young Welke, *Recasting American Liberty: Gender, Race, Law, and the Railroad Revolution, 1865–1920*

Michael Vorenberg, *Final Freedom: The Civil War, the Abolition of Slavery, and the Thirteenth Amendment*

Robert J. Steinfeld, *Coercion, Contract, and Free Labor in the Nineteenth Century*

David M. Rabban, *Free Speech in Its Forgotten Years, 1870–1920*

Jenny Bourne Wahl, *The Bondsman's Burden: An Economic Analysis of the Common Law of Southern Slavery*

Michael Grossberg, *A Judgment for Solomon: The d'Hauteville Case and Legal Experience in the Antebellum South*

The Forgotten Emancipator

*James Mitchell Ashley and the Ideological
Origins of Reconstruction*

REBECCA E. ZIETLOW

The University of Toledo College of Law

CAMBRIDGE
UNIVERSITY PRESS

CAMBRIDGE
UNIVERSITY PRESS

University Printing House, Cambridge CB2 8BS, United Kingdom

One Liberty Plaza, 20th Floor, New York, NY 10006, USA

477 Williamstown Road, Port Melbourne, VIC 3207, Australia

314-321, 3rd Floor, Plot 3, Splendor Forum, Jasola District Centre, New Delhi - 110025, India

79 Anson Road, #06-04/06, Singapore 079906

Cambridge University Press is part of the University of Cambridge.

It furthers the University's mission by disseminating knowledge in the pursuit of education, learning and research at the highest international levels of excellence.

www.cambridge.org
Information on this title: www.cambridge.org/9781107479234
DOI: 10.1017/9781316155059

First published 2018
First paperback edition 2019

A catalogue record for this publication is available from the British Library

Library of Congress Cataloging in Publication data
NAMES: Zietlow, Rebecca E., author.
TITLE: The forgotten emancipator : James Mitchell Ashley and the ideological origins of Reconstruction / Rebecca E. Zietlow, The University of Toledo College of Law.
DESCRIPTION: Cambridge ; New York, NY : Cambridge University Press, 2017. |
Series: Cambridge historical studies in American law and society |
Includes bibliographical references and index.
IDENTIFIERS: LCCN 2017035060 | ISBN 9781107095274 (hardback : alk. paper) |
ISBN 9781107479234 (pbk. : alk. paper)
SUBJECTS: LCSH: Ashley, James Mitchell, 1824–1896. |
Legislators–United States–Biography. | United States. Congress. House–Biography. |
Reconstruction (U.S. history, 1865–1877)
CLASSIFICATION: LCC E415.9.A77 Z54 2017 | DDC 328.73/092 [B] –dc23
LC record available at https://lccn.loc.gov/2017035060

ISBN 978-1-107-09527-4 Hardback
ISBN 978-1-107-47923-4 Paperback

Cambridge University Press has no responsibility for the persistence or accuracy of URLs for external or third-party internet websites referred to in this publication, and does not guarantee that any content on such websites is, or will remain, accurate or appropriate.

To David, Alice, and Zoe

and

To the memory of Sally Ashley

Contents

Acknowledgments

Over ten years ago, I had the pleasure of organizing a symposium on the Thirteenth Amendment. I was inspired by the work of Alexander Tsesis and Lea Vandervelde on the history of that amendment, as well as the work of James Gray Pope and Risa Goluboff on the relevance of the Thirteenth Amendment to the labor and civil rights movements in the twentieth century. I thank all of these scholars for inspiring me and drawing me toward this fascinating and fulfilling project. Alex, Lea, Jim, and Risa all participated in the Toledo symposium, along with the inimitable Chip Carter and Les Benedict. Since then I have developed deep friendships with these scholars of the Thirteenth Amendment, who form a warm and welcoming community. With Jim, Lea, Avi Soifer, and Ruben Garcia, I am on the steering committee for the Thirteenth Amendment project, a project of scholars, students, activists, and practitioners who are exploring the history promise of the Thirteenth Amendment. On panels at existing conferences and special symposia on the Thirteenth Amendment, we have had a great opportunity to network and exchange ideas and insights. Working on the Thirteenth Amendment Project has been a fulfilling and rewarding experience. I thank all of my Thirteenth Amendment friends for their support and guidance and look forward to our future work together.

Other warm and welcoming scholarly workshops have enabled me to share my ideas as I developed this project. Thanks to Mark Graber for his support and help at crucial moments, and for including me in his "schmoozes" on the Thirteenth Amendment and the meaning of citizenship. Thanks to Martha Fineman and her legendary vulnerability workshops, where I always gain crucial insights from creative and interesting people. Thanks to Randy Barnett for his interactive and engaging workshops on Lysander Spooner, Salmon Chase, and the Thirteenth Amendment, and for generally supporting and encouraging me. Thanks to Alex Tsesis for organizing Thirteenth Amendment conferences at the University of Chicago and Columbia University, and for initiating the constitutional law colloquia at Loyola University Chicago.

Richard Aynes invited me to an important symposium on John Bingham and the Fourteenth Amendment early in my career, where I also had the pleasure of meeting Michael Kent Curtis and Paul Finkelman for the first time. I'll never forget the dinner at that symposium, where I was surrounded for the first time by people who spoke of the Reconstruction Congress in the present tense. Since then, Richard regularly contacts me whenever he finds a newspaper article or other historical document that mentioned James Ashley, and I have the highest regard for him and his humble fount of knowledge about Bingham and the Reconstruction Congress.

Thanks to the many labor and employment law scholars, especially Katherine Fisk, Charlotte Garden, Michael Z. Green, Ann McGinley, and Marley Weiss for including me in their labor and employment colloquia and law and society CRN8, which gave an opportunity to present my labor-related theories and to learn from their insights. Thanks to the participants in all of the symposia, and to those who attended my numerous presentations at the Law and Society annual meetings, Constitutional Law Colloquia, and Thirteenth Amendment conferences and symposia, for your comments and insights, which greatly enriched my work.

One of the best parts of working on the history of Reconstruction has been the chance to get to know the historians who specialize in this area, some of whom revolutionized the study of Reconstruction a generation before me. First and foremost among them is my former college professor, Eric Foner, who is not only an incredible scholar and teacher, but also a kind person. Les Benedict attended my first legal history talk at Ohio State University many years ago and since then I have valued his feedback and friendship. Michael Vorenberg and James Oakes have also encouraged me and given me important feedback from the start of this project. Risa Goluboff, Sophia Lee, Christopher Schmidt, and Paul Finkelman have also given me crucial feedback and help, and their writing has been essential to aiding my understanding of the Reconstruction Era and the history of the labor and civil rights movements. Thanks to all of you for keeping me honest and on track, and for your generosity of spirit toward me.

Thanks to my editors, Christopher Tomlins and Debbie Gershenowitz. You are both so thoughtful, efficient, kind, and insightful. It has been such a pleasure and an honor to work with you. Thanks to the numerous people who have read over drafts of chapters and related articles, including Les Benedict, Risa Goluboff, David Koeninger, Maria Ontiveros, Jim Pope, Joe Slater, Lee Strang, Lea Vandervelde, and Mary Ziegler. Thanks to Jack Balkin for encouraging me to write this book, and to Reva Siegel for her support and encouragement.

Thanks to my dear friends and colleagues at the University of Toledo College of Law, especially Joe Slater, Llew Gibbons, Dan Steinbock, and Nicole Porter, for your friendship and understanding as I have worked on this project. Thanks to the University of Toledo College of Law for funding my research and my time writing this book. Thanks also to my research assistants, Ashley Blas, David Cowen, Sarah Kurfis, and Brianna White.

Thanks to Tom Dolgenos for telling me about his great-great-grandfather James Mitchell Ashley, and to his mother, Sally Ashley, who enthusiastically embraced my scholarship about her great grandfather.

Finally, thanks to my loving and supportive husband, David Koeninger, and my beautiful and intelligent daughters, Alice and Zoe. While I was working on this book, Alice and Zoe grew up, and they have become passionately engaged in the cause of justice. They even like to hear about history sometimes.

Prologue

In the fall of 2003, I attended a conference on the Fourteenth Amendment in Philadelphia. Not far from our conference, I saw a historical marker commemorating the Republican Party's first nominating convention in 1856. That evening, I mentioned the marker to my friends from law school, Sarah Ricks and Tom Dolgenos. Tom responded that if I was learning about members of the early Republican Party, I might be interested in his great-great-grandfather, James Ashley, the first member of Congress to propose a constitutional amendment to end slavery. Tom pulled out a book with a picture of Ashley, and I saw for the first time the wild mane of hair and dark penetrating eyes of the radical Republican from Toledo, Ohio. According to Tom, his great-great grandad's version of the Thirteenth Amendment would have prohibited all bondage, including that of convicted prisoners.[1] I was intrigued by Tom's story. Yes, I said, I am very interested.

When I first heard of Ashley, I already knew about other leaders of the Reconstruction Congress, and was already engaged in learning about their accomplishments. Earlier that year, I had the pleasure of meeting

---

[1] This bit of family lore turned out to be inaccurate. Though Ashley's version of the Thirteenth Amendment differed slightly from that eventually adopted, it did include an exception for people duly convicted of a crime. ("Article. Slavery or involuntary servitude, except in punishment of crime, whereof the party shall have been duly convicted, is hereby forever prohibited in all the States of this Union, and in all Territories now owned or which may be hereafter be acquired by the United States." See Letter from James Ashley to Benjamin Arnett, December 22, 1892, Benjamin Arnett, ed., *Duplicate Copy of the Souvenir from the Afro-American League of Tennessee to Hon. James M. Ashley of Ohio* (Philadelphia: Publishing House of the AME Church, 1894), 329, 331.

Richard Aynes and Michael Kent Curtis at a conference celebrating John
Bingham and the Fourteenth Amendment. I was struck by Richard's and
Michael's depth of knowledge about Bingham as well as their passion
for educating people about the remarkable contributions that Bingham
made to our constitutional history.[2] Later, I met Lea Vandervelde and
learned about her work on Senator Henry Wilson, another influential
member of the Reconstruction Congress and supporter of the Thirteenth
Amendment.[3] I grew to share these scholars' passion for the members of
the Reconstruction Congress. I admire the Reconstruction Congress
members' work to end slavery, enact the first civil rights measures, and
amend the Constitution to establish federal rights that are enforceable
against state and federal governments. James Ashley was a leader among
them, yet most constitutional scholars and many historians had never
heard of him.[4]

My interest in Ashley deepened as I learned the extent of his radicalism
and idealism. Ashley joined the antislavery movement as a young man,
and he helped to found the Republican Party as an antislavery party.
Ashley led initiatives to end slavery and other exploitative labor practices,
establish fundamental rights for free blacks, and expand suffrage rights.
As early as 1856, Ashley called for voting rights for free blacks. During
Reconstruction he proposed a constitutional amendment that would have
established voting rights for women. James Ashley's story is one of
leadership and activism, of political engagement to advance the cause
of human rights. He recognized that slavery was based on an ideology
of white supremacy and racial subordination that facilitated the exploitation of slave labor and gross violations of their human rights. Ashley was

[2] John Bingham, another member of the House of Representatives from Ohio, was a leading
member of the Reconstruction Congress, and a strong advocate for the rights of freed
slaves. Bingham is best known as the principal author of Section 1 of the Fourteenth
Amendment, with its Equal Protection, Due Process and Privileges or Immunities Clauses.
See Richard L. Aynes, "On Misreading John Bingham and the Fourteenth Amendment,"
Yale Law Journal 103 (1993); Gerard Magliocca, *American Founding Son: John Bingham
and the Invention of the Fourteenth Amendment* (New York: NYU Press 2013).
[3] See, e.g., Lea S. VanderVelde, "The Labor Vision of the Thirteenth Amendment," *University of Pennsylvania Law Review* 138 (1989): 437; Lea S. Vandervelde, "Henry Wilson,
Cobbler of the Frayed Constitution, Strategist of the Thirteenth Amendment," *Georgetown Journal of Law and Politics* 15 (2017): 173.
[4] See Les Benedict, "James M. Ashley, Toledo Politics and the Thirteenth Amendment,"
University of Toledo Law Review 38 (2007): 815, 815 ("Although he was well known
during the Civil War era, [Ashley] has largely faded from the historical record. Even
historians of the Civil War and Reconstruction are not very familiar with him, and legal
scholars are even less so.")

truly on the forefront of the fight for liberty as he developed a vision of rights that included racial equality and economic rights for workers.

Ashley's story is an inspiring one, and it aids in understanding a crucial period in our country's constitutional development, the Reconstruction Era. It is a fascinating time in the transformation of our nation's law and politics. However, my interest in the Reconstruction Era is not only historical. Although Reconstruction occurred 150 years ago, this crucial era of constitutional development still resonates in the United States today. In many ways, our national still has not resolved the conflicts that characterized that era. As my friend Leslie Goldstein once said at a constitutional law workshop, when it comes to understanding essential constitutional principles, "we always keep coming back to Reconstruction." This insightful statement also applies to understanding our nation's politics.

One hundred fifty years after the Reconstruction Era, racial divisions still plague our nation, and our country still depends on the exploitation of labor, especially workers of color. After Reconstruction ended, southern states resurrected slavery "in all but name" with the convict leasing and sharecropping systems.[5] Jim Crow laws not only treated blacks as second-class citizens lacking human rights, but also facilitated the exploitation of their low-wage and unpaid labor. Today, black men are incarcerated at such a high rate that legal scholar Michelle Alexander has referred to the mass incarceration phenomenon as the New Jim Crow.[6] Our national economy depends on the labor of millions of undocumented immigrants who are easily exploited by unscrupulous employers because they are afraid of being discovered.[7] The crackdown on immigration in early 2017 prompted many undocumented immigrants to flee to Canada,

---

[5] See Douglas A. Blackmon, *Slavery by Another Name: The Re-enslavement of Black Americans from the Civil War to World War II* (New York: Anchor Books, 2009).

[6] Michelle Alexander, *The New Jim Crow: Mass Incarceration in the Age of Colorblindness* (New York: New Press, 2010). Ava Du Vernay's highly acclaimed film "13th" links the modern-day prison industrial complex directly to the institution of slavery. See Bethonie Butler, "Ava DuVernay's Netflix Film "13th" Reveals How Mass Incarceration Is an Extension of Slavery," *Washington Post*, October 6, 2016. Du Vernay's film focuses on the "exceptions clause" of the Thirteenth Amendment (which prohibits slavery and involuntary servitude "except as a punishment for crime whereof the party shall have been duly convicted"). Ibid.

[7] See Maria Ontiveros, "Immigrant Workers' Rights in a Post-Hoffman World: Organizing Around the 13th Amendment," 18 *Georgetown Immigration Law Journal* 18 (2004): 651; Maria Ontiveros, "Is Modern Day Slavery a Private Act or a Public System of Oppression?," *Seattle University Law Review* 39 (2016): 665.

following in the footsteps of fugitive slaves from the antebellum era. The Black Lives Matter movement has developed in response to police violence against the black community. A new group of black authors and artists have recently explored anew the meaning of slavery and racism to our national identity.[8] Their work highlights the importance of studying the Reconstruction Era to understand some of the most pressing legal and political issues confronting our society today.

Ashley's story was also important to me because it aids in revealing the history and promise of the Thirteenth Amendment. As a student at Yale Law School in the late 1980s, I was inspired by the Warren Court's enforcement of Fourteenth Amendment–based rights against state government.[9] We worshipped what I call the "*Brown* story" of civil rights – court enforcement of the Equal Protection Clause. By the time I learned about Ashley, however, I had grown skeptical of the *Brown* story and disillusioned by the Court's formal approach to equality under the Equal Protection Clause.[10] My dear friend Denise Morgan and I developed an alternative vision of rights that we called "rights of belonging," those rights that promote an inclusive vision of who belongs to the national community of the United States and that facilitate equal membership in that community.[11] Rights of belonging included both the right to be free

---

[8] See, e.g., Paul Beatty, *The Sell Out* (New York: Farrar, Strauss and Giroux, 2015); Ta-Nehisi Coates, *Between the World and Me* (New York: Spiegel & Grau, 2015); Yaa Gyasi, *Homegoing* (New York: Alfred A. Knopf, 2016); Colson Whitehead, *The Underground Railroad* (New York: Doubleday, 2016); and the art of Kerry James Marshall. See Darryl Pinckney, "Kerry James Marshall: Mastry," *New York Review of Books*, January 2, 2017.

[9] In *Brown v. Board of Education*, the US Supreme Court held that racially segregated public schools violated the Equal Protection Clause of the Fourteenth Amendment. *Brown v. Board of Education*, 347 U.S. 483 (1954). Many of my professors viewed this decision as the catalyst for the civil rights movement of the 1960s. Indeed, it seemed to me that every professor at Yale Law School could remember the day that the US Supreme Court decided the landmark case of *Brown v. Board of Education*. Historians see a more complex relationship. See, e.g., Michael J. Klarman, "Rethinking the Civil Rights and Civil Liberties Revolutions," *Virginia Law Review* 82 (1996): 1 (describing the differing views held by law professors and historians of the relationship between the *Brown* decision and the civil rights movement).

[10] Under the formal equality approach, the Court applies the same level of scrutiny to legislation that is intended to help racial minorities as that which discriminates against minorities. See, e.g., *Parents Involved in Community Schools v. Seattle District No. 1*, 551 U.S. 701 (2007).

[11] See Denise C. Morgan and Rebecca E. Zietlow, "The New Parity Debate: Congress and Rights of Belonging," *Cincinnati Law Review* 73(2005): 1347; I discuss rights of belonging at length in my first book. See Rebecca E. Zietlow, *Enforcing Equality: Congress, the Constitution, and the Protection of Individual Rights* (New York: NYU

of discrimination based on immutable characteristics and the positive economic rights needed to be an active member in one's community. However, the Supreme Court had refused to find any economic rights in the Equal Protection Clause.[12] In Risa Goluboff's classic book, *The Lost Promise of Civil Rights*, I learned the history of the New Deal era labor-focused vision of civil rights based primarily on the Thirteenth Amendment.[13] As I learned more about Ashley, I discovered the ideological continuity between Ashley's ideology and that of the New Deal era movement. I turned to the Thirteenth Amendment, with its promise of economic and racial equality.

My interest in economic rights grew out of the four years I spent as a legal services attorney in the South Side of Chicago, representing clients who were primarily African American. Many of my clients had migrated from the Deep South, hoping to escape the virulent racism and violence of the Jim Crow era and find a better life in the North. Unfortunately, in the North they encountered racial segregation, the lack of economic opportunity, gang violence, and a police force that was indifferent, if not hostile, to their needs. Clearly, the civil rights revolution of the 1960s had achieved minimal gains for my clients. They were engaged in a daily struggle for economic survival and physical safety. Many of my clients were descended from slaves, and they still suffered from slavery's legacy of race discrimination and economic subordination.

Later, I became a law professor in James Ashley's home town, Toledo, Ohio. There I learned first-hand about the importance of rights for workers, black and white, who worked for the automobile industry. The city of Toledo has a special place in labor history because of the 1934 Toledo Auto-Lite strike, a catalyst for congressional approval of the National Labor Relations Act. The Auto-Lite workers fought for the right to organize, strike, and bargain collectively.[14] They succeeded, and their

---

Press, 2006). Tragically, Denise Morgan died in 2006 and we were unable to complete our work together.

[12] See *Dandridge v. Williams*, 397 U.S. 471 (1970) (holding no right to a minimum income under the Equal Protection Clause of the Fourteenth Amendment). See Julie A. Nice, "Whither the Canaries? On the Exclusion of Poor People from Equal Constitutional Protection," *Drake Law Review* 60 (2012): 1023.

[13] Risa L. Goluboff, *The Lost Promise of Civil Rights* (Cambridge, MA: Harvard University Press, 2007).

[14] James Gray Pope and Rebecca E. Zietlow, "The Auto-Lite Strike and the Fight against 'Wage Slavery,'" *University of Toledo Review* 38 (2007): 839, reprinted in Kenneth M. Casebeer, ed., *American Labor Struggles and Law Histories* (Durham, NC: Carolina Academic Press, 2011).

union jobs earned good wages, enough to buy a home and a car, raise children, and send them to college. By the 1990s when I moved to Toledo, however, union density was on the decline, as was the automotive indus-try. General Motors was once the leading employer of workers in Ohio, but now Walmart has far surpassed GM. The new, nonunionized, jobs available to high school graduates pay minimum wage and lack benefits and job security. Moreover, workers are often scheduled on demand, which makes it impossible for them to plan from day to day. The decline in wages and quality of life for low wage workers has contributed to the despair reflected in increased drug and alcohol abuse and declining life expectancy of the working class in the United States.[15] The Reconstruc-tion Era promise of free labor also has failed for these workers.

Reconstruction is not generally viewed as relevant to the white working class. However, James Ashley drew a connection between the plight of southern slaves and northern white workers. James Ashley recognized the link between racial and economic justice. He saw com-monality of interest between white workers and black slaves. He drew a connection between the exploitation of slaves and poor wages and working conditions for white workers. Many northern workers participated in the antislavery movement and joined the antislavery Republican Party. Northern workers fought for the Union Army, and helped fugitive slaves to escape across enemy lines. After the war, Ashley's Thirteenth Amendment abolished not only slavery but also involuntary servitude, ending the northern institution of indentured servitude and establishing a paradigm of free labor. In fact, the Reconstruction Era transformed the all of work for all workers, including my clients in Chicago and the automobile workers in Toledo. As I wrote this book, I always had both groups of people in mind.

Finally, the Reconstruction Era still resonates in the political arena. In 2008, white workers helped to elect the first black president of the United States, Barack Obama. Working with the Obama campaign in Toledo, I saw how Obama inspired workers of all races who were suffering during the Great Recession. The night that Obama was elected, I listened to The Band song, "The Night They Drove Old Dixie Down." I joked (well, half

[15] See Jessica Body, "The Forces Driving Middle-Aged White People's 'Deaths of Despair,'" NPR, March 23, 2017, www.npr.org/sections/health-shots/2017/03/23/521083335/the-forces-driving-middle-aged-white-peoples-deaths-of-despair; Anne Case and Sir Angus Deaton, "Mortality and Morbidity in the 21st Century," www.brookings.edu/bpea-articles/mortality-and-morbidity-in-the-21st-century/.

joked) that the Union had finally won the Civil War. Eight years later, however, many of those same workers voted for the openly racist Donald Trump for president. In part, the election of Trump reflected a general disillusionment with politicians and a desire for change. However, it is undeniable that Trump's election coincided with an increase in racist hate speech and racial violence and that voters were largely divided across racial lines. Electoral College maps superimposed over the map of the Confederate states showed a striking overlap between the states that voted for Trump and those that seceded to protect slavery. The margin of victory, however, depended on the northern industrial states marked by the decline in well-paying union manufacturing jobs. Race had divided the working class, and white workers voted against both their economic interests and those of their co-workers of color.

Thus, as I was writing about the political battles of the past and the idealism of James Ashley and his Reconstruction Era allies, I witnessed the polarized and challenging political battles of the early twenty-first century and thought about the parallels between the past and the present. Ashley and his allies grew up in a country with an economy dependent on the brutal, inhuman, racist institution of chattel slavery. They formed coalitions and engaged in constitutional politics to outlaw an institution that they saw as incompatible with our nation's fundamental values. Ashley and his allies used the upheaval of the Civil War to further their mission to outlaw slavery and establish fundamental human rights. Their mission was successful, but in some ways their success was fleeting. One hundred fifty years later, our economy continues to depend on underpaid and exploited labor, mostly performed by racial minorities. On the other hand, the laws that embodied Ashley's vision largely remain on the books too, including most notably the Thirteenth Amendment and its promise of free labor. Ultimately, I hope that my book can serve as a resource for those, like Ashley, who are working for the cause of racial and economic justice.

I

James Ashley, the Forgotten Emancipator

On November 20, 1865, the Colored People's Convention of the State of South Carolina convened "for the purpose of deliberating upon the plans best calculated to advance the interests of our people."[1] After five days of deliberation, this convention of newly freed slaves issued a resolution calling for the end of race discrimination, the right to vote, the right to equal citizenship, and the repeal of laws that reduced free slaves to "serfdom."[2] A century later, the Negro American Labor Council met to plan a march "For Jobs and Freedom" in Washington, DC. Their leader, noted civil rights advocate A. Philip Randolph, hoped that the march would "ensure that Americans of all races had access to quality education, affordable housing, and jobs that paid a living wage."[3] Although these activists lived almost one hundred years apart from each other, they shared a vision of rights that combined antidiscrimination norms, rights of citizenship, and economic rights for workers. In the years leading up to the Civil War, antislavery and proworker activists articulated a similar vision as they sought to end slavery and improve workers' rights. Participants in the antislavery movement advocated not only against slavery, but also in favor of racial equality and worker's rights. Participants in the labor movements advocated not only for the rights of

---

[1] Proceedings of the Colored People's Convention of the State of South Carolina (Charleston, South Carolina), November 1865, reprinted in Philip Foner and George E. Walker, eds. *Proceedings of the Black State Conventions, 1840–1865* (Philadelphia: Temple University Press, 1980), vol. 2: 288–302.
[2] Ibid.
[3] William P. Jones, *The March on Washington: Jobs, Freedom, and the Forgotten History of Civil Rights* (New York: W. W. Norton, 2013), ix, xvii.

northern workers, but also against slavery in the southern states. This
book tells their story through the lens of a leading member of the
Reconstruction Congress, Ohio Representative James Mitchell Ashley.[4]
James Ashley was an active participant in the antislavery movement and a
strong advocate for the rights of all workers. Ashley and his allies in
Reconstruction Congress worked to enforce a positive right to free labor,
including the right to work free of undue coercion, for a living wage, and
without discrimination based on race. They also sought to establish a new
republic based in liberty and equality.

Despite James Ashley's prominence in the Reconstruction Congress
and notable contributions to our Constitution and the expansion of
rights, Ashley is practically unknown to legal scholars and little mentioned by historians.[5] Though he worked hand in hand with President
Abraham Lincoln, "the Great Emancipator," Ashley's role has been
largely forgotten. This book seeks both to restore Ashley's memory and
to resurrect his progressive vision.

The nineteenth century was a time of great change in the United States.
The nation's economy was transformed from one that was primarily
agricultural and artisanal, and dependent on the institution of slavery,
to a largely industrialized economy in which slavery was illegal. Our
Constitution was transformed from a proslavery document, written by
the owners of slaves, to a document that promised freedom and individual
rights to all people within its jurisdiction. Finally, the institution of work

[4] There is some confusion about Ashley's actual middle name. Robert F. Horowitz, *The
Great Impeacher: A Political Biography of James M. Ashley* (New York: Brooklyn College
Press, 1979), 1, note 3. The official congressional biography listed it as "Mitchell." Ibid.
However, the *New York Times* obituary listed Ashley's middle name as "Monroe," as did
a recent congressional resolution renaming the Federal Courthouse in Toledo as the
"James M. Ashley and Thomas W. L. Ashley United States Courthouse." *New York
Times*, September 4, 1896. See Designation of James A. Ashley and Thomas W. L. Ashley
United States Courthouse, H.R. 3712, P.L. 110–284, Report (Amended) by the Committee
on Transportation. H. Rept. 110–455 (November 15, 2007). Ashley himself always signed
his name "James M. Ashley." Horowitz at 1 note 3. According to his great-great-grand-
son, Tom Dolgenos, "'Mitchell' is the most likely possibility. His grandfather, a Baptist
minister named Benjamin Ashley, was close to another Baptist minister named James
Mitchell; his son (the brother of our g-grandfather Charles) called himself James Mitchell
Ashley, Jr.; and articles in several reputable biographical dictionaries, whose authors
presumably talked to family members and/or other persons close to JMA I, do give the
name as Mitchell." Tom Dolgenos, email message to author, January 17, 2017.
[5] For example, Ashley was omitted from Manisha Sinha's recent encyclopedic (768-page-
long) book on the antislavery movement. Manisha Sinha, *The Slave's Cause: A History of
Abolition* (New Haven: Yale University Press, 2016). See James M. McPherson, "America's Greatest Movement," *New York Review of Books*, October 27, 2016.

was transformed from a common law system characterized by master–servant relations, apprenticeship, and indentured servitude to one based on free labor and freedom of contract between employers and employees. All of these developments are interconnected and are largely the result of political advocacy by antislavery and labor activists. This book considers those antislavery and proworker activists, and the politicians who were influenced by their views and represented them in changing the law. Those politicians were members of the Republican Party, a party formed in the mid-1850s as an antislavery party that dominated Congress during the Reconstruction Era. James Ashley played an active role founding the Republican Party and was one of its early leaders.

James Ashley was a large man with an imposing presence. Six feet tall, he had "abundant and curly" hair that he wore "combed up and back, so that it lay on his head in curly masses."[6] Ashley represented northwest Ohio as a member of the US House of Representatives from 1858 to 1868. As chair of the House Committee on the Territories, Ashley presided over abolition of slavery in the District of Columbia and spearheaded the Reconstruction effort. During the Civil War, Ashley used every opportunity to weaken slavery, supporting the "confiscation" and liberation of slaves who crossed enemy lines. Ashley was the first member of Congress to propose a Reconstruction Act and the first to propose amending the Constitution to abolish slavery. At the side of President Abraham Lincoln, Ashley led the battle for the Thirteenth Amendment's approval in the House of Representatives. Said the noted abolitionist Frederick Douglass, "In every phase of the great conflict over slavery, [James Ashley] bore a conspicuous and honorable part. He was among the foremost of that brilliant galaxy of statesmen who reconstructed the Union on a basis of liberty."[7]

The book also examines the end of Ashley's political career. Ashley became embroiled in the failed attempt to impeach President Andrew

---

[6] Charles S. Ashley, "Governor Ashley's Biography and Messages," in *Contributions to the Historical Society of Montana* (Helena, MT: Rocky Mountain Publishing, 1907), 210. Pointing out that Ashley's hairstyle was unique, his son Charles observed, "In this and other peculiarities of personal habits we may see an illustration of Herbert Spencer's theory of the correspondence between radicalism in politics and non-conformity in manners." Ibid.

[7] Frederick Douglass, "Introduction," *Duplicate Copy of the Souvenir from the Afro-American League of Tennessee to Hon. James M. Ashley of Ohio* (Benjamin Arnett, ed.) (Philadelphia: Publishing House of the AME Church, 1894) (hereafter referred to as *Souvenir*), 3.

Johnson, and that led to his political downfall. In 1868 Ashley lost his battle for reelection to Congress and President Ulysses S. Grant appointed him governor of the Montana Territory. As governor, Ashley sought to perpetuate his free labor vision by supporting workers' rights and opposing the slavery-like coolie system. Ashley was caught in the divisions of the late Reconstruction Republican party, as the party leadership turned away from protecting the rights of freed slaves and toward serving the needs of big business. President Grant removed Ashley from his governorship in 1870, and Ashley entered private life. Ashley spent the last fifteen years of his career as the owner of a small railroad. In that role, he continued to advocate for the rights of workers, even his own employees.

James Ashley recognized that slavery violated fundamental human rights, including what he viewed as the positive right to free labor. Ashley recognized the interrelationship between race discrimination and economic subordination. Ashley argued that slavery corrupted democracy because in slave states the concentration of wealth was in the hands of a landed oligarchy. Nonetheless, Ashley and his allies succeeded in using democratic means to abolish slavery. Of course, Ashley and his allies would not have succeeded, and slavery would not have been abolished, had it not been for the Civil War. However, the war was merely a precondition of their success – it did not ensure the end of slavery. Ashley was among those members of Congress and military leaders who seized the opportunity that the war presented to bring an end to slavery. As Chair of the Committee on the Territories, Ashley was poised to capitalize on the conflict to achieve his political ends. Ultimately, Ashley succeeded, and he also failed. Ashley and his allies ended slavery, and they established a constitutional and statutory framework to protect the fundamental rights that they had identified during their political struggle. However, they did not manage to reform democracy because of the federal government's ultimate failure to enforce voting rights of freed slaves. Moreover, the Republican party gradually strayed from its Reconstruction Era free labor commitment. After the 1876 presidential election, the federal government abandoned any commitment to protecting the rights of freed slaves in southern states. That commitment was not revived until the 1960s, as a result of the twentieth-century civil rights and labor movements.

This book is primarily a book about ideology. It is an intellectual history of the political antislavery movement and the antebellum labor movement. Antislavery constitutionalists argued that slavery violated constitutional provisions that protected individual rights. Workers' rights activists argued that workers who were underpaid and poorly treated were "wage slaves." There were many tensions between participants in the two movements, and sometimes they conflicted. However, there was also a significant amount of convergence between the two movements. After all, slavery was above all an exploitative system of labor relations based on racial subordination. James Ashley believed that slavery was a moral abomination that violated the natural rights of man. In his draft memoir, Ashley explained that he believed that "[e]very child born of a slave mother in America, was by the law of nature and of nature's God, born free. All such children seized and held as slaves by American slave masters involved the moral crime of kidnapping human beings and depriving them, by force and fraud, of their natural right to liberty, and denying to them the protection which the law of nature and the human race are entitled."[8] But Ashley was also a materialist, who drew connections between the exploitation of slaves and other workers. He explained, "In all my speeches, beginning with our early anti-slavery struggle, you will find that I uniformly made my appeals for the rights of all labor, black and white, and demanded for each an equitable share in the property which his toil created."[9] Most important, Ashley was a political pragmatist who effectively worked with allies to implement his ideology with the Reconstruction measures that altered our Constitution and expanded human rights.

Reconstruction was the second founding of our nation, a crucial time to recreate our national identity. The Reconstruction Amendments transformed our Constitution from a document that perpetuated the institution of slavery to one that expanded citizenship rights and promised liberty and equality for all people within our nation. The Reconstruction Constitution expanded the power of the federal government and, for the first time, authorized the federal government to enforce federal rights against state interference. Thus, the Reconstruction Constitution established the United States of America for the first time as one nation that was truly "One nation ... indivisible, with liberty and justice for all." The Constitution of our imagination, which Americans revere and respect, would not exist if it were not for the efforts of James Ashley and his Reconstruction colleagues. Ashley's Thirteenth Amendment abolished slavery and involuntary servitude and established the fundamental rights

[8] John M. Morgan papers relating to James M. Ashley, University of Toledo libraries, Ward M. Canaday Center Manuscript Collection, Box 1, Folder 7.
[9] James Ashley, Centennial Oration, Wood County Centennial Celebration, July 4, 1876, *Souvenir*, 578, 599.

of free people for the newly freed slaves and other people in the United States. The Fourteenth Amendment established birthright citizenship, extending citizenship rights to newly freed slaves and all other people born in the United States, and promised due process and equal protection of the laws to all people. The Fifteenth Amendment prohibited race discrimination in suffrage rights. These rights were originally advocated by the political antislavery movement that Ashley joined as a young adult. In his speeches advocating for these Reconstruction measures, Ashley articulated those rights, and he used his political skills to help enshrine them into law.

The Reconstruction Constitution also redefined citizenship and established the United States as a new republic. In his monumental Gettysburg Address, President Abraham Lincoln promised "a new birth of freedom," describing the US government as one that was "for the people, by the people, and of the people." At the time that Lincoln gave his address, his description of our government was aspirational, and objectively inaccurate. Millions of slaves were excluded from participating in the political process and, indeed, were not even treated as people under the state laws that governed them. Women were also denied the right to vote and subjected to legal disabilities that restricted their rights. As a former Democrat, Ashley believed strongly in the institutions of democracy. As early as 1856, Ashley argued that free blacks should have the right to vote, and during Reconstruction he was one of the foremost advocates of suffrage rights for freed slaves. Ashley envisioned a new republic, extending the populism of Jacksonian democracy to the racial minorities whom it had excluded. He also supported the voting rights of women and proposed a constitutional amendment that would have established universal voting rights. Along with suffrage rights, Ashley promoted free and universal public education to educate the children of the working class and prepare them to participate in democratic institutions.

Finally, and crucially important, Reconstruction measures transformed workers' rights, not only ending slavery but also establishing a free labor paradigm for all workers. The Reconstruction Era is widely recognized as a time when our Constitution was amended to include the promise of racial equality and individual rights vis-à-vis state governments. Ashley's story reveals that this conventional view of Reconstruction is accurate but incomplete. Slaveholders used racial subordination as a means to exploit the labor of unpaid slaves, and this had a negative impact on the lives of all low wage workers. Thus, ending slavery also had a monumental impact on workers' rights in this country. In the early nineteenth century, the majority of workers in our country were not truly free. Indentured servitude, under which employees were bound to their employers and served solely their employers' will, was still common in the northern states.[10] While slaves were obviously treated the worst of any workers, the prevalence of indentured servitude made it easier to justify the inhumane conditions of slavery. The Thirteenth Amendment transformed a society that had been based in unfree labor to one in which the paradigm was a free worker with individual autonomy and rights with respect to his employer, a positive right to free labor. Without James Ashley, this paradigm might never have become law.

This is also a book about constitutional politics. Although constitutional scholars tend to focus on court rulings, much of constitutional development occurs within the political process. In the years leading up to the Civil War, antislavery activists asserted their own authority to interpret the Constitution even when the courts rejected their arguments. Throughout our history, political movements have framed their rights claims in constitutional terms. This book tells their story and thus joins the burgeoning movement of constitutional scholars who study how constitutional interpretation outside the courts and how political movements affect our constitutional law.[11]

In 1892, the Afro-American League of Tennessee decided that they wanted to publish a compilation of Ashley's writing and orations. The League's leader was Benjamin W. Arnett, a man who had had been in the House gallery when they voted for the Thirteenth Amendment and was now president of Wilberforce University. Arnett was a leading figure in the African Methodist Episcopal church.[12] Many years ago, Ashley had helped to establish an AME Church in his hometown of Toledo. Now, Arnett wanted to honor Ashley. Arnett wrote to Ashley and asked for his papers and statements, and copies of his Reconstruction Acts and draft constitutional amendments. Ashley happily complied, and Arnett compiled

---

[10] Robert J. Steinfeld, *The Invention of Free Labor: The Employment Relation in English and American Law and Culture, 1350–1870* (Chapel Hill: University of North Carolina Press, 1991), 7, 11.

[11] See, e.g., Larry D. Kramer, *The People Themselves: Popular Constitutionalism and Judicial Review* (New York: Oxford University Press, 2004); Robert C. Post and Reva B. Siegel, "Legislative Constitutionalism and Section Five Power: Policentric Interpretations of the Family and Medical Leave Act," *Yale Law Journal* 112 (2003): 1943; Keith E. Whittington, *Constitutional Construction: Divided Powers and Constitutional Meaning* (Cambridge, MA: Harvard University Press, 1999).

[12] Leonard L. Richards, *Who Freed the Slaves? The Fight over the Thirteenth Amendment* (Chicago: University of Chicago Press, 2015), 255.

the papers into a single volume.[13] Noted black abolitionist Frederick Douglass wrote the introduction to the volume and praised Ashley's contributions to ending slavery and furthering workers' rights.[14] The compilation was presented to Ashley at the Columbian Exhibition in Chicago on September 22, 1892, the anniversary of Lincoln's announcement of the preliminary emancipation proclamation. It was a day devoted to the black churches. Over five thousand people attended the ceremony, most of whom were black. Bishop Arnett gave a speech and his son handed the book to Ashley. It was a fitting tribute to Ashley, a man who had devoted his entire life to ending slavery and improving the lives of workers in the United States.[15]

In the draft memoir that he wrote at the end of his life, Ashley predicted that "future historians will honor" the border state members of Congress who voted for the Thirteenth Amendment, "to whom this nation owes a debt of eternal gratitude." Doubtless, Ashley also expected that he, too, would be honored by those historians. Ashley did not anticipate the extent to which historians in the Dunning school would work to denigrate him and his allies as corrupt carpetbaggers, and how successful they would be during the first half of the twentieth century. For example, in 1929, historian Claude G. Bowers called Ashley "depraved," "disreputable," and "low and corrupt."[16] In the 1960s, a generation of historians reframed the members of the Reconstruction Congress and their project to protect the rights of the newly freed slaves.[17] Inspired by the civil rights movement of their time, historians such as Hans Trefousse, Les Benedict, and Eric Foner focused primarily on Reconstruction's promise of racial equality.[18] When legal scholars also sought to resurrect the true meaning

---

[13] *Souvenir.*   [14] Frederick Douglass, Introduction, *Souvenir*, 3–6.
[15] Richards, *Who Freed the Slaves?*, 257.
[16] Claude G. Bowers, *The Tragic Era: The Revolution after Lincoln* 157, 158, 240, 459 (1929); cited in Horowitz, *Great Impeacher*, xi.
[17] See Michael Les Benedict, *A Compromise of Principle* (New York: W. W. Norton, 1974); Eric Foner, *Reconstruction: American's Unfinished Revolution, 1863–1877* (New York: Harper Collins, 1988); Eric Foner, *Free Soil, Free Labor, Free Men: The Ideology of the Republican Party before the Civil War* (New York: Oxford University Press, 1995); Hans L. Trefousse, *The Radical Republicans: Lincoln's Vanguard for Racial Justice* (New York: Alfred A. Knopf, 1968).
[18] Historians also discussing labor issues during the Civil War and Reconstruction include Eric Foner, *Politics and Ideology in the Age of the Civil War* (New York: Oxford University Press, 1980); David Montgomery, *Beyond Equality: Labor and the Radical Republicans 1862–1872* (Urbana and Chicago: University of Illinois Press, 1967); David Montgomery, *Citizen Worker: The Experience of Workers in the United States with Democracy and the Free Market during the Nineteenth Century* (New York: Cambridge

of Reconstruction, they focused primarily on the Fourteenth Amendment's Due Process and Equal Protection clauses, and not on his Thirteenth Amendment.[19] While historians have written about the northern workers who contributed to the antislavery movement, until now most legal scholars of the Reconstruction Era have virtually ignored them.[20]

After Ashley died, some members of his family tried to preserve his memory. Ashley's son, Charles Sumner Ashley, wrote his own biography as part of a multivolume history of the Montana Territory. In 1916, a woman named Margaret Ashley who may have been his daughter Mary wrote a master's thesis on James Ashley at Columbia University. But their efforts were by and large to no avail. Since then, only one biography has been written about James Mitchell Ashley, and it focuses on his role in the failed attempt to impeach President Andrew Johnson.[21] In 2006, a conference at the University of Toledo College of Law celebrated James Ashley and the Thirteenth Amendment. Attending the conference, Ashley's great-grand-daughter, Sally Ashley, remarked at how happy her father (Ashley's grandson) would have been to know about the conference. Sally noted that her father often bemoaned the fact that his grandfather's contributions had been forgotten and nobody know who he was.

University Press, 1993); Heather Fox Richardson, *The Death of Reconstruction: Race, Labor and Politics in the Civil War North, 1865–1901* (Cambridge: Harvard University Press, 2001). For other important accounts of labor practices in the antebellum era, see Steinfeld, *Invention of Free Labor*; Christopher L. Tomlins, *Law, Labor and Ideology in the Early American Republic* (New York: Cambridge University Press, 1993). Other historians have discussed labor issues in their work about the Freedman's Bureaus. See, e.g., Amy Dru Stanley, *From Bondage to Contract: Wage Labor, Marriage, and the Market in the Age of Slave Emancipation* (New York: Cambridge University Press, 1998); Donald G. Nieman, *To Set the Law in Motion: The Freedman's Bureau and the Legal Rights of Blacks* (Millwood, NY: KTO Press, 1979).

[19] Notable works include Judith A. Baer, *Equality under the Constitution: Reclaiming the Fourteenth Amendment* (Ithaca: Cornell University Press, 1983); Pamela Brandwein, *Reconstructing Reconstruction: The Supreme Court and the Production of Historical Truth* (Durham: Duke University Press, 1999); Michael Kent Curtis, *No State Shall Abridge: The Fourteenth Amendment and the Bill of Rights* (Durham: Duke University Press, 1986).

[20] Notable exceptions the work of James Gray Pope, Avi Soifer, and Lea VanderVelde. See, e.g., James Gray Pope, "Labor's Constitution of Freedom," *Yale Law Journal* 106 (1997): 941; Avi Soifer, "Federal Protection, Paternalism, and the Virtually Forgotten Prohibition of Voluntary Peonage," *Columbia Law Review* 112 (2012): 1607; Lea S. VanderVelde, "The Labor Vision of the Thirteenth Amendment," *University of Pennsylvania Law Review* 138 (1989): 437; Lea S. VanderVelde, "Henry Wilson, Cobbler of the Frayed Constitution, Strategist of the Thirteenth Amendment," *Georgetown Journal of Law and Politics* 15 (2017): 173.

[21] Horowitz, *Great Impeacher*.

Recently, historians and legal scholars have rediscovered the Thirteenth Amendment and have revitalized the debate about its meaning and promise.[22] James Ashley has also received some attention. In July 2008, a congressional resolution renamed the federal courthouse in Toledo, Ohio, the James M. Ashley and Thomas W. L. Ashley U.S. Courthouse.[23] In 2015, historian Leonard Richards featured Ashley prominently in his account of the antislavery effort during the Civil War and the Thirteenth Amendment, "Who Freed the Slaves?" In a 2016 book review, historian James McPherson called Ashley "the real-life hero of the drama that finally ended slavery."[24] In 2014, Ashley appeared as a character in Steven Spielberg's film *Lincoln*, about the campaign for approval of the Thirteenth Amendment in the House of Representatives.

In *Lincoln*, Ashley was portrayed inaccurately as a mealy mouthed moderate. In real life, James Ashley was an ideological radical who was passionate about his beliefs. Historian Hans Trefousse described Ashley as "extreme and emotional in his approach to almost every question."[25] Indeed, it is precisely Ashely's radicalism that may account for his disappearance in constitutional history. Ashley's extreme approach to the impeachment effort harmed his reputation, as did his rejection of the Grant administration. Historians have also been stymied by the fact that

---

[22] Excellent works on the history of the Thirteenth Amendment include Michael Vorenberg, *Final Freedom: The Civil War, the Abolition of Slavery, and the Thirteenth Amendment* (New York: Cambridge University Press, 2001); James Oakes, *Freedom National: The Destruction of Slavery in the United States, 1861–1865* (New York: W. W. Norton, 2013); Richards, *Who Freed the Slaves?* Legal scholarship includes Alexander Tsesis, *The Thirteenth Amendment and American Freedom: A Legal History* (New York: NYU Press, 2004); Alexander Tsesis, ed., *Promises of Liberty: The History and Contemporary Relevance of the Thirteenth Amendment* (New York: Columbia University Press, 2010): Pope, "Labor's Constitution"; Soifer, "Federal Protection"; VanderVelde, "Labor Vision." See also Maria Ontiveros, "Is Modern Day Slavery a Private Act or a Public System of Oppression?," *Seattle University Law Review* 39 (2016): 665; Lea Vander-Velde, "The Thirteenth Amendment of Our Aspirations," *University of Toledo Law Review* 38 (2007): 855. Symposia on the Thirteenth Amendment are published in volume 39 of the *Seattle University Law Review* (2015), volume 112 of the *Columbia Law Review* (2012), volume 71 of the *Maryland Law Review* (2011), and volume 38 of the *University of Toledo Law Review* (2006).

[23] A Bill to Designate the United States courthouse located at 1716 Spielbusch Avenue in Toledo, Ohio as the "James M. Ashley and Thomas W. L. Ashley United States Courthouse;" H.R. 3712, P.L. 110–284 (July 23, 2008). Thomas W. L. ("Lud") Ashley was Ashley's great-grandson. Lud Ashley represented Toledo, Ohio, in the US House of Representatives from 1955 to 1980. Report on H.R. 3712, H. Report. 110–455 (November 15, 2007).

[24] McPherson, "America's Greatest Movement."

[25] Trefousse, *Radical Republicans*, 13.

Ashley's papers were destroyed in a fire before his death. Constitutional law scholars tend to prefer Ashley's moderate colleague from Ohio, John Bingham, a well-respected member of Congress and the principal author of Section 1 of the Fourteenth Amendment. Constitutional historians have done great work reviving the memory of John Bingham and celebrating his impact on the Reconstruction Congress.[26] But Bingham was a moderate and a former Whig. Ashley, a former Democrat, had a different outlook and a more radical approach to politics. Learning about Ashley as well as Bingham leads to a more nuanced understanding of the Reconstruction Era.[27]

Toward the end of his life, Ashley was aware of the ongoing reframing of the Confederacy as the "lost cause" with its sanitized and romanticized view of slavery. In his draft memoir written in the early 1890s, Ashley condemned the Confederate memorials that were then being erected throughout the South. Ashley observed that "lost cause" monuments then being erected in southern states overlooked the fact the slave barons wanted to erect a slave-holding empire.[28] He exclaimed, "To vindicate the truth of history and to serve as a lesson and warning, one monument ought to be erected by the champions of the 'lost cause' in Jamestown, Virginia, with the design on it, in bold relief, of a ship landing the first cargo of African slaves on the continent in 1620!"[29] According to Ashley, those monuments should have included images of slaves on a slave block and fugitive slaves being chased by hounds. In Ashley's view, "It would be appropriate to build cheap monuments for those men, out of old red sand stone or some such cheap material, so that they might soon crumble and be forgotten."[30] Of course, most of those Confederate monuments remain in all their glory. More important, our nation still struggles with

---

[26] See Richard L. Aynes, "On Misreading John Bingham and the Fourteenth Amendment," *Yale Law Journal* 103 (1993): 57; Michael Kent Curtis, "John A. Bingham and the Story of American Liberty: The Lost Cause Meets the 'Lost Clause,'" *Akron Law Review* 36 (2003): 617; Gerard Magliocca, *American Founding Son: John Bingham and the Invention of the Fourteenth Amendment* (New York: NYU Press, 2013).

[27] Learning about the differences in ideology of key members in the Reconstruction Congress such as Bingham and Ashley also challenges the claim of originalists that it is possible to identify a single meaning in any provision of the Constitution. See James W. Fox, Jr., "Publics, Meanings and the Privileges of Citizenship," *Constitutional Commentary* 30 (2015): 567, 569 (pointing out that "a far more robust idea ... of the Reconstruction Amendments was articulated by white Republicans, African Americans, and feminists").

[28] John M. Morgan papers relating to James M. Ashley, University of Toledo libraries, Ward M. Canaday Center Manuscript Collection, Box 1, Folder 5, 2.

[29] Ibid., 3.   [30] Ibid., 4.

the meaning of the Reconstruction Era for our national identity, our constitutional rights, and our system of federalism.

In striking contrast to the grandiose Confederate monuments in the South are the monuments to Union soldiers that proliferated in northern towns and cities, from White House, Ohio, to Lyme, New Hampshire.[31] These memorials are symbolic of a nineteenth-century movement that sought to universalize fundamental human rights for freed slaves and the northern working class. Among those soldiers were thousands of workers who joined the Union Army and fought for the world's leading democracy.[32] Many of these soldiers were drafted, and by and large they primarily sought to restore the Union rather than pursue a broad rights agenda. However, soldiers on the front line also engaged in early efforts to confiscate and free the slaves. Those soldiers who survived returned from battle to an economy that was rapidly industrializing, and many joined the burgeoning labor movement. The changes wrought by the Civil War affected the entire nation, from freed slaves in the South to northern white workers. In Congress, James Ashley sought to improve all of their lives with a broad free labor agenda.

[31] See Harold A. George, *Civil War Monuments of Ohio* (Mansfield, OH: Book Masters, 2006); Mildred C. Baruch and Ellen J. Beckman, *Civil War Union Monuments* (Washington, DC: Daughters of Union Veterans of the Civil War, 1978).
[32] See Montgomery, *Beyond Equality*, 73.

2

Antislavery Constitutionalism and the Meaning of Freedom

> Mr. Chairman, I do not believe that the Constitution of my country
> recognizes property in man.
>> – Speech of Hon. James Ashley of Ohio, Delivered in the
>> U.S. House of Representatives, May 29, 1860[1]

James Mitchell Ashley was born in 1824, in Allegheny, Pennsylvania.[2] He grew up in a tumultuous time in American history. Ashley was born four years after the Missouri Compromise launched the constitutional anti-slavery movement,[3] and in the midst of the beginning of the US labor movement.[4] As the antislavery movement grew, so did tension between free and slave states. Ashley spent his early life near the Ohio River, which formed a border between the free state of Ohio and the slave state of Virginia, and he later attributed his deep opposition to slavery to the fact that he had witnessed the cruelty of slavery first hand so early in life. The son of an evangelical minister, Ashley hated slavery with a religious fervor. Like his country, however, Ashley's family was divided, with his

---

[1] *Duplicate Copy of the Souvenir from the Afro-American League of Tennessee to Hon. James M. Ashley of Ohio* (Benjamin Arnett, ed.) (Philadelphia: Publishing House of the AME Church, 1894) (hereafter referred to as *Souvenir*), 44, 79.

[2] The exact date of Ashley's birth is unknown. His son, Charles, insisted that his father was born in 1822, but Ashley always claimed to have been born in 1824. See Robert F. Horowitz, *The Great Impeacher: A Political Biography of James M. Ashley* (New York: Brooklyn College Press, 1979), 1, note 3.

[3] William M. Wiecek, *The Sources of Antislavery Constitutionalism in America, 1760–1848* (Ithaca: Cornell University Press, 1977), 111.

[4] Eric Foner, *Politics and Ideology in the Age of the Civil War* (New York: Oxford University Press, 1980), 58.

father favoring slavery and his mother opposing it. Ashley adored his mother but hated his father. When he was fourteen, he ran away from home and went to live with a Quaker abolitionist family.[5] There, he enjoyed standing on a table and reciting the antislavery speeches of Kentucky Senator Cassius Clay to entertain his friends. Ashley worked then as a cabin boy on the Ohio River, where he had frequent contact with slaves and their owners.[6]

At the age of seventeen in 1841, James Ashley traveled to Washington, DC, with a letter of introduction from a family friend to Richard M. Johnson, the outgoing vice president. While in Washington, Ashley witnessed the inauguration of President William Henry Harrison. Though Ashley did not find a job in Washington, the trip inspired him to seek a direction in life, toward a future political career. In 1851, Ashley ran unsuccessfully for mayor of Portsmouth, Ohio. He lost in part because of his antislavery views, and because he was known to be involved with the Underground Railroad, an informal network of people who helped fleeing slaves.[7] His failed attempt in the race for mayor was just the beginning of what became a successful political career. Ashley spent most of his life in politics, including ten years as a member of the US House of Representatives. Throughout his career, Ashley was a fierce antislavery advocate who also supported workers' rights and the rights of free blacks. During his years as a politician, Ashley developed a theory of rights that was influenced by the antislavery constitutionalists, the nascent labor movement, and his background as a populist Jacksonian Democrat.

Ashley was licensed to practice law, but he rarely practiced, saying it was dull. Instead, he dabbled in journalism and tried unsuccessfully to run a pharmacy. Ashley married Emma G. Smith, of Portsmouth, Ohio, in November 1851. Emma was a strong advocate for women's suffrage who shared James's strong religious and political beliefs. Shortly after their marriage, the couple moved to Toledo, Ohio, a city that was more hospitable to their antislavery convictions.[8] Ashley became involved in Toledo politics and sold his business to run for political office. Ashley became involved in politics just as the political antislavery movement was ascendant and the issue of slavery in the territories was causing the

---

[5] Horowitz, *Great Impeacher*, 2, 5–6.
[6] Address of Hon. James M. Ashley before the "Ohio Society of New York," at the Fifth Annual Banquet, Wednesday evening, February 19, 1890, *Souvenir*, 692, 695.
[7] Horowitz, *Great Impeacher*, 8, 10.   [8] Ibid., 9–11.

disintegration of the political party system. He became a protégé of Salmon Chase, a leading antislavery constitutionalist and Ohio politician.

As Ashley developed from a young boy into a man, the antislavery movement also came of age, in a political sense. During the 1830s, antislavery activists debated whether to join politics or shun the political realm as tainted by slavery. Abolitionist leader William Lloyd Garrison famously shunned politics, but other antislavery activists believed that it was necessary to engage in politics to end slavery. In 1833, these activists formed the American Anti-Slavery Society (AASS), arguing that slavery was immoral and demanding immediate abolition. Eventually, the leaders of the AASS decided to use the political process to fight the peculiar institution. Antislavery constitutionalists claimed that the Constitution should be interpreted consistently with the egalitarian principles of the Declaration of Independence and the Northwest Ordinance. They insisted that ambiguities in the Constitution should be resolved consistently with those egalitarian principles.[9] These antislavery activists made their arguments in constitutional terms to enhance and reinforce the legitimacy of their political claims. Antislavery constitutionalism was central to the strategy of the political antislavery movement.

According to Eric Foner, the antebellum era was "an age which cared deeply about constitutional interpretation, and regarded the Constitution as the embodiment of legal wisdom." In the antebellum era, it was not unusual for political arguments to be framed in constitutional terms. People revered the Constitution, and constitutionalizing political arguments gave them added weight. Congressman John Bingham later recalled that "everything was reduced to a Constitutional question, in those days." Moreover, as Foner notes, while the antislavery constitutionalists' position may not have been as legally accurate as Garrison's, "they were politically and tactically far superior." During the antebellum era, Americans revered their Constitution.[10] Antislavery arguments had more force if they were consistent with the Constitution. Eventually, the emerging Republican Party embraced some of their constitutional arguments. Thus, the antislavery constitutionalists contributed to the antislavery debate and

[9] Wiecek, *Antislavery Constitutionalism*, 167–168; Richard H. Sewell, *Ballots for Freedom: Antislavery Politics in the United States 1837–1860* (New York: Oxford University Press, 1976), 37.

[10] Eric Foner, *Free Soil, Free Labor, Free Men: The Ideology of the Republican Party before the Civil War* (New York: Oxford University Press, 1995), 85; Sewell, *Ballots for Freedom*, 306.

enriched our constitutional culture. They also developed a theory of rights that Ashley and his allies eventually enshrined in the Constitution.

Many of the prominent antislavery constitutionalists were from Ashley's state of Ohio, including James Birney, Theodore Dwight Weld, Joel Tiffany, and Salmon Chase. Birney and Weld were members of the American Anti-Slavery Society (AASS) and founders of the Ohio Anti-Slavery Society (OASS). Chase and Tiffany were lawyers who went on to engage in antislavery politics. In 1840, Birney joined New Yorkers Alvan Stewart and Gerrit Smith to form the first antislavery political party, the Liberty Party. Salmon Chase joined the party a year later and wrote the first party platform. Smith served in the US House of Representatives as a member of the Free Soil Party from 1852 to 1854. Other prominent antislavery constitutionalists include New York's journalist William Goodell, the 1852 Liberty Party presidential nominee, and Boston journalist Lysander Spooner. In the late 1850s, noted black abolitionist Frederick Douglass also adopted the antislavery constitutionalist arguments.[11]

The Liberty Party was widely viewed as a party of extreme abolitionists, and the party garnered little support outside of those committed to the antislavery cause. However, the leaders of the Liberty Party gained momentum during the turbulent 1850s. Liberty Party members helped to form the Free Soil Party in 1848 and the Republican Party in 1856. The 1856 Republican Party platform reflected the influence of the antislavery constitutionalists, stating that "it is both the right and the imperative duty of Congress" to prohibit slavery in the territories, and implying that slavery violated the Due Process Clause.[12] At the same time, other antislavery constitutionalists developed and refined constitutional arguments to address other issues of the day. Those issues included the pressing controversy over the rights of fugitive slaves and the relationship between local control, popular sovereignty, and slavery in the territories. In all of these debates, antislavery constitutionalists claimed that their policy arguments were also a matter of constitutional law.

The argument that the pre-Reconstruction Constitution prohibited slavery may sound strange to the twenty-first-century observer. Nonetheless, from the beginning of the antislavery movement, activists struggled

[11] Sewell, *Ballots for Freedom*, 57–63; Foner, *Free Soil*, 78. For an excellent, in-depth analysis of Frederick Douglass's antislavery constitutionalism, see Hoang Gia Phan, *Bonds of Citizenship: Law and the Labors of Emancipation* (New York: NYU Press, 2013).

[12] Foner, *Free Soil*, 80, 83; Republican Platform of 1856, www.ushistory.org/gop/convention_1856republicanplatform.htm.

with the question of whether the Constitution was a proslavery or antislavery document. Slavery had existed within the United States since well before the Founding Era. Many of the Framers of the Constitution, including James Madison, owned slaves.[13] Moreover, provisions of the Constitution, including the Fugitive Slave Clause, the Three-Fifths Clause, and the prohibition on banning the importation of slavery before 1805, protected the institution of slavery. Thus, noted abolitionist William Lloyd Garrison argued, in an influential and widely publicized speech, that the Constitution was so tainted by slavery that it represented a "covenant with Death" and an "agreement with Hell."[14]

The overwhelming evidence supports Garrison's view that the Constitution was a proslavery document. Nonetheless, it is also true there was a great paradox between the institution of slavery and the broad language of equality and human rights in the Declaration of Independence and the Preamble to the Constitution. Moreover, provisions of the Constitution, including the Article IV Privileges and Immunities Clause, the Fifth Amendment Due Process Clause, and other measures, protected fundamental human rights. Antislavery constitutionalists seized on this rights-protecting language, arguing that slavery was not only morally wrong, but also unconstitutional.[15] Although their arguments varied, three broad theories of human rights are discernible from the writings and speeches of antislavery constitutionalists. Antislavery constitutionalists argued that natural law had a legally binding force that superseded manmade law. The natural rights argument rested primarily on the Declaration of

---

[13] See Eric Foner, *Free Soil*, 86 (Republicans often referred to two opposite theories of the Constitution); Paul Finkelman, *Slavery and the Founders: Race and Liberty in the Age of Jefferson* (Armonk, NY: M. E. Sharp, 1996) (arguing that the original Constitution is a fundamentally proslavery document).

[14] William Lloyd Garrison, "The Constitution: A Covenant with Death and an Agreement with Hell," *Liberator* 12 (1842): 71, reprinted in Oliver Joseph Thatcher, *The Library of Original Sources* (New York and Chicago: University Research Extension, 1907), 97. See Michael Vorenberg, *Final Freedom: The Civil War, the Abolition of Slavery, and the Thirteenth Amendment* (New York: Cambridge University Press, 2001), 8.

[15] Notwithstanding their influence on the Reconstruction Congress, very little has been written about the antislavery constitutionalists. For a comprehensive history of early antislavery constitutionalism, see Wiecek, *Antislavery Constitutionalism*. See also Alexander Tsesis, "Antislavery Constitutionalism," in *Encyclopedia of the Supreme Court*, David A. Schultz, ed. (New York: Facts on File, 2005). For a discussion of the influence of antislavery constitutionalism on the Fourteenth Amendment, see Michael Kent Curtis, *No State Shall Abridge: The Fourteenth Amendment and the Bill of Rights* (Durham: Duke University Press, 1986), 42–56, and Richard L. Aynes, "On Misreading John Bingham and the Fourteenth Amendment," *Yale Law Journal* 103 (1993) (describing John Bingham's theory of Section 1).

Independence and the Preamble to the Constitution. Many antislavery constitutionalists argued that slavery was illegal because it violated the natural rights of man. Others made a more textually based argument that slavery violated the Article IV Guaranty and Privileges and Immunities Clauses and Due Process Clause of the Fifth Amendment. Finally, some antislavery constitutionalists advocated a broad egalitarian view of the Constitution, one in which neither race nor class would diminish one's individual rights.

Antislavery constitutionalists also argued in favor of rights for free blacks. The AASS constitution provided that free blacks should "according to their intellectual and moral worth, share an equality with the whites, of civil and religious privileges," and urged whites to "encourage their intellectual, moral and religious improvement, and ... remove public prejudice." The 1835 OASS convention's "Report on the Free Colored People of Ohio" found that "[t]he government under which we live was formed upon the broad and universal principles of equal and inalienable rights, principles which were proclaimed at the first formation, which were incorporated into our compact under which our own state claims a right of membership in the Union." The Report cited access to education, the right to free labor, the right to testify in court, and freedom of religion as fundamental human rights which were denied to free blacks.[16] While denying that they supported political rights (such as the right to vote) for free blacks, the OASS resolved, "But we do mean that instead of being under the unlimited control of a few irresponsible masters they shall receive the protection of the law, that they shall be employed as free laborers, fairly compensated and protected in their earnings, that they shall have secured to them the right to obtain secular and religious knowledge, and to worship God according to his word." Thus, the antislavery societies sought not only to end slavery, but also to establish fundamental human rights for free people.

Theodore Dwight Weld was one of the founding members of the OASS. Weld began his antislavery activism as a ministry student in Cincinnati, Ohio. In 1834, after transferring to Oberlin College in Ohio, Weld left his studies and became an agent for the AASS. In his capacity as an AASS agent, Weld is credited with recruiting James Birney, Harriet Beecher Stowe, and Henry Ward Beecher to abolitionism. He was an

---

[16] Proceedings of the Anti-Slavery Convention, held at Putnam, on the twenty-first, twenty-second, and twenty-third of April, 1835 at 36 (Beaumont and Wallace, Printers) (hereafter referred to as "OASS proceedings").

advisor to antislavery members of Congress, including John Quincy Adams and Thaddeus Stevens.[17] In April 1835, Weld and Birney attended the founding convention of the OASS in Putnam, Ohio. That same year, Weld published a treatise arguing that Congress had the power to abolish slavery in the DC territory and that the Constitution required it to do so. According to Weld, Congress's plenary power over the District of Columbia enabled it to abolish slavery in that territory. Weld cited the Northwest Ordinance, claiming that it proved that the American Revolution was animated by a strong antislavery, proliberty ideology. He claimed that the Ordinance was a precedent that proved that Congress had the power to abolish slavery in any territory, including the District of Columbia.[18]

James Birney was another of the founding members of the OASS and a chief proponent of an antislavery political party. A former slave owner from Kentucky, Birney moved to Cincinnati and began to operate an antislavery paper called *The Philanthropist*. Because he was a former slave owner who had served on the state legislatures in Kentucky and Alabama, Birney's views carried special weight. In 1837, Birney was elected executive secretary of the American Antislavery Society, shortly before it split between the followers of Garrison and the Liberty Party. Birney served as the Liberty Party presidential nominee in 1840 and 1844.[19] In his 1847 treatise, Birney invoked the Declaration of Independence to support his argument that slavery violates the "right to liberty that can never be alienated" by preventing the slave "from pursuing his happiness as he wished to do." According to Birney, slavery thus violated the rule that "governments were instituted among men to secure their rights, not to destroy them."[20]

When a mob attacked James Birney's printing press in 1836, the young lawyer Salmon P. Chase came to his defense. Soon Chase and Birney were working together. In a well-known case, Chase defended runaway slave

---

[17] "Theodore Dwight Weld," in *Britannica Biographies*, October 10, 2010, available at MAS Ultra – School Edition, Accession No. 32426453; see Foner, *Free Soil*, 109.

[18] OASS proceedings; Theodore Dwight Weld, "The Power of Congress over the District of Columbia," *The Antislavery Examiner No. 6*, reprinted from the *New York Evening Post*, with additions by the author, published by the *American Antislavery Society* (New York, 1838), vol. 5, p. 11.

[19] Wiecek, *Antislavery Constitutionalism*, 191–192; Foner, *Free Soil*, 74. Betty Fladeland, *James Gillespie Birney, Slaveholder to Abolitionist* (Ithaca: Cornell University Press, 1955), 188, 227.

[20] James G. Birney, "Can Congress, Under the Constitution, Abolish Slavery in the States?," *The Albany Patriot*, May 12, 19, 20, 22, 1847.

Matilda and argued that the federal Fugitive Slave Act was unconstitutional. Chase also represented a client accused of the 1793 Fugitive Slave Act before the US Supreme Court. In his brief, Chase claimed that "slaveholding is contrary to natural law and justice" and argued that the Fifth Amendment Due Process Clause prevented Congress from enacting any legislation in favor of slavery.[21] He joined the Liberty Party in 1841, and by 1844 had become one of its leaders. Chase served twice as US senator, and twice as governor of the state of Ohio, and repeatedly contemplated running for president. President Abraham Lincoln appointed Chase first as Secretary of the Treasury and then Chief Justice of the US Supreme Court. Throughout his career prior to the Civil War, Chase championed an antislavery vision of the Constitution. Chase was successful at convincing the Republican Party to adopt his view in the 1856 and 1860 platforms.[22]

Perhaps the most prolific writer of the four Ohioans was the journalist Joel Tiffany. Tiffany was a lawyer who grew up in the "abolitionist hotbed" of Lorain County, Ohio, and later worked as a reporter for the New York Supreme Court. In 1849, Joel Tiffany published his *Treatise on the Unconstitutionality of Slavery*. Tiffany said that the argument that the Constitution guarantees slavery is "absurd and ridiculous." Said Tiffany, "[H]ere we affirm, and will maintain, that the Constitution of the United States contains no guaranty in favor of slavery, and makes no compromise with it whatsoever." Tiffany claimed that the Constitution is "intended to *withhold* all countenance and support of that institution."[23]

Like Weld, Tiffany argued that Congress had the power to end slavery, at least in the federal territories. According to Tiffany, the federal government had the duty to enforce the privileges of the writ of habeas corpus, and protect the rights of citizens, by abolishing the institution of slavery. Tiffany seized on Justice Story's statement in the case of *Prigg v. Pennsylvania*, upholding the constitutionality of the 1793 Fugitive Slave Act. In his *Prigg* opinion, Story held that the existence of a right implied congressional

[21] Foner, *Free Soil*, 74–77; Salmon P. Chase, An Argument for the Defendant, Submitted to the Supreme Court of the United States, as the December Term, 1846: In the Case of Wharton Jones vs. John Vanzandt 89, 101 (1847).

[22] Ibid. at 75; Republican Platform of 1856, www.ushistory.org/gop/convention_1856 republicanplatform.htm; Republican Party Platform of 1860, www.presidency.ucsb .edu/ws/?pid=29620.

[23] Joel Tiffany, *A Treatise on the Unconstitutionality of Slavery, Together with the Powers and Duties of the Federal Government in Relation to That Subject* (Cleveland: D. J. Calyerk, 1849), 8–9.

authority to enforce it.[24] While Tiffany understandably hated *Prigg*, he relied on the ruling to argue that Congress had the power to enforce the Privileges and Immunities Clause against the institution of slavery. Tiffany explained that "taking the rules adopted by the Supreme Court of the United States, for construing that instrument to be correct (and who can show that they are not correct?), the Federal Government has ample power to enforce those guarantees in every state of the Union."[25]

Thus, antislavery constitutionalists championed a broad vision of congressional power to eliminate slavery. The question of whether Congress had the power to abolish slavery remained a potent political issue. From Theodore Dwight Weld to Joel Tiffany, antislavery constitutionalists articulated a broad theory of congressional power that was eventually adopted by the Reconstruction Congress. Another influential treatise claiming congressional power over slavery was William Goodell's *Views of American Constitutional Law, in Its Bearing upon American Slavery*. In his treatise, Goodell also insisted that the entire Constitution was profoundly antislavery. Goodell rejected the argument that the Constitution represented a compromise between pro- and antislavery forces. In his view, "To represent, as do others, that the Constitution is partly in favor of liberty, and partly in favor of slavery, is to represent that it is a house divided against itself which cannot stand."[26] Pointing out that the Preamble to the Constitution states as its purpose securing the blessings of liberty, Goodell maintained that "*Liberty cannot be secure in a country where there is slavery.*" Goodell agreed that the Preamble to the

[24] Ibid., 99. In *Prigg v. Pennsylvania*, the Court ruled on the constitutionality of the 1793 Fugitive Slave Act, which required state officials to cooperate in returning fugitive slaves. The case arose when Pennsylvania officials challenged the act, arguing that it violated the Personal Liberty Act. Joel Tiffany rejected the Court's ruling in *Prigg*, saying, "If the position of the Supreme Court be correct, then the writ of Habeas Corpus is suspended in any and all of States of this Union at the pleasure of a slave claimant." Ibid., 74. However, he also cited the *Prigg* ruling in support of congressional power to enact antislavery measures. According to Tiffany, the federal government has the duty to enforce the privileges of the writ of habeas corpus, and protect the rights of citizens, by abolishing the institution of slavery. Ibid., 99.

[25] Ibid., 138–141.

[26] William Goodell, *Views of American Constitutional Law, in Its Bearing upon American Slavery* (Utica, NY: Jackson & Chaplain, 1844), 10. William Goodell was the editor of the *Radical Abolitionist*, a member of the New York Antislavery Society, and the most prominent advocate of Congress's power to abolish slavery in the existing states. Sewell, *Ballots for Freedom*, 95. Goodell's treatise was circulated widely with more than 13,000 copies sold in 1844 and a second edition published in 1845. The treatise introduced the "principal ideas of the radical constitutionalists." Phan, *Bonds of Citizenship*, 122.

but why?

Constitution *required* the overthrow of slavery. According to Goodell, the Necessary and Proper Clause of Article I authorized Congress to enforce the Preamble by legislating to end slavery. Like Tiffany, Goodell drew on the broad test for congressional power in the Supreme Court's ruling in *Prigg*. Said Goodell, "Judge Story wields this power of the Federal Government in favor of SLAVERY and consequently against LIBERTY; – we would wield *the same* federal power in favor of LIBERTY and consequently against SLAVERY."[27] Thus, the antislavery constitutionalists tried to convince members of Congress to abolish slavery in the District of Columbia. During the Civil War, Ashley chaired the House Committee on the Territories when Congress finally accomplished this task.

Many antislavery constitutionalists argued that slavery violated natural law. They rooted their natural law arguments in the Declaration of Independence and the Preamble to the Constitution. Tiffany started with the Declaration of Independence's guarantee that "all men are possessed of the same natural rights, secured by the same natural guarantys." He argued that the Declaration was legally enforceable because representatives of the thirteen colonies, elected by the people, had adopted it. Tiffany explained, "It is our theory, that all government power emanates from the people, is delegated to be used for the protection of natural and inalienable right of men ... [and] predicated ... upon the equal, common rights of man." According to Tiffany, governments lack the power to enslave people because "they can have no rightful power, not delegated to them by the people: and the *people* can delegate to them no power which they, as individuals, do not possess." This is so because "the law of nature – *natural justice*, is superior in obligation to every other law."[28] Under this broad natural law approach, slavery could not be legal anywhere, including in the states.

Theodore Dwight Weld also drew on the Declaration of Independence and the Preamble to the Constitution. He explained, "In the recognition of slaves as persons, the United States' constitution caught the mantle of the glorious Declaration, and most worthily wears it. It recognizes all human beings as 'men' persons and thus as equals." Weld claimed that the Preamble of the Constitution "declares it to be a fundamental object of the organization of government to ESTABLISH JUSTICE." He argued that Congress had the power to enforce the preamble by abolishing slavery. "To abolish slavery, is to take from no rightful owner his

---

[27] Goodell, *Views*, 85, 112–113. [28] Tiffany, *Treatise*, 26, 29, 30, 36.

property; but to *establish justice* between two parties." Thus, according to
Weld, the Preamble not only contained an antislavery mandate, but also
empowered Congress to enforce that mandate. William Goodell was
another who relied on the Declaration and the Preamble to support
his thesis that the Constitution was an antislavery document. Goodell
pointed to the Preamble's promise to "form a more perfect union,"
"establish justice," and "ensure the blessings of liberty." According to
Goodell, the Preamble's promises are antagonistic to the institution of
slavery. Thus, said Goodell, proper constitutional interpretation must
pronounce judgment in favor of liberty and against slavery.[29]

Some antislavery constitutionalists argued that slavery was forbidden
by the Guaranty Clause of Article IV, which obligates the United States to
guarantee to each state a republican form of government.[30] For example,
Joel Tiffany argued that a government that authorizes slavery is not a
republic. According to Tiffany, the Clause protects individual rights – it is
a guarantee to individuals that their state governments shall be republics.
"No, it was not the *state*, but the *individual* crushed, and overwhelmed by
an insolent, and tyrannical majority, that needed such a guaranty; and to
him, as a citizen of the United States, whether in the majority or minority,
is that guaranty given, to secure him, not only from *individual*, but also
from *governmental* oppression." Tiffany called the Guaranty Clause a
"bulwark of liberty, which ensures that state governments be those of free
citizens, not slaves. "And if there be a single citizen who is, or has been
robbed of full and ample protection in the enjoyment of his natural and
inherent rights, by the authority, or permission of the State in which he
lives, this solemn guaranty has been violated." Thus, Tiffany argued that
the Guaranty Clause required the federal government to protect individual rights. Goodell also cited the Guaranty Clause of Article IV, arguing
that slavery is antithetical to a republic. "Whether therefore, we define a
republic by its principles, its usages, its protection of human rights, or its
sovereignty of the People, or of a majority of them, the slave States can
not be called *republics*." The importance of this argument is reflected in
the name of the political party formed by antislavery constitutionalists
and their allies in 1856: the Republican Party. It provided a constitutional
basis for the Republicans' belief that "the most cherished values of the

---

[29] Goodell, *Views*, 43, 44, 40–41.
[30] U.S. Constitution, Art. IV, §4. ("The United States shall guarantee to every state in this
Union a republican Form of Government.")

free labor outlook – economic development, social mobility, and political democracy – all appeared to be violated in the south."[31]

Antislavery constitutionalists also invoked the civic republican concept of citizenship and articulated a broad theory of the rights of citizenship. Many claimed that free blacks were citizens, entitled to the protection of the federal government by their allegiance to that government. They maintained that the Article IV Privileges and Immunities Clause prohibited states from violating the rights of citizenship. In their view, the rights of citizenship were extremely broad, including the rights to life, liberty, and property, but also the fundamental rights of free persons.

The most prominent advocates of citizenship rights were journalists Lysander Spooner and Joel Tiffany. A lifelong resident of Boston, Massachusetts, Spooner published a treatise entitled *The Unconstitutionality of Slavery* in 1845. Spooner argued that if states were to abolish slavery, then slaves would immediately become US citizens. He continued, "[I]f they would become citizens then, they are equally citizens now – else it would follow that the State governments had had an arbitrary power of making citizens of the United States." Spooner championed the concept of full and equal national citizenship, which entitled each citizen to the protection of the law and informed the applicability of the Privileges and Immunities Clause of Article IV.[32] To Spooner, a slave became a citizen when he was freed.

Joel Tiffany went even further than Spooner, articulating the most comprehensive theory of citizenship rights. According to Tiffany, all persons born within the United States, including slaves, were US citizens and thus are entitled to the protection of the US government. "As citizens of the United States, we stand mutually pledged to each other, to see that all the rights, privileges, and immunities, granted by the constitution of the United States, are extended to all, if need be, by the force of the whole Union." The federal government was formed to protect the rights of its citizens, including the rights in the Bill of Rights and the right to habeas corpus. "What is it, then, to be a citizen of the United States? It is to be invested with a title to life, liberty, and the pursuit of happiness, and to be protected in the enjoyment thereof, by the guaranty of twenty millions of

---

[31] Tiffany, *Treatise*, 107, 110, 114; Goodell, *Views*, 57; Foner, *Free Soil*, 40.
[32] See Wiecek, *Antislavery Constitutionalism*, 256–257; Randy E. Barnett, "Whence Comes Section One? The Abolitionist Origins of the Fourteenth Amendment," *Journal of Legal Analysis* 3 (2011): 165, 203; Lysander Spooner, *The Unconstitutionality of Slavery* (Boston: B. Marsh, 1845), 94.

people." Tiffany thus claimed that all slaves born within the United States were citizens, deprived of their rights as citizens by the institution of slavery.[33] This argument was by far the most expansive description of the citizenship rights, because Tiffany expressly included slaves among those entitled the protections due to citizens.

A corollary to the citizenship argument was the claim that slaves were entitled to the protection of the federal government. Using the language of civic republicanism, Theodore Weld linked the government's obligation to protect those, including slaves, who show allegiance to the government by obeying the law. "Is the government of the United States unable to grant *protection* where it exacts *allegiance?* It is an axiom of the civilized world, and a maxim even with savages, that allegiance and protection are reciprocal and correlative ... *Protection is the* CONSTITUTIONAL RIGHT *of every human being under the exclusive legislation of Congress who has not forfeited it by crime.*"[34] Thus, Weld drew on the themes of protection and equality when arguing in favor of Congress's power to abolish slavery in a federal territory. As had his colleagues in the OASS, Weld drew on a strong vision of rights protected by the Constitution to argue against the constitutionality of slavery.

James Birney agreed with Weld that Congress could abolish slavery in exchange for slaves' allegiance and willingness to obey the law. He claimed that the slaves' duty to obey the law entitled them to protection and maintained that "without this protection – this security – we have no right to try him for violation of the laws of the country which deprives him of both."[35] According to Birney, to be a citizen of the United States is to be like a Roman citizen, entitled to the equal protection of the government. This argument gained strength after freed slaves proved their loyalty and commitment to the Union during the Civil War. Members of the Reconstruction Congress often cited this argument during the debate over the 1866 Civil Rights Act.

Many antislavery constitutionalists argued that slavery violated the Due Process Clause of the Fifth Amendment. Theodore Weld responded to the proslavery arguments that abolishing slavery would amount to a deprivation of property without due process of law, or a taking without just compensation. Weld denied that the slaveholder had any property interest in his slaves. According to Weld, slaves were not property but persons, and slavery itself was a taking of private property from the

[33] Tiffany, *Treatise*, 57, 86, 56, 99.   [34] Weld, "The Power of Congress," 45.
[35] James G. Birney, *The Philanthropist*, January 13, 1837.

enslaved people. The premise of his argument was that slaves had a natural right to liberty and a property interest in the fruit of their labor, which could not be taken away without a ruling from a court of law. As James Birney asked rhetorically, "By what 'due process of law' is it, that two millions of 'persons' are deprived every year of the millions of dollars produced by their labor? By what due process of law is it that 56,000 'persons,' the annual increase in the slave population, are annually deprived of their liberty?" Birney conceded that the Due Process Clause was not intended to address slavery. Nevertheless, he claimed that the Clause embodied "principles which are at an entire enmity with the spirit and practice of slavery."[36]

Salmon Chase relied on the Due Process Clause to challenge the federal Fugitive Slave Act. He insisted that the Due Process Clause prohibited Congress from authorizing slavery in the federal territories. Thus, the Due Process Clause supported Chase's stance against slavery in the territories. This was consistent with the longstanding "federal consensus" that federal power over slavery would be limited. Others argued that the Due Process Clause prohibited slavery everywhere. Alvan Stewart claimed that Congress's power to enforce the Fifth Amendment Due Process Clause extended to abolishing slavery "in every state and territory in the Union."[37]

William Goodell also cited the Due Process Clause in his antislavery arguments. Goodell insisted that the spirit of the Constitution's protections of individual rights and liberties was antislavery. He explained that slavery is a system "in which all rights of its victims are trampled down and denied, and the liberties of all others made insecure." Acknowledging that those who adopted the Due Process Clause may not have expected that it would apply to slavery, Goodell insisted, "The question here is *not* what *they intended*, but what the *People have done*, by adopting that clause." According to Goodell, other provisions protecting individual rights, including First Amendment and the Fourth Amendment, were

---

[36] Weld, "Power of Congress," 42, 41. ("Who has a better right to the *product* than the producer?" "To the hands and arms, than he from whose shoulders they swing?" "Congress not only impairs but annihilates the right of private property, while it withholds from the slaves of the District their title to *themselves*."). James G. Birney, *The Philanthropist*, January 13, 1837.

[37] Wiecek, *Antislavery Constitutionalism*, 78; Alvan Stewart, "A Constitutional Argument on the Subject of Slavery," in *The Friend of Man* (Utica, 1937), vol. 2, 286, reprinted in Jacobus tenBroek, "Thirteenth Amendment to the Constitution of the United States: Consummation to Abolition and Key to the Fourteenth Amendment," *California Law Review* 39 (1951): 171, 282.

"provisions that are utterly at war, both in their letter and their spirit, with the usages that constitute slavery and that are requisite to sustain it." These provisions augmented Goodell's argument that the entire Constitution was an antislavery document.

Joel Tiffany also articulated an egalitarian vision of the Constitution. According to Tiffany, no class of people was excluded from we "the people," so that all persons are entitled to their rights as citizens, regardless of their race. Thus he concluded, "The government belonged to no class of citizens; it was the property of all, and designed for the equal protection of all, individually and collectively." Tiffany stressed the lack of racial distinction in the Constitution. "The people of the United States" ordained and established the Constitution, "not by the States, not by the white people, or black people, not by the rich people, or poor people; not by the voting or non-voting people . . . but expressly, and emphatically by *all*, who, in the common acceptation of the term, might be denominated *the people* of the United States."[38] Thus, well before the adoption of the Equal Protection Clause of the Fourteenth Amendment, Tiffany linked equal protection to the structure of the government and championed it as a fundamental right.

Similarly, Lysander Spooner claimed that the Preamble referred to "all the people then permanently inhabiting the United States" because it did not distinguish between types of people. "It does not declare . . . 'we, the *white* people,' or 'we, the *free* people.'" Spooner concluded that the invocation of "we the people" in the Preamble "is equivalent to a declaration that those who actually participated in its adoption, acted in behalf of others, as well as for themselves."[39] To Spooner, the Preamble established that all the rights protecting provisions of the Constitution applied to all people in the United States, regardless of their race.

Other antislavery constitutionalists also claimed that the Constitution was an anticlass, anticaste document. They argued that the lack of race-based distinctions in the Constitution precluded governments from making race-based distinctions. Pointing out that "[n]o distinction of *color*, of *race*, or *parentage*, is specified in the Constitution," William Goodell concluded, "Thus especially certain is it that the 'SPIRIT OF THE CONSTITUTION' is the spirit of human equality, directly and specifically hostile for the spirit of caste, especially to a caste founded on the circumstance of *color*, of *blood*, of *race*, or of *descent*." Goodell insisted that if

[38] Tiffany, *Treatise*, 91, 86, 89.   [39] Spooner, *Unconstitutionality*, 90–91.

the Constitution guaranteed slavery, it would include the word "white" and limit rights to white persons. That the Constitution did not do so belies the argument that the *same* "spirit of the Constitution" has "guaranteed" the "perpetual degradation and chattelhood of the colored man." No, said Goodell, the whole structure and organizing frame of the Constitution agrees that it establishes a *free* government, "founded on the supremacy of THE PEOPLE, the exclusion of MONOPOLIES, the annihilation of PRIVILEGED ORDERS, and the absence of CASTE."[40] Here, Goodell advocates for economic equality as well as equality of legal rights.

Goodell went even further with his anticaste argument, also invoking Article I, Section 10, which prohibits states from granting titles of nobility. According to Goodell, slave owners obtain the status of nobility by virtue of the laws that authorize them to own slaves. "Like other political institutions of a similar character, it is wielded for the exclusive benefits of the *privileged caste* at the expense of *all others*. It operates to withdraw political power from the mass of the people, the laboring population, and confer it upon a select few, which is the very description or definition of aristocracy, or government of *nobles*." Significantly, the title of nobility clause expressly limited the power of *state* governments. Thus, Goodell maintained, slavery was therefore unconstitutional in any state. This radical position went well beyond that of his other colleagues, who focused primarily on slavery in the federally controlled territories. Eventually, Goodell refused to support the Republican Party, saying that he could not support a party that recognized the constitutionality of slavery anywhere in the Union.[41]

Of course, the antislavery constitutionalists needed to respond to the argument articulated by both the abolitionists and the proslavery forces – that the Constitution was really a proslavery document. For example, antislavery constitutionalist Lysander Spooner engaged in a well-publicized debate with Garrison's ally, Wendell Phillips. Phillips insisted that Spooner was turning a blind eye to the real, proslavery nature of the Constitution. Phillips based his arguments primarily on Madison's notes from the constitutional convention, which described the compromises between representatives from slave and free states.[42] For textual support,

[40] Goodell, *Views*, 87–88.
[41] Goodell, *Views*, 72; Foner, *Free Soil*, 302. Instead, Goodell formed his own party, the Radical Abolition Party. Sewell, *Ballots for Freedom*, 287.
[42] Wendell Phillips, *A Review of Lysander Spooner's Essay on the Unconstitutionality of Slavery* (Boston: Andrew Prentiss, 1847); Wendell Phillips, *The Constitution:*

Phillips and others who argued that the Constitution was a proslavery document relied on the Fugitive Slave Clause and other measures protecting the institution of slavery. They also raised the undeniable fact that many of the Constitution's framers owned slaves and thus had an interest in protecting slavery.

Some antislavery constitutionalists insisted to the contrary, that the Framers were not in favor of slavery, but hoped that it would die out. Antislavery constitutionalists often claimed that the Framers of the Constitution opposed slavery. This argument was included in the Republican Party platforms of 1856 and 1860. It was a bedrock principal of Salmon Chase's antislavery constitutionalism. For proof of this proposition, Chase pointed out that the Framers had taken care to omit the word "slavery" from the original Constitution. Chase pointed out that the proclamations of liberty in the Northwest Ordinance and the Declaration of independence anteceded the Constitution and had inspired the Framers. Theodore Dwight Weld also cited the Ordinance as proof that the founders of the nation were opposed to slavery. According to Weld, it was "the universal expectation that the moral influence of Congress, of state legislatures[,] ... of ministers of religion, and of the public sentiment widely embodied in abolition societies, would be exerted against slavery."[43]

Similarly, Joel Tiffany insisted that the Framers intended to establish a government that would uphold the principles of the American Revolution, "instituted for the *protection* of the natural and inalienable rights of man." According to Tiffany, "At the time of the framing and adoption of the Constitution, few, if indeed any, could be found to defend slavery, either in principle or in practice. As an institution public sentiment was against it." As evidence of this, Tiffany cited the fact that Congress unanimously approved the antislavery Northwest Ordinance shortly after the Constitution's ratification. According to Tiffany, the Constitution merely allowed time for states to abolish slavery, time that was running out. The southern states had violated the understanding with their attempts to expand slavery and suppress any dissent to that expansion.[44]

A Proslavery Compact, or Selections from the Madison Papers (New York: American Anti-Slavery Society, 1844); See Barnett, "Whence Comes Section One?," 203.

[43] See Foner, *Free Soil*, 75; Salmon Chase, "Liberty Party Address," in J. W. Schuckers, *The Life and Public Services of Salmon Portland Chase* (New York: D. Appleton, 1874), 48–49; Weld, "Power of Congress," 39.

[44] Tiffany, *Treatise*, 10, 17, 20, 21, 22. ("They have denied to the Freemen of the North the right of petition; and there is no wrong, insult or injury they have not practiced upon the advocates of freedom.")

Other antislavery constitutionalists acknowledged that many of the Framers were proslavery, but insisted that Framers' intent was irrelevant to interpreting the Constitution. They argued that only the text of the Constitution, and not the intent of the Framers, should determine constitutional meaning. For example, Gerrit Smith maintained that the meaning of the Constitution "is to be gathered from the words of the Constitution, and not from the words of its framers, for it is the text of the Constitution, and not the talk of the Convention, that the people adopted." Similarly, William Goodell insisted that courts are precluded from considering the intent of the Framers when interpreting the Constitution. As for the alleged compact, he asked rhetorically, "Are we to be bound by their secret and *unrighteous purposes*, rather than by the *righteous words they were obliged to employ*, in order to make their document acceptable to the People?" According to Goodell, the Court had no authority to presume the intent of the Framers, but could only "*collect* them from the words, taken in their *ordinary import*."[45]

Goodell described his method of constitutional interpretation in detail. Goodell claimed that there were only two proper methods of interpretation, "strict construction" and following the "spirit" of the Constitution. "Strict construction" limited the interpreter to considering the "*words* of the instrument, the *literal words*, according to their commonly received and authorized *import*." Under this method, "*nothing but* the words, shall be allowed to tell us the meaning of the Constitution." The other proper method was to rely on the "spirit" of the Constitution. Neither method allowed for consideration of extraneous evidence, including the intent of the Framers. Under either method, claimed Goodell, it was clear that slavery was unconstitutional. If one is to interpret the Constitution according to its spirit, Goodell claimed, "The spirit of the paragraph is, if possible, still more emphatically and unmistakably belligerent in its aspect, against slavery and imperative in its demands for its overthrow."[46]

---

[45] Gerrit Smith, Speech in opposition to the Kansas Nebraska Act, Cong. Globe, 33rd Cong., 1st Sess., Appendix 520 (April 6, 1854). Smith appealed to the democratic legitimacy of the Constitution, pointing out that only the document itself had been approved by the people. See also Byron Paine, *Unconstitutionality of the Fugitive Slave Act: Argument of Byron Paine, Esq. and Opinion of Hon. A. D. Smith, Associate Justice of the Supreme Court of the State of Wisconsin* (Milwaukee: Free Democrat Office, 1854), 8 (citing Spooner for the proposition that "the intention of an instrument is to be gathered from its words"); Goodell, *Views*, 27, 123–124.

[46] Goodell, *Views*, 21, 81, 84.

Lysander Spooner also argued that conversations between Framers were irrelevant to determining the meaning of the Constitution. What mattered was that the Constitution itself contained not a single mention of the institution of slavery. Spooner maintained that the text of the Constitution should be interpreted according to its meaning at the time of the enactment, and the "original meaning of the Constitution itself" is binding regardless of the intent of the Framers. Spooner explained, "It is not the intentions men actually had, but the intentions they constitutionally expressed; they make up the Constitution." Moreover, Spooner maintained, "no intention, in violation of natural justice and natural right ... can be ascribed to the Constitution, in violation of natural justice and natural right."[47] The choice of the Framers to avoid the word "slavery" precluded their arguments that the document sanctioned slavery.

The fact that the Constitution did not mention the word "slave" was the central reason for textualist interpretation. The provisions that allegedly sanctioned slavery used other terms to refer to slaves. The importation of slaves clause referred to slaves as "such persons,"[48] the Three-Fifths Clause refers to slaves as "other persons," contrasted with "free persons,"[49] and the so-called Fugitive Slave Clause refers to "persons held to service or labor."[50] Noted black abolitionist Frederick Douglass pointed out that if a man from another country were to read the Constitution, he could not imagine that it applied to slaves. Salmon Chase used this textualist approach in his lawsuits challenging the constitutionality of the Fugitive Slave Act. Though his lawsuits were unsuccessful, his arguments were far from frivolous. To evaluate the strength of Chase's claims, it is important to understand that in the early nineteenth century, slaves were not the only workers who were "held to service or labor." Indentured servitude was common, as was the practice of multiyear apprenticeships in which the apprentice was bound to the same master regardless of the master's treatment of the apprentice.[51] Indentured servants and apprentices were bound to their employers by contracts, however unconscionable those contracts may have been. However, the laws of slave states prohibited slaves from entering into contracts, and therefore could not be bound by contract "to service or labor." The issue

---

[47] Barnett, "Whence Comes Section One?," 28–29; Spooner, *Unconstitutionality*, 117–118, 58–59, 218.
[48] U.S. Constitution, Art. I, §9, cl. 1.   [49] U.S. Constitution, Art. I, §2, cl. 3.
[50] U.S. Constitution, Art. IV, §2, cl. 3.
[51] Phan, *Bonds*, 3; Foner, *Free Soil*, 83; Steinfeld, *Free Labor*, 7.

of labor and workers' rights, underlying all debates over slavery, is explored in more detail in the following chapter.

Not all of these advocates agreed on every issue. The issue that most divided the antislavery constitutionalists was the question of whether slavery was unconstitutional everywhere (including in the existing states) or only in the federal territories. If slavery violated natural law, as many of them claimed, and if natural law was legally enforceable, then slavery was unconstitutional everywhere. This argument demanded the immediate of abolition throughout the country, including the southern states. For years, Alvan Stewart sought to convince the Liberty Party leaders that it should adopt the position that slavery was unconstitutional everywhere. Although many leaders agreed with Stewart, the party rank and file was not persuaded. Party members debated strategy – whether to merely advocate nonextension of slavery or to support the abolition of slavery in the states. They chose more moderate position, consistent with the federal consensus, that slavery was unconstitutional in federally controlled territories and that Congress had the power to abolish slavery in those territories. Thus the Liberty Party chose not to advocate for immediate abolition in the South, but instead insisted that the federal government should divorce itself from slavery.[52]

Radicals such as Goodell continued to insist that slavery was unconstitutional everywhere.[53] However, the moderate position was less threatening to southern states and thus more politically palatable. While they adopted their position for reasons of political expediency, it is also true that many activists believed that Congress lacked the power to restrict slavery in the states. The federal consensus was firmly entrenched in the national consciousness. Only the most radical activists believed that slavery could be abolished in the existing states. Neither Weld nor Birney went so far as to claim that Congress had power to abolish slavery in the existing states. According to Weld, although slavery did not exist under the common law, "the grand element of the United States Constitution," it could be created by positive law. Weld conceded that states could authorize slavery by statute. Weld's argument was directed exclusively to preventing the expansion of slavery within the territories. Moreover, those more moderate activists believed that slavery would die out if it could not expand.[54] This became the position of the Liberty, Free Soil, and Republican parties.

---

[52] Sewell, *Ballots for Freedom*, 91–93.   [53] Ibid., 91.
[54] Ibid., 91, 46, 282, 13; Wiecek, *Antislavery Constitutionalists*, 190; see Foner, *Free Soil*, 96.

The Supreme Court rejected all of the arguments of the antislavery constitutionalists in the *Dred Scott* decision. In *Dred Scott v. Sanford*, the Court ruled against a slave who claimed that he had been liberated when he traveled to the free state of Illinois and a portion of the Louisiana Territory that is now the state of Minnesota. Both the state and the territory were free as a result of the Missouri Compromise. The Court held that it lacked jurisdiction over the case because Dred Scott was not a citizen and could not be a citizen due to his African heritage.[55] Notwithstanding this jurisdictional ruling, Chief Justice Taney went on to hold that the Missouri Compromise itself was unconstitutional. In the Northwest Ordinance, Congress had purported to abolish slavery in the Louisiana Territory. The Court held that Congress lacked the power to do so because slaveholders had a constitutional right to own slaves. The *Dred Scott* ruling was a huge blow to all antislavery activists because it foreclosed federal action to abolish slavery. However, the antislavery constitutionalists eschewed court rulings that were inconsistent with their theories. They directed their arguments primarily toward the public sphere and the court of public opinion. In their speeches and writings, antislavery constitutionalists rejected the argument that courts were the primary interpreters of the law. They asserted their own authority to determine the meaning of the Constitution. They viewed the political bodies, including Congress, as an important potential source for the protection of rights. Thus, antislavery constitutionalists truly engaged in popular constitutionalism.

Antislavery constitutionalists sought to convince the public at large and their political representatives that slavery could be and must be abolished and that the Constitution not only allowed this to occur, but required it to happen. Antislavery constitutionalism strongly influenced members of the Reconstruction Congress, including James Ashley.[56] The antislavery constitutionalists developed theories of constitutional interpretation and a broad theory of the human rights that are protected by the document. During the congressional debates over Reconstruction measures, members of Congress, including Ashley, echoed the antislavery constitutionalists as

---

[55] *Dred Scott v. Sanford*, 60 U.S. (19 How.) 393, 399, 404, 407 (1857).

[56] See Curtis, *No State Shall Abridge*, 43 (arguing that Joel Tiffany's views were similar to those adopted by the 39th Congress); Wiecek, *Antislavery Constitutionalists*, 274 (pointing out that antislavery constitutionalists were "the first to introduce concepts of substantive due process, equal protection, paramount national citizenship and the privileges and immunities of citizenship").

they explained what they believed to be the constitutional rights of a free person, and enacted measures to protect those rights.

The Court's ruling in *Dred Scott* did not preclude antislavery activists from their antislavery constitutionalism. In 1857, Frederick Douglass, the most influential black leader among the abolitionists, gave a speech that illustrates this response and illuminates the political salience of antislavery constitutionalism just before the Civil War. Douglass was one of the last prominent activists to join the antislavery constitutionalists prior to the Civil War, but he played a significant role in raising the prominence of antislavery constitutionalist arguments. Douglass originally joined Garrison in his condemnation of the Constitution. He caused a sensation when he changed his mind and adopted the position that slavery was unconstitutional. As an antislavery constitutionalist, Douglass gave several prominent speeches that fired up the debates over slavery, the Constitution, and political strategy among abolitionists. In his 1857 speech condemning the Supreme Court's decision in *Dred Scott*, Douglass presented an unapologetic response to the Court's ruling.[57]

In his speech, Douglass argued that the Preamble, the Due Process Clause, the Fourth Amendment, and the prohibition on bills of attainder all "strike at the root of slavery" and, if "faithfully carried out, would put an end to slavery in every State in the American Union." Douglass acknowledged the influence of Spooner and Goodell when he invoked the Preamble and the Declaration of Independence to support his view that "we the people" referred to "not we, the white people – not we, the citizens or the legal voters – not we, the privileged class and excluding all other classes, but we the people ... the men and women, the human inhabitants of the Unites States." He concluded, "The Constitution, as well as the Declaration of Independence, and the sentiments of the founders of the Republic, give us a platform broad enough, and strong enough, to support the most comprehensive plans for the freedom and elevation of all the people of this country, without regard to color, class, or clime."[58]

---

[57] See Frederick Douglass, "Comments on Gerrit Smith's Address," *The North Star*, March 30, 1849; Frederick Douglass, "A Change of Opinion Announced," *The North Star*, May 15, 1851, reprinted in *The Liberator*, May 23, 1851; Frederick Douglass, Speech on the Dred Scott Decision, delivered in New York, on the occasion of the Anniversary of the American Abolition Society, May, 1857, in Frederick Douglass, *Two Speeches* (New York, 1857).

[58] Frederick Douglass, Speech on the Dred Scott Decision, delivered in New York, on the Occasion of the Anniversary of the American Abolition Society, May, 1857, in Douglass, *Two Speeches*, 40, 41. 45.

42   *The Forgotten Emancipator*

In this speech, Douglass applied a textualist approach to Justice Taney's interpretation of the Constitution as a proslavery document. Douglass pointed out, "Neither in the preamble nor in the body of the Constitution is there a single mention of the term slaves or slaveholder." Indeed, he insisted, "a plain and common sense meaning" of the text lacked any guarantee for slavery. He condemned Taney's reliance on the intent of the Framers as wrongly "assuming that the written Constitution is meant to be interpreted in light of a secret and unwritten understanding." Moreover, Douglass insisted that the leading religions were antislavery at the time of the Framing, and the prevailing sentiment was antislavery. Thus, he denounced the *Dred Scott* decision as "a most scandalous and devilish perversion of the Constitution."[59]

Over time it became evident that the Liberty Party, with its outspoken stance on slavery and in favor of the rights of free blacks, was simply too extreme to garner much support. In the 1844 presidential election, Liberty Party candidate James Birney garnered only 65,508 votes. In 1848, the most prominent Barnburner Democrats decided to leave their party and form a new antislavery party, the Free Soil Party. Some members of the Liberty Party, including Salmon Chase, joined the new Free Soil Party. Like the Liberty Party platform, the Free Soil Party platform was written primarily by Salmon Chase. The Free Soil platform largely echoed that of the Liberty Party, but lacked a plank advocating for the rights of free blacks. This omission was due to the fact that Freesoilers could not agree on a position. The party included some members who were strong supporters of black rights, but also those who opposed them. The goal of the Free Soil platform was to unify the antislavery elements in all parties, in order to achieve electoral success, so they were more willing to compromise than their Liberty Party predecessors. The Free Soil Party also adopted the more moderate position on the constitutionality of slavery. They adopted the slogan "Freedom National," arguing that the presumption would be in favor of freedom and that only state law (not federal law) could authorize slavery.[60]

Nonetheless, Frederick Douglass's speech reflects the fact that by 1857, the arguments of the antislavery constitutionalists had become mainstream, central to the debate over slavery. Moreover, Douglass's speech reflects the unrepentant nature of the antislavery activists. "Freedom

---

[59] Douglass, *Two Speeches*, 40, 41, 43.
[60] Sewell, *Ballots*, 107, 110, 137–139, 156; Eric Foner, *Politics and Ideology in the Age of the Civil War* (New York: Oxford University Press, 1980), 80, 87, 92.

national" was their response to *Dred Scott,* a cause that became the motto for the Republican Party. Years later, Douglass called James Ashley "among the foremost of the brilliant galaxy of statesmen who reconstructed the Union on the basis of liberty," who "puts the rights of humanity above every other right and, as inseparably connected with the rights of all races of men."[61] James Ashley came of age listening to and admiring what he called "the old antislavery guard," that is, the antislavery constitutionalists. Eventually, Ashley was a leader in the fight to incorporate their theories into constitutional law.

[61] Foner, *Free Soil,* 97; *Souvenir,* 3, 6.

Just b/c slaves + Northern laborers are both working, are both causes aligned in antebellum America?

think of the difference in labor performed

— Is the connection with slavery an appeal to morality?

It left ingenuous for labor to adopt the slavery cause b/c it wasn't the central concern

3

Free Labor and Wage Slavery

The Labor and Antislavery Movements

> I am opposed to all forms of ownership of men, whether by the state, by corporations, or by individuals ... If I must be a slave, I would prefer to be the slave of one man, rather than a slave of a soulless corporation, or the slave of a state.[1]

The above remarks are from a stump speech that James Ashley delivered in Montpelier, Ohio, in 1856. At first glance, they may seem surprising. Why would Ashley talk about any form of slavery other than southern chattel slavery? What does it mean to be a "slave of a soulless corporation?" Ashley's language seems at first to be foreign to the antislavery effort. On the other hand, one can see the influence of the labor movement on Ashley's broad definition of slavery in this speech, an influence that enriched his vision of free labor. According to historian Eric Foner, "Reconstruction was a national phenomenon – the north was reconstructed as well as the south. The center of Reconstruction was the transformation of labor relations."[2] Slaves were workers, and the southern system of chattel slavery entailed the uncompensated exploitation of labor. Thus, it is not surprising that activists in the northern labor movement used the imagery of slavery to describe their own working conditions, and that many of them became involved with the antislavery

---

[1] James Ashley, Closing Portion of Stump Speech Delivered in the Grove near Montpelier, Williams County, Ohio, September, 1856, in *Duplicate Copy of the Souvenir from the Afro-American League of Tennessee to Hon. James M. Ashley of Ohio* (Benjamin Arnett, ed.) (Publishing House of the AME Church, Philadelphia 1894) (hereafter referred to as *Souvenir*), 601, 622.

[2] Eric Foner, *Politics and Ideology in the Age of the Civil War* (New York: Oxford University Press, 1980), 98.

44

effort. In turn, antislavery activists such as James Ashley invoked the language of the labor movement and advocated an expansive approach to the rights of workers. While historians have studied the ties between the labor and antislavery movements, until now legal scholars have largely overlooked those ties, and thus missed a central facet of the Reconstruction Era.[3] In fact, Reconstruction was a crucial point of transition for workers' rights throughout the United States. James Ashley and his allies in Congress understood this connection and advocated for the rights of all workers in the country. With the Thirteenth Amendment, they ended not only slavery but involuntary servitude, and they enacted measures to empower workers and give them rights. This chapter explores the labor roots of a positive right to free labor.

In 1848, many antislavery activists left the Liberty Party to form the Free Soil, Free Labor Party. They sought to reach out to white northern workers, whom they saw as a natural constituency in the antislavery effort and challenged the ties between workers and northern Democrats that had been established during the Jacksonian Era. The Free Soil Party achieved some success, considerably more than had the Liberty Party. In 1848, twelve Free Soilers were elected to Congress, including Ashley's mentor, Salmon Chase, who was elected to the US Senate. Eventually Free Soilers joined with antislavery Democrats (and former Whigs) to form the Republican Party. Ashley allied with the Free Soilers to form the Republican Party, but came from the populist, proworker wing of the Democratic Party. Antislavery activists often called free labor a fundamental right. For example, in 1935 the Ohio Antislavery Society promised that "instead of being under the unlimited control of a few irresponsible masters [freed slaves] shall ... be employed as free laborers, fairly compensated and protected in their earnings." James Birney and others argued that slaves were deprived of their labor without due process of law. William Goodell condemned slavery's negative impact on the "political power ... [of the] laboring population."[4] The Free Soil, Free Labor

---

[3] Notable exceptions include Lea S. VanderVelde, "The Labor Vision of the Thirteenth Amendment," *University of Pennsylvania Law Review* 138 (1989): 437; Avi Soifer, "Federal Protection, Paternalism, and the Virtually Forgotten Prohibition of Voluntary Peonage," *Columbia Law Review* 112 (2012): 1607; James Gray Pope, "Contract, Race, and Freedom of Labor in the Constitutional Law of 'Involuntary Servitude,'" *Yale Law Journal* 119 (2010): 1474.

[4] Richard H. Sewell, *Ballots for Freedom: Antislavery Politics in the United States 1837–1860* (New York: Oxford University Press, 1976), 168; Proceedings of the Anti-Slavery Convention, Held at Putnam, on the twenty-first, twenty-second, and twenty-third

Party proclaimed a doctrine of free labor to justify the end of slavery and improve the condition of northern workers. To understand more deeply the meaning of "free labor" in the antebellum era, one must examine the relationship between the antislavery activists and the nascent labor movement.

In the beginning of the nineteenth century, workers in the United States were largely not free. The most obvious example of unfree labor was chattel slavery. However, throughout the country, workers had little control over their lives. While colonial labor practices had varied from region to region, indentured servitude was common in colonial America. In the early days of the Republic, the practice of indentured servitude, "a specific condition identified with persons entering the colony bound to multiyear indentures," and apprenticeship lingered from the country's colonial days.[5] Many workers who immigrated to this country at the end of the eighteenth century were indentured servants. Between 1773 and 1776, 50 percent of English and Scottish immigrants were indentured servants, and from 1785 to 1804, 45 percent of German immigrants shared the same status. Indentured servitude carried over well into the nineteenth century. Servants were paid low wages, not taught a skill, and usually bound to their employers for periods of three to five years. Artifices and laborers were often bound to contracts that prohibited them from leaving their employers. Colonial statutes did not distinguish between slaves and servants, and neither did the Constitution's Fugitive Slave Clause.[6]

As Hong Gia-Phan points out, slavery is the "absent presence" in the Constitution, but indentured servitude is expressly mentioned in its text. The so-called Fugitive Slave Clause refers to workers "held to service or labor," a phrase that "originated in intercolonial efforts to prohibit the

of April, 1835 (Beaumont and Wallace, Printers); James G. Birney, *The Philanthropist*, January 13, 1837; William Goodell, *Views of American Constitutional Law, in Its Bearing upon American Slavery* (Utica, NY: Jackson & Chaplain, 1844).
[5] Robert J. Steinfeld, *The Invention of Free Labor: The Employment Relation in English and American Law and Culture, 1350–1870* (Chapel Hill: University of North Carolina Press, 1991), 7; VanderVelde, "Labor Vision," 441; Christopher L. Tomlins, *Law, Labor and Ideology in the Early American Republic* (New York: Cambridge University Press, 1993), 239, 242, 249, 254.
[6] Steinfeld, *Invention of Free Labor*, 11, 41, 34 102; the Fugitive Slave Clause provides that "No person held to service of labour in one state under the laws thereof, escaping into another, shall ... be discharged from such service or labour." U.S. Const. art. IV, §2, cl. 3. Antislavery constitutionalists argued that the clause applied not to slaves but to other indentured servants. See Chapter 2, supra.

absconding of white servants." The Three-Fifths Clause also refers to indentured servants, "those bound to service for a period of years" among those to be counted as whole persons. Slaves are "other persons" who would be counted as only three-fifths of a person. The distinction between indentured servants and slaves in the Three-Fifths Clause reflects the understanding that the immigrant who arrived as an indentured servant would eventually be assimilated as a "citizen," and thus "undersore[s] the framers' understanding of slavery as a peculiar form of labor bondage in a broader system of labor exploitation." Racial lines separated the two categories of unfree labor, as chattel slaves were virtually all of African descent.[7] The Constitution thus drew racialized distinctions to divide the working class in the United States. Slavery was different in kind from all other labor practices, including servitudes. Southern laws treated slaves as property, not persons. Slaves lived in unspeakably inhumane conditions and were denied the most basic of human rights. Nonetheless, fugitive slaves and indentured servants shared a commonality of interest in the ability to escape exploitative labor conditions.

The customary practice of indentured servitude was reflected in the law of labor in the early nineteenth century. At the beginning of the nineteenth century the law of employment relationships was still largely based in master/servant law that had its roots in the age of feudalism. The employer, or master, was the head of the household, his workers dependents with "status contracts." Rather than belonging to the worker, the worker's labor was considered a resource belonging to the community in which he lived. The master had the property right to the servant's labor, which enabled the master to dictate the conditions of employment.[8] Thus, many northern workers lacked control over their working lives because they were entirely subordinate to their employers. Through the early 1840s, even industrial workers were forced to sign year-long contracts that bound them to their employer. Northern workers did not suffer the degradation and violent exploitation of chattel slavery but they did lack autonomy and mobility. The most privileged workers on the continuum of unfree labor were apprentices, who entered into agreements with employers to work in exchange for learning a craft. Even apprentices were bound to employers for periods of up to seven years, and could be

---

[7] Hoang Gia Phan, *Bonds of Citizenship: Law and the Labors of Emancipation* (New York: NYU Press, 2013), 12 (founding law thus "establishes" one of the central categories through which "freedom" would be imagined, and racialized).

[8] Steinfeld, *Invention of Free Labor*, 16, 56, 62 (like feudal society), 67 (from medieval law).

prosecuted if they left before the term was over. In the early nineteenth century, then, workers were on a continuum of laborers, from most free to least free: hired servants, apprentices, indentured servants, and slaves.[9] The institution of slavery was easier to justify when so many workers were not fully free.

By midcentury, the practice of indentured servitude had fallen out of favor. Americans began to think of indentured servitude "as a form of involuntary rather than voluntary servitude and as essentially indistinguishable from slavery." At the beginning of the Civil War, indentured servitude was no longer allowed in most states. Instead, labor came to be viewed as a commodity that could be bought and sold. Proworker advocates claimed workers should have the liberty to choose their employers and to exercise control over the conditions of the employment relationship. The paradigm had shifted to one of free labor.[10] Antislavery and prolabor advocates had changed the fundamental expectations of workers, who chafed at the restrictions that had once seemed inevitable. The "free market" had replaced what radical reformer Cornelius Blatchley referred to as "ancient usurpation, tyranny, and conquest."[11] The transformation of the law of labor was due to a number of factors, including industrialization, the resultant transformation of work, and the democratic mobilization of the working class in Jacksonian democracy. Importantly, activists in the antislavery and labor movements facilitated the transformation by putting forth their doctrine of free labor. As workers involved themselves in politics, they helped to transform the law that governed their lives. Political engagement was central to the republican ideology that workers embraced, helping to define free labor.

The labor movement in the United States began in the late 1820s, as groups of tailors and weavers in New York City organized strikes to improve their working conditions. At the time, most workers were agricultural and artisanal, and most were self-employed. These men enjoyed considerable autonomy in their working lives, and they "provided the

---

[9] David Montgomery, *Citizen Worker: The Experience of Workers in the United States with Democracy and the Free Market during the Nineteenth Century* (New York: Cambridge University Press, 1993), 42 (discussing mill workers in Lowell, Massachusetts); Steinfeld, *Invention of Free Labor*, 41, 104.

[10] Steinfeld, *Invention of Free Labor*, 7, 8 (pointing out that indentured servitude disappeared by the 1830s), 87, 78–79 ("What makes a man human is his freedom from other men. Man's essence is freedom"), 15 (arguing that the modern idea of employment as contract "between juridical equals" is an invention of the nineteenth century).

[11] Ibid., 113; See Montgomery, *Citizen Worker*, 38.

meaningful point of reference for Jeffersonian republicans." However, conditions of work were changing dramatically. While in 1820, only one-third of US workers were employed by others, that percentage had increased to 50 percent by midcentury, and in eastern industrializing states, as many as three-fourths of workers were nonagricultural workers employed by others.[12] Early industrialization caused the increasing mechanization of work, and industrial jobs enticed workers to migrate from rural to urban areas. In the South, the invention of the cotton gin revived the institution of slavery by vastly increasing the capacity to process the cotton that was grown and picked by slaves. In the North, New England clothing mills provided factory jobs for workers who sometimes referred to themselves as "white slaves." These changes gave rise to the early labor movement, which, like the antislavery movement, sought to improve the conditions of workers. In the 1830s, antislavery activists "vigorously disseminated ... the ideology of free labor ... throughout the country as part of an emotional campaign against slavery."[13] In the 1840s and 1850s, northern labor activists sought to further disseminate this ideology as part of their campaign for reforms to improve the lives of free workers.

Free northern workers who benefited from the decline of indentured servitude suffered other perils in the nineteenth-century workplace. Industrialization brought about new workplace rules that limited the workers' autonomy and depersonalized the worker's relationship with his or her employer. The nineteenth-century employment relationship failed to comport with the "liberal illusion" of formal legal equality. Instead, the workplace was structured on inequality. Though employers formally no longer held a property interest in the labor of their employees, they maintained wide latitude to direct and control the labor that the worker delivered. Vestiges of master/servant doctrine helped to underpin workplace discipline and legitimate supervisory prerogative, creating a "contradictory co-existence of freedom and subordination" in the law of employment.[14] Thus, employment contracts reinforced asymmetries of power between the worker and his or her employer. Moreover, as industrial wage earners, many workers felt as if their work was being degraded

---

[12] Foner, *Politics and Ideology*, 59–60; Sean Wilentz, *Chants Democratic: New York City and the Rise of the American Working Class, 1788–1850* (New York: Oxford University Press, 1984), 167, 169; Tomlins, *Law, Labor and Ideology*, 259.

[13] David Montgomery, *Beyond Equality: Labor and the Radical Republicans 1862–1872* (Urbana and Chicago: University of Illinois Press, 1967), 4; Steinfeld, *Invention of Free Labor*, 177.

[14] Montgomery, *Citizen Worker*, 55; Tomlins, *Law, Labor and Ideology*, 227–228.

and debased. They often expressed concern about not being treated with dignity. Thus the changes in labor conditions in the first half of the nineteenth century were problematic for workers. It is true that servants were no longer legally bound to their masters through indentures, but employers, not workers, still controlled the workplace.[15] Longing for autonomy and control over their lives, many US workers turned to the nascent labor movement.

Another factor that contributed to the early US labor movement was immigration. The transformation from a paradigm based on the feudal model of servitude to one of free labor occurred not only in the United States, but throughout the western world. As Foner urges, "We must place the Civil War in the context of the general abolition of unfree labor systems in the nineteenth century, from slavery in the western hemisphere, to serfdom in Russia and robot in the Austrian Empire." The US labor movement was influenced by world events and ideologies brought from across the globe. The end of slavery in the United States was part of a worldwide movement toward free labor, which included the end of serfdom in Russia and failed workers' revolutions in Britain, Germany, and France.[16]

A wave of immigration swelled the ranks of northern workers from 1815 to 1865. About a third of these immigrants came from Ireland, fleeing the Irish potato famine. In the 1840s, almost half of US immigrants hailed from Ireland. The Irish immigrants settled primarily in East Coast cities such as New York and Boston.[17] Largely unskilled, they formed a strong base of support for the nascent labor movement, many influenced by the chartist working-class movement in Britain. After Ireland, Germany was the second largest source of nineteenth-century immigration. Many of the German immigrants moved to the Midwest, including the Western Reserve area of James Ashley's Ohio. The German immigrants were also highly supportive of the labor movement.[18] Some of the

---

[15] Tomlins, *Law, Labor and Ideology*, 261, 386, 390.

[16] Foner, *Politics and Ideology*, 22; VanderVelde, "Labor Vision," 476, pointing out that Charles Sumner read the Russian Czar's proclamation freeing the serfs during the debate over Freedman's Bills. Cong. Globe, 39th Cong., 1st Sess., 111 (1865); ibid., 471. Cong. Globe, 38th Cong., 1st Sess., 2955 (1864).

[17] Michael C. LeMay, *Transforming America: Perspectives on U.S. Immigration* (Santa Barbara: Praeger, 2013), 1: 158; Marta Mestrovic Deyrup and Maura Grace Harrington, *The Irish-American Experience in New Jersey and Metropolitan New York: Cultural Identity, Hybridity, and Commemoration* (Lanham: Lexington Books, 2014), 79.

[18] LeMay, *Transforming America*, 71, 35; Farley Grubb, *German Immigration and Servitude in America, 1709–1920* (New York: Routledge, 2013), 384; Alison Clark Efford,

British and German immigrants fled to the United States after their respective failed workers' revolutions in 1848, and those workers brought their radical ideology with them. These immigrant workers lent significant support and guidance to the US labor movement. Many of them, especially the German immigrants, engaged in the antislavery movement as well.[19]

In 1848, a wave of failed revolutions spread through Europe, inspired in part by the writings of Karl Marx. Proworker immigrants flocked to the United States, including some who were quite radical. Many of those immigrants were German immigrants who came to the Western Reserve and formed an important part of Ashley's constituency. While it is difficult to know the extent of their influence on Ashley, he often referred to his German allies in campaign speeches. The antislavery movement in the United States coincided with the effort to end serfdom in Russia, an effort that succeeded in 1861, during the Civil War. In his speeches, Ashley expressed solidarity with the Russian effort to end serfdom. He made it clear that he opposed all forms of servitude, including the Chinese "coolie" system that prevailed in the West at the time. He also used more radical language, insisting that he would not want to be a slave or a corporation.[20] What is clear is that Ashley viewed a positive right to free labor as part of a worldwide commitment to expanding individual rights.

German Immigrants, Race, and Citizenship in the Civil War Era (New York: Cambridge University Press, 2013), 35.

[19] See Philip Sheldon Foner, *History of the Labor Movement of the United States* (New York: International Publishers, 1947), 1: 266–296 (pointing out that the followers of Karl Marx who came to the United States after 1848 became effective opponents of slavery); Philip S. Foner and Herbert Shapiro, eds. *Northern Labor and Antislavery: A Documentary History* (Westport, CT: Greenwood Press, 1994), xxiii–xxiv (pointing out that Frederick Douglass spoke favorably about the 1848 revolution in France and praised the "rebellious spirit of workers in 1848 England"); LeMay, *Transforming America*, 35; Efford, *German Immigrants*, 56.

[20] James M. Ashley, Letter on President Lincoln's Emancipation Proclamation (Jan. 1, 1863), *Souvenir*, 240, 241–242 (drawing parallels between the emancipation of slaves in the United States and the abolition of serfdom in Russia); Ashley, Address at German Township, Fulton County, Ohio (Nov. 1, 1859), *Souvenir*, 31, 35 (Ashley condemned the Chinese "coolie" system in an 1859 speech claiming that the Republican Party "favors the prohibition of slavery in all the national territories, and more stringent laws to suppress not only the African slave trade but the enslavement of Chinese coolies, or any other race of men, under whatever pretense the attempt may be made"). James M. Ashley, Closing Portion of Stump Speech Delivered in the Grove Near Montpelier, Williams County, Ohio (Sept. 1856) in *Souvenir*, 622; See also Leonard L. Richards, *Who Freed the Slaves? The Fight over the Thirteenth Amendment* (Chicago: University of Chicago Press, 2015), 255, 244.

It is important to note, however, that not all immigrant workers had the liberty to participate in the labor movement. Although Congress had abolished the importation of slaves at the beginning of the nineteenth century, slave importation continued clandestinely in the South until the Civil War. On the West Coast, Chinese immigrants were lured by the California gold rush and stayed to help build the western railroads. The Chinese were the target of severe race discrimination, subject to the slave-like "coolie" system. These immigrants were captured in the system of slavery or slavery-like conditions.[21]

Before the late 1820s, a "labor movement" did not exist in the United States. Journeymen formed associations, but they were mostly civic minded, single-trade organizations. However, changes taking place in work patterns and authority prompted workers to begin to form groups to improve the conditions of their workplaces. Initially, the labor movement was concentrated in the urban northeast, especially in New York City, Philadelphia, and the mill towns of Massachusetts.[22] Workingmen's organizations formed in Philadelphia as early as 1827, and in New York and Massachusetts in the late 1830s.[23] While the workingmen's associations did not explicitly endorse worker's collective action, by the 1830s, there was "a growing and explicit emphasis on the extension of organization and permanence of unions was the *only* basis upon which working people could expect to have any impact on the polity." In 1833 and 1834, urban federations of craft unions formed in eastern seaboard cities, including a General Trade Union with up to 20,000 members. Well-established trade unions formed in numerous other cities, including Boston, Albany, Buffalo, Washington, and Cincinnati. By 1872, there were 1500 trade unions in the United States. National unions, including the Brotherhood of Locomotive Engineers, began forming during the Civil War.[24]

[21] 9 Cong. 22 (Mar. 2, 1807), 2 Stat. 426; Paul Finkelman, Gary W. Gallagher, and Margaret E. Wagner, *The Library of Congress Civil War Desk Reference* (New York: Simon and Schuster, 2002), 94; Najia Aarim-Heriot, *Chinese Immigrants, African Americans, and Racial Anxiety in the United States* (Urbana: University of Illinois Press, 2003), 66–67, 77–78.
[22] Tomlins, *Law, Labor and Ideology*, 152–153; Foner, *Politics and Ideology*, 58; Wilentz, *Chants Democratic*, 220 (trade unions in New York City, 1836).
[23] Wilentz, *Chants Democratic*, 175; Tomlins, *Law, Labor and Ideology*, 153–154. In 1827, Philadelphia journeymen and factory workers formed a citywide federation of journeymen's trade societies, known as the Mechanics Union of Trade Associations. Tomlins, *Law, Labor and Ideology*, 153.
[24] Tomlins, *Law, Labor and Ideology*, 156–157; Montgomery, *Beyond Equality*, 173.

Throughout the antebellum era, workers engaged in strikes and other forms of direct action. They also engaged in politics, attempting to use the state to improve their conditions of work and repealing laws that prohibited workers' "combinations." The issue that galvanized the first labor organizations in the late 1820s was their attempt to limit length of the working day. In the 1840s and 1850s, labor's first priority continued to be legislation limiting the workday to eight hours.[25] The labor movement achieved some political success before the Civil War. The movement thrived in Massachusetts, electing prolabor politicians such as the "Nattick cobbler" Senator Henry Wilson. In New York City, Tammany Hall Democrats depended on labor support for their political success. During the war, labor allied with the Radical Republicans, who pushed for labor priorities such as eight-hour workday legislation.[26]

Northern labor's approach to southern chattel slavery varied widely. Some labor spokesmen argued that northern free workers were treated as poorly as their southern enslaved counterparts. They claimed that northern workers were as much at the mercy of their "masters" as southern slaves, lacking any control over their lives. Argued one labor newspaper, "'Tis a gross error to suppose that I must claim a man's body as my property in order to hold him as my slave ... Give me the air a man must breathe, the water he must drink, or THE LAND from which he must draw his subsistence, and you give me THE WHOLE MAN. He must obey me, serve me, or die." Horace Greeley, publisher of the influential *New York Tribune*, also promulgated an expansive theory of slavery that linked the fates of northern workers and southern slaves. The *New York Tribune* was "the most important newspaper in antebellum America," with nearly 280,000 subscribers in 1856. Its national weekly edition was particularly popular in New England and areas of "New England migration," including Ashley's northwest Ohio. Influenced by the French socialist Fourier, Greeley advocated a social democratic critique of the market.[27] Greeley's *Tribune* functioned as a bridge between the midcentury labor reform

---

[25] Wilentz, *Chants Democratic*, 249–250 (female tailors' strike); Tomlins, *Law, Labor and Ideology*, 153, 158–159; Montgomery, *Beyond Equality*, 163, 186 (NLU priority); 261 (noting that after the fall elections of 1866, labor reformers urged the successful radicals to add an eight-hour workday to their program).

[26] Montgomery, *Beyond Equality*, 125 (Massachusetts labor movement strong in 1865), 102, 244–245 (New Orleans Reconstruction government reforms), 113–114.

[27] Foner and Shapiro, *Northern Labor and* Antislavery, 187; see Adam Tuchinsky, *Horace Greeley's New York Tribune: Civil War Era Socialism and the Crisis of Free Labor* (Ithaca: Cornell University Press, 2009), 2–3, 11–12.

movement and partisan politics. A key Whig ideologue, Greeley was also
one of the main architects of the Republican Party. In that role, Greeley
also sought to forge alliances between the labor movement and the antislavery movement.

According to Greeley, slavery existed "wherever service is rendered
from one human being to another, on a footing of one-sided and not of
mutual obligation." Greeley *Greeley* defined slavery broadly to include
both southern chattel slaves and some northern workers. Greeley argued
that any person who was coerced to obey and serve others and considered
part of an inferior class might be a slave. Other factors indicating a
slave-like relationship included ownership of soil by a small part of the
community and a shortage of jobs that enabled the employing class to
unilaterally set the terms of employment. Greeley argued that these characteristics of slavery described not only the lives of southern chattel slaves,
but also those of some northern workers.[28] Greeley drew a continuum
between slaves and northern workers to promote connections between
the antislavery and labor movements.

Some labor spokesmen argued that northern workers were treated
worse than southern slaves. According to New York Democrat Tommy
Walsh, "in the South, the Negro had a master without asking for one, while
in the North, the wage earner had to 'beg for the privilege' of becoming a
slave." He explained that "the liberty of the white worker was only such
liberty as the employer chose to extend to him." The slave was pictured as
having a master who cared for him; but the northern worker did not, "and
was forced, therefore, to sell his labor by the day to any employer who
would hire him." The employer was pictured as being able at any moment
to "abandon his victim, and consign him to everlasting poverty and
wretchedness, though he devoted the best days of his life to the service of
his master." An 1845 declaration of the National Reform Association
(NRA) argued that wage slaves were more oppressed than chattel slaves,
because unlike slaves, wage-earners had no one to care for them.[29]

Southern defenders of slavery eagerly seized on labor's critique of the
plight of the northern worker. They emphasized the obligation of slave
owners to care for their slaves. For example, noted South Carolina
Senator John Calhoun claimed that "the liberty of the northern wage

---

[28] *The Awl*, August 23, 1845, Foner and Shapiro, *Northern Labor*, 20.
[29] Wilentz, *Chants Democratic*, 333; William H. Lofton, "Appeal of the Abolitionists to the
Northern Working Classes," *The Journal of Negro History* 33, no. 3 (July 1948): 249,
266; Foner and Shapiro, *Northern Labor*, 181.

earner ... amounted to little more than the freedom to sell his labor for a fraction of its value, or to starve." In 1854, sociologist George Fitzhugh published the influential book *Sociology of the South*, in which he insisted that in a free society labor and capital are always antagonistic, and workers are always vulnerable. Fitzhugh criticized the individualism and materialism of northern society and argued that northern laborers were no better off than slaves. Some labor leaders allied themselves with the southern defenders of slavery. These were mostly northern Democrats, including New York Representatives Tommy Walsh and Fernando Wood. Some labor publications agreed, even giving positive reviews to a "work by an apologist for slavery" in 1836.[30]

Conventional accounts of the relationship between labor and the antislavery movement focus on the tension between the two movements. The northern labor movement was dedicated primarily to improving the conditions of white, free workers in the northern states, not to opposing slavery in the South. Many abolitionists were wealthy and not interested in the plight of their working-class neighbors. This led to resentment and sometimes violence directed against abolitionists. However, some historians have noted that the ties between the antislavery and labor movements were stronger than conventionally acknowledged. They argue that the antislavery movement would not have succeeded without the support of the working classes. By the late 1830s, abolitionists started to try to recruit labor. At the same time, some leaders in the labor movement began to argue that opposing slavery was part of the overall struggle against the oppression of workers.[31] However, there was a significant overlap between the antislavery and the labor movements. Leaders of both movements engaged in an ongoing conversation about the meaning of slavery and free labor, and the relationship between the two. Some

---

[30] Foner, *Politics and Ideology*, 57 (southern critique of capitalism – Fitzhugh and Calhoun); Lofton, "Appeal," 255 (Calhoun); see George Fitzhugh, *Sociology of the South, or The Failure of Free Society*, cited in Foner, *Free Soil*, 66. According to Eric Foner, Abraham Lincoln carefully read this book. Foner, *Free Soil*, 66; Wilentz, *Chants Democratic*, 333–334; National Trades Journal, March 12, 1836, in Foner and Shapiro, *Northern Labor*, 216 (reviewing *Slavery in the United States* by James Kirke Paulding).

[31] Foner, *Politics and Ideology*, 67, 63 ("In contrast to the labor movement, most abolitionists accepted social inequality as a natural reflection of individual differences in talent, ambition and diligence, and perceived the interests of capital and labor as existing in harmony rather than conflict"). For example, in 1834, an angry mob attacked abolitionist and antiunion Lewis Tappan's house in New York City. Wilentz, *Chants Democratic*, 265 (Tappan in New York City); Lofton, "Appeal," 273, 277 (some workers in mobs).

labor activists, and their counterparts in the antislavery movement, argued that ending slavery would be necessary to improve the conditions of all workers. The connection between the welfare of slaves and workers throughout the country was the foundational principle of the Free Soil Party, and a principle eventually adopted by the Republican Party.

There is indeed ample evidence of tension and conflict between labor and antislavery activists. Abolitionists such as William Lloyd Garrison denounced slavery in moral, religious terms, insisting that no other wrong compared to the wrong of slavery, implicitly downplaying the concerns of northern workers. Indeed, Garrison's relationship with the labor movement was fraught with conflict. On the one hand, Garrison wrote a column in 1832 supporting the effort to limit the workday to ten hours. After slavery was abolished by the Thirteenth Amendment, Garrison explained that he supported labor reforms on "the same principle which has led me to abhor and oppose the unequalled oppression of the Black laborers of the South."[32] Nonetheless, Garrison's critics charged that the abolitionist had too narrow a view of the concerns of the working man. For example, William E. Channing, a self-described socialist, addressed the New England Anti-Slavery Convention in Boston in May 1850, accusing the abolitionists of overlooking the northern urban workers who should be recruited for the antislavery fight. Channing accused Garrison of "not going far enough in showing that man is man everywhere." He agreed with Garrison that slavery was a great abomination, but insisted that there was no logical distinction between the antislavery movement and that directed "to raise labor universally." Garrison responded defensively, arguing that he had accomplished more than Channing's socialism could.[33]

Some labor activists argued that the abolitionists had their priorities backward, that improving the conditions of northern workers was necessary before ending southern slavery. An 1850 union publication insisted that "only when workingmen had freed themselves of monopoly" would they "consider the propriety of unfettering those who are better off than to be let loose under the present Competitive System of labor." Similarly,

---

[32] Foner and Shapiro, *Northern Labor*, x, xxi (citing early *Liberator* columns by Garrison in which he condemned the labor movement); W. L. Garrison to Ira Steward, March 20, 1866, in *Daily Evening Voice*, May 2, 1866, cited in Montgomery, *Beyond Equality*, 123.

[33] Foner and Shapiro, *Northern Labor*, 168–169; Lofton, "Appeal," 250. Garrison insisted that Channing was unfairly blaming the abolitionist movement for being misunderstood, claiming that his movement had accomplished significantly more than Channing's socialists. Foner and Shapiro, *Northern Labor*, 170.

during the 1852 elections one group of workers argued that it was important "to abolish Wage Slavery before we meddle with Chattel Slavery." They viewed the slavery fight as a struggle between northern and southern capitalists, one that did not concern the working class. As noted above, some argued that northern workers were worse off than slaves, justifying workers' abstention from the antislavery effort.[34]

Moreover, some workers were simply racist. They feared competition from free blacks if slavery were to end, and some politicians fed on this fear. For example, a leaflet to the working men of New Haven argued that if white workers had to compete with blacks, it would undermine the dignity of labor, dignity contingent on "Free laboring white men do[ing] the working." The leaflet argued that "in states where Negroes are made to do the labor, all white men and their children, except the rich planters, are worse off and lower the slaves themselves." A few labor leaders urged recruitment of black workers, but others went on strike to avoid having to work with a black man at their side.[35]

While it is true that there were divisions between organized labor and the antislavery movement, then, it is also undeniable that over time, "the labor movement was increasingly drawn to the antislavery position." Ultimately, working men and women "played a direct and decisive role in bringing chattel slavery to an end." Despite the barriers to cooperation between the labor and antislavery movements, there was a significant overlap between the two. Some labor activists saw slavery as part of the continuum of exploitative labor practices, and viewed the abolition of slavery as an essential step to improve the conditions of workers throughout the country. They argued that the institution of slavery hurt all workers, including white workers, north and south.[36] Together, leaders of the antislavery and labor movements formed a free labor ideology that was essential to the political success of the antislavery movement and shaped the promise of free labor guaranteed by the Thirteenth Amendment.

Antislavery activists came to realize that they needed the support of the working class in order to succeed. One of the most prominent

---

[34] Lofton, "Appeal," 262; "Brotherhood of the Union," *New York Tribune*, August 15, 22, October 8, 1850, cited in Wilentz, *Chants Democratic*, 382; Lofton, "Appeal," 266, 262.

[35] Sewell, *Ballots*, 172–173; Wilentz, *Chants Democratic*, 236 (most craft workers and white laborers distrusted black workers); leaflet in Yale University Library, reprinted in Foner and Shapiro, *Northern Labor*, 245–246; Montgomery, *Beyond Equality*, 180.

[36] Foner and Shapiro, *Northern Labor*, x–xi; Wilentz, *Chants Democratic*, 184 (Thomas Skidmore argues slavery pits property-less whites against enslaved blacks).

abolitionists to do so was Nathaniel P. Rogers, editor of the *Herald of Freedom* from Concord, New Hampshire. In his paper, Rogers "proposed a grand alliance of the producing classes North and South, free and slave, against all exploiters of labor." He insisted that abolitionists must be looking to the northern workers for support. Edward West, a leading reformer of the day, agreed that the antislavery movement's success depended on showing to the "Commercial and Working Classes of America, not only that slavery is unjust and inconsistent with Christian Dispensation, but also show how their private interest is really injured by slavery" by pointing out the negative effect that slavery had on their wages. Antislavery constitutionalist William Goodell supported the expansion of the franchise because he believed it would enable an alliance between northern and southern workers.[37]

Many labor leaders were sympathetic to emancipation, as were the workers whom they represented. As early as 1836, the Rhode Island Anti-Slavery Society issued an appeal to its supporters, saying that slavery "degrades the laboring population assimilating them to slaves. It leads our statesmen to imagine ... that the laboring people are incompetent to self-government." In 1846 the Lowell, Massachusetts, antislavery convention called for the support of "workingmen and mechanics" because "they themselves are victims of oppression and are thereby especially called upon to remember that those who are in bonds are bound by them ... so long as the vast body of southern laborers as held and driven as beasts of burden; because there must be chains for allow liberty for all ..." Studies of antislavery petitions between 1829 and 1837 reveal that artisans were among the largest occupational group to sign antislavery petitions.[38] Thousands of Massachusetts mill workers did the same. In December, 1845, the labor publication *Voice of Industry* reported a mile-long line of factory girls in Lowell, Massachusetts, waiting to sign an antislavery petition. "Many hundreds" of them were reported to be members of antislavery societies. The antislavery sentiment in the labor movement was strongest in New York and Massachusetts, where labor reformers were "at the heart of the antislavery movement." Shoemakers in Lynn, Massachusetts, were strong supporters of abolition.[39]

---

[37] Foner, *Politics and Ideology*, 67–68; *Liberator*, November 10, 1848, cited in Lofton, "Appeal," 251; Montgomery, *Citizen Worker*, 20.

[38] Lofton, "Appeal," 276, 253 (1836, the Rhode Island Anti-Slavery Society); *Liberator*, May 8, 1846, cited in Lofton, "Appeal," 257; Foner, *Politics and Ideology*, 61.

[39] Montgomery, *Beyond Equality*, 117, 118–119; *Voice of Industry*, December 26, 1845, cited in Foner and Shapiro, *Northern Labor*, 214; Lofton, "Appeal," 278 (citing Joseph

Notable antislavery labor activist Ira Steward was a leader of the machinists' and blacksmiths' league and a founder of the Boston Eight Hour League. Steward drew parallels between the antislavery and labor movements, arguing that "the anti-slavery idea was that every man had a right to come and go at will. The labor movement asks how much this abstract right is actually worth, without the power to exercise it." Antislavery and prolabor journalist Horace Greeley insisted that he opposed slavery in all of its forms, and all forms of worker oppression, including "the shameful, atrocious civil disabilities under which the African race now generally labor."[40] This, Greeley and Stewart served as influential voices to unite the antislavery and labor movements.

Workers' conventions during the decades leading up to the Civil War increasingly embraced the antislavery cause. In July 1845, the NRA and the New England Workingmen's Association (NEWA) called for a general convention in New York to discuss the problems of northern workers and plan a general labor movement. In the call, L. W. Ryckman, president of the NEWA, stated that one of the purposes of the meeting was to "abolish slavery." At a meeting before the larger meeting of the Industrial Congress, the secretary of the NRA declared freedom of public lands for "the slaves of wages and all other slaves forever." Even though the NRA drafters believed that wage slaves were worse off than chattel slaves, they opposed all forms of slavery. They declared, "The National Reformers seek a free soil for humanity, the whole of it, without regard to sex or color, and when that object is accomplished, all kinds of slavery must die a natural death."[41]

In January 1847, the New England Labor Reform League adopted an antislavery resolution that argued that "American slavery must be uprooted before the elevation sought by the laboring classes can be effected." In 1849, mechanics and working men in Louisville, Kentucky, adopted an antislavery resolution that stated the following: "Resolved that the institution of slavery is prejudicial to every interest of the state." "We hold that the laboring man has as full a right to his occupation and the profits of his labor, as the master to his slaves." In 1850, radicals in

Sturge, "A Visit to the United States in 1841 or of Slavery and Servitude, and the formal extermination of this hideous ulcer which is still as it ever has been, preying upon the vitals of humanity," June 18, 1845); Foner, *Politics and Ideology*, 61.

[40] Montgomery, *Beyond Equality*, at 249 (citing Ira Steward, Poverty, Mass Bureau of Labor Statistics 1873, 411–439 at 412).

[41] Lofton, "Appeal," 279 (citing *Liberator*, July 4, 1845, *The Harbinger*, June 21, 1845, and *Commons*, 549–550); Foner and Shapiro, *Northern Labor*, 181.

the Industrial Congress in New York passed a resolution stating that they "utterly detest slavery, black and white."[42]

In the decade preceding the Civil War, working men's organizations became increasingly strident in their opposition to slavery. On March 1, 1854, the German worker's society (the Arbeiterbund) held a public meeting in New York City and declared that they should "protest most emphatically against both black and white slavery." In 1856, several hundred working men in Pittsburgh signed a petition stating, "In another section of our country, exists a practical aristocracy, owning Labor, and made thereby independent of the United States. With them, Labor is servitude, and freedom is only compatible with mastership ... Low wages for freemen that slaves may be profitable – is this equality?" At an assembly of New York City workers opposing the Kansas-Nebraska Act in 1856, a man named Hale argued that the working men of America wanted the country to be "free for your grandchildren ... a place where the honest labourer may labour in the dignity of his own manhood – a labour which shall not be degraded by working side by side with the slave ... this fair inheritance of freedom shall not be drenched by the sweat of the unpaid toil of slavery." And in 1859, in James Ashley's state of Ohio, the Social Working Man's Association of Cincinnati held an assembly to honor John Brown. They issued a statement calling slavery the result of "force and fraud" without any foundation in justice, and "differing in no respect of principle from the early bondage of western Europe, or from the serfdom of Russia, which are condemned by the voice of history against human nature." Slavery conflicted "with the cause for which the fathers of the Republic fought." "That such an interpretation of the constitution as to acknowledge the rightfulness of the existence of slavery is an infamy, and an insult to the fathers of the Republic."[43]

Due to the ongoing dialogue between the antislavery and the labor movements and the eventual ties between the two movements, the ideology of the labor movement contributed significantly to meaning of "free labor" in the antebellum era. First, the labor movement advocated

[42] Lofton, "Appeal," 281 (citing Norman Ware, *The Industrial Worker, 1840–1860* (Boston, 1924) at 221, quoting *The Voice of Industry*, February 9, 1847); *The North Star*, May 25, 1849, in Foner and Shapiro, *Northern Labor*, 213; Wilentz, *Chants Democratic*, 382.

[43] Lofton, "Appeal," 282 (citing Herman Schluter, *Lincoln, Labor, and Slavery* (New York, 1913), 76); *New York Tribune*, October 31, 1856; Foner and Shapiro, *Northern Labor*, 242; *National Antislavery Standard*, February 25, 1854; Foner and Shapiro, *Northern Labor*, 248, 250.

republicanism – a belief in the liberty, equality, and individual worth of the working man. Labor spokesmen shared a "passionate attachment to [economic] equality," a belief in independence and the ability to resist personal and economic coercion, and a commitment to the labor theory of value.[44] Leaders of the labor movement often cited the Declaration of Independence, arguing that the Declaration established individual rights for working people. The 1834 founding Declaration of the Rights of the Trades Union in Boston declared "that it is the right of working men, and a duty they owe each other, to associate together." New York City Democrat Tommy Walsh, who had strong ties to the labor movement, claimed that the Declaration "guaranteed every person who was willing to labor the right to do so."[45]

Notably, racial equality was largely absent from this language of equality. Most northern workers ranged from hostile to indifferent in their attitudes toward racial minorities. The question of race was thus a "vexing" one for Free Soilers. To attract them, members of the Free Soil party downplayed the issue of racial equality and focused primarily on economic equality. Some Free Soilers were prejudiced and argued that the end of slavery would not necessarily bring about black equality.[46] However, other Free Soilers "found slavery a moral evil and shared Liberty notions on race." Many Free Soilers, including James Ashley's mentor Salmon Chase, shared a record of advocacy for black equality. As the first Free Soil Party senator, Chase sought to make blacks eligible for homestead grants. Supporters of the rights of free blacks believed that downplaying racial issues would be more effective at attracting political support, especially the working-class vote, to the antislavery cause.[47]

---

[44] Steinfeld, *Invention of Free Labor*, 105 (seventeenth-century "contractarian individualism" and republicanism were the new traditions in American life); Foner, *Politics and Ideology*, 59 (dates back to Tom Paine's republicanism); Wilentz, *Chants Democratic*, 157–158, 161, 274 (labor adds value), 332 (Tommy Walsh voiced the labor theory of value).

[45] Tomlins, *Law, Labor, and Ideology*, 159; Wilentz, *Chants Democratic*, 332.

[46] Foner, *Free Soil*, 261; the Free Soil platform lacked a plank advocating for the rights of free blacks and condemning the Fugitive Slave Act. See Sewell, *Ballots*, 159 (politically, Free Soilers knew that they were more likely to be successful if they downplayed concerns about racial injustice); Sewell, *Ballots*, 316, 307 (racial prejudice was virtually universal at the time, and Democrats routinely used race baiting as part of their platform).

[47] Sewell, *Ballots*, 160, 176, 178–180, 183–185; Foner, *Free Soil*, 281 (Western Reserve elected officials against black laws; Free Soilers in Massachusetts repealed the ban on interracial marriage in 1843).

Second, from Tom Paine to Jefferson to Lincoln, the main tenet of republican ideology was that "freedom entailed ownership of productive property." They championed the labor theory of value – "Labour is the sole portant of all property – the land yealdeth nothing without it, & there is no food, clothing, shelter, vessel or any nesecary of life but what costs Labour & is generally esteemed valuable according to the Labour it costs." Republican ideology held that freedom entailed economic independence and ownership of productive property "because such independence was essential to participating freely in the public realm, an ideal which dated back to the American Revolution."[48] Economic independence and independence as a citizen were thus intertwined in the prevailing ideology of the antebellum labor movement.

Finally, labor spokesmen argued that workers were suffering from a loss of status, a decline in the "dignity" of labor.[49] In part, this view reflected nostalgia for the artisanal days of the early Republic in a world that was rapidly changing due to industrialization. Workers saw that their ideal of self-ownership and economic independence was increasingly difficult to obtain. They feared that the dignity of labor was eroding because they lacked control over their working lives.

Labor activists invoked the concept of "wage slavery" to describe the plight of the northern worker. To some, working for wages itself was equivalent to slavery. Because they associated liberty with the ownership of productive property, they considered any worker who depended on another person for his livelihood to be a "wage slave." This reflected the middle-class aspirations of many in the labor movement, who hoped that workers would be able to earn enough to eventually purchase their own business and no longer work for others. Selling one's labor to another was the equivalent of voluntarily entering into slavery, "a day's bondage for a day's wages." Massachusetts Senator Henry Wilson made this analogy, arguing, "The difference between [the South and the North] is, that our slaves are hired for life – yours are hired by the day ... your slaves are white – of your own race."[50]

---

[48] William E. Forbath, "The Ambiguities of Free Labor and the Law in the Guilded Age," *Wisconsin Law Review* 1985 (1985): 767, 768; William Billerica, "The Key of Liberty," cited in Tomlins, *Law, Labor, and Ideology*, 4; Foner, *Free Soil*, 64.

[49] Foner, *Politics and Ideology*, 59.

[50] Wilentz, *Chants Democratic*, 332 (Tommy Walsh says that "wage slavery and the tyranny of capital had reduced republican producers to dependent menials"); Montgomery, *Beyond Equality*, 25–26, 31, 30 ("Americans associated liberty with ownership of productive property, the opposite of "wage slavery"); 238–239 (this was the concept of

Some reformers, such as Henry Evans, argued that workers could never be free unless they owned their own land. Evans argued that in the United States, as in England, "usurpation of the soil" gives rise to wage slavery. He insisted that "there is slavery everywhere there is land monopoly," explaining, "There is servile dependence wherever a lording class stands between the cultivator and the soil." Therefore, Evans maintained that no reform would be effective unless it was preceded by land reform. He insisted that land reform had to occur before chattel slavery ended. If not, ending slavery would "merely ... convert the chattel slave into a laborer for wages."[51] Evans believed that working men needed to own their own land in order to sustain themselves and avoid having to work for wages. In this respect, Evans agreed with the republicans in the labor movement.

Over time, however, it became increasingly clear that many workers would be wage earners for their entire lives. By 1870, two-thirds of productive workers in the United States were wage-earners. The changing nature of work made it difficult to argue that working for wages alone was sufficient to transform a free worker into a "wage slave." Labor reformers began to critique the wages, hours, and conditions of work. They saw that workers in northern manufacturing plants were working long hours under poor conditions and argued that those who toiled under the worst conditions were "wage slaves."[52] Female textile workers in Lowell, Massachusetts, began to refer to themselves as "the white slaves of New England" because of the poor wages and conditions in the mills. Labor activists often analogized the condition of northern workers to southern slaves. In February 1836, striking tailors were convicted of conspiracy and used imagery of slavery to protest their conviction. They accused the judge of "an unhallowed attempt to convert the working men

---

"wage slavery"); Foner, *Free Soil*, 17; Cong. Globe, 35th Cong., 1st Sess., App. at 71 (1858); cited in VanderVelde, "Labor Vision," 464.

[51] Wilentz, *Chants Democratic*, 336–342; Foner and Shapiro, *Northern Labor*, 180, 174, 175. Abolitionists were outraged by Evans's claims. Said noted abolitionist Wendell Phillips, "The idea that a man robbed of land is worse off than one robbed of himself, ought almost to subject any intelligent man, who professes it, to the suspicion of catering to corrupt public sentiment and sacrificing the rights of the race in the vain hope of more easily securing those of another." Wendell Phillips letter to Henry Evans, in Foner and Shapiro, *Northern Labor*, 179.

[52] Montgomery, *Beyond Equality*, 30, 238; Wilentz, *Chants Democratic*, 332 (Tommy Walsh said that "no man devoid of all other means of support but that which has labor affords him can be a freeman, under the present state of society. He must be a humble slave of capital"; *Subterranean*, November 8, 1845).

of this country to slaves," and issued an anonymous handbill that claimed that "a deadly blow has been struck at your Liberty! The prize for which your fathers fought has been robbed from you! The freemen of the North are now on a level with slaves of the South! With no other privileges than laboring that drones may fatten on your life blood!"[53] These workers argued that without the right to organize to improve their conditions, they were no better than slaves.

By the 1840s, some leaders had adopted a more forward-looking, radical stance toward the status of workers. In 1840, the "Grand Rally" of the Workingmen of Charlestown, Massachusetts, issued a statement declaring the direct opposition between their interests and those of the "purchasers of labor." The declaration said that they were "men obliged to labor for our daily accept the wages they offer . . . The capitalist had no other interest in us, than to get as much labor out of us as possible." These activists saw workers as a natural majority and capitalists as a minority, an aristocracy. They overtly used the language of class. They called on workers to organize in associations, "to combine in our own defense" to countermand the power of their employers.[54] These activists focused more directly on the power relationship between workers and their employers, and sought to alter that relationship to address the asymmetry of power.

What does learning about the labor movements and the Free Soilers tell us about the meaning of free labor in the antebellum era? First, that "free labor" was the antithesis to slavery and involuntary servitude. Slaves, peons, and indentured servitude were not considered to be free workers, even if they had initially entered into their employment relationship voluntarily. Christopher Tomlins notes, "To the antebellum labor movement free labor ideally meant economic independence through the ownership of productive property, or proprietorship," or at the very least, "a far more substantive conception of contractual freedom than the abstract formalism of mere self ownership would allow." To antislavery men, "free labor" entailed working because of incentive instead of coercion, labor with education, skill, the desire for advancement, and the freedom to move from job to job according to the changing demands of the marketplace. "Free labor" required some degree of autonomy, so the

---

[53] Foner, *Politics and Ideology*, 60; Wilentz, *Chants Democratic*, 291.

[54] Third Grand Rally of the Workingmen of Charlestown, Mass, Held October 23d, 1840, Kress Library, Harvard Business School, Cambridge, 8, 12, cited in Tomlins, *Law, Labor, and Ideology*, 9, 10.

worker would have as much control as possible over the worker's own life, including the ability to limit the hours of the workday.[55] Free labor included mobility, the ability to leave one's employer at will, and the liberty to contract with one's employer. Both the moderate and more radical strands of the movement worried about the growing concentration of power in the hands of employers and capitalists, and the concomitant lack of wealth and power of the workers. Both sought to use the state to address that imbalance.

The alliance between labor and antislavery activists led to the first major breakthrough in the success of the political antislavery movement, the Free Soil Party. In the mid-1840s, founders of the Free Soil Party seized on the connection between the plight of northern workers and southern slaves to expand support for the antislavery movement. The Free Soil Party was formed by Liberty Party members who were frustrated by its lack of political success. They were joined by former Democrats and Whigs who were upset at their own parties' positions on slavery. The Free Soil Party sought to appeal to northern workers by emphasizing the link between slavery and the exploitation of northern workers. Free Soilers argued that slavery caused labor to lose its dignity and pointed out that white workers were indirectly competing with slave labor. Free Soilers insisted that the very existence of slavery in the South enabled employers in the North to act abusively toward their employees, including physical abuse. They claimed that slavery had a downward impact on the conditions of work, and the wages, of free workers. According to Free Soiler Representative Thaddeus Stevens of Pennsylvania, "the people will ultimately see that laws which oppress the black man and deprive him of full safeguards of liberty, will eventually enslave the white man."[56]

Free Soilers spoke to the class consciousness of northern workers, maintaining that the interests of southern aristocratic slaveholders were directly opposed to that of the workers. Representative Francis Kellogg of Michigan expressed this view in 1864 when he said that "[southerners] would degrade the laboring classes to a condition below that of the peasantry of Europe and render it impossible for them to rise in society." In 1858, even the relatively moderate *New York Times* compared

---

[55] Tomlins, *Law, Labor, and Ideology*, 289; Foner and Shapiro, *Northern Labor*, 24; VanderVelde, "Labor Vision," 438.

[56] Sewell, *Ballots*, 156, 199, 157 (Free Soil platform); Foner, *Free Soil*, 153; VanderVelde, "Labor Vision," 442, 443 (citing letter), 470, 474.

slaveholders to feudal barons, who would prefer to own all of their employees. The Free Soilers stressed the class-based connection between northern workers and slaves. Former Free Soiler Massachusetts Senator Henry Wilson later explained, "[W]e have advocated the rights of the black man because the black man was the most oppressed type of the toiling men of this country." As Republican Ohio Representative John Bingham said in 1857, workers were entitled to more than "crumbs from their masters' table," but would not receive what they deserved as long as slavery existed.[57] Bingham was a moderate who had not been a member of the Free Soil Party. His remarks here illustrate the extensive influence of the Free Soil, Free Labor ideology on prominent members of the Republican Party.

The Free Soil ideology reflected the influence of the labor movement on antislavery advocates and represented a fusion of antislavery and prolabor views. Said Gemaliel Bailey, "Free Soilers are opposed to the spirit of caste ... because its inevitable tendency is to create or perpetuate inequality of natural rights." They argued that labor should be performed not by slaves but by free men. Many Free Soilers viewed the ideal worker through a middle-class lens. They believed in a mobile society where labor would pay off, with the goal of economic independence. They championed the dignity and opportunities of free labor, social mobility, and "progress." They valued materialism, social fluidity, and the "self made man."[58] These views reflected the republicanism of the early labor movement and were based on their increasingly outdated experience with a primarily agricultural population. The Jacksonian Democrats were more radical and saw an inevitable conflict between capital and labor. They criticized the industrial state and expressed concern for the well-being of wage-earning industrial workers. However, even the radicals were wary of making class-based arguments. Some

[57] VanderVelde, "Labor Vision," 467, 461; Cong. Globe, 38th Cong., 1st Sess., 2955 (1864), cited in Vandervelde, "Labor Vision," 471; *New York Times*, June 10, 1858, cited in Foner, *Free Soil*, 89; Cong. Globe, 39th Cong., 1st Sess., 343 (1866).

[58] Gemaliel Bailey, *National Era*, June 28, 1849, cited in Sewell, *Ballots*, 176; Vandervelde, "Labor Vision," 470 (citing Iowa Rep. James Wilson, "What member of our free labor force could stand in the presence of this despotism which owns men and combat the atrocious assertion that 'slavery is the natural and normal condition of society,' with the noble declaration that 'labor being the sure foundation of the nation's prosperity should be performed by free men'"; Cong. Globe, 38th Cong., 1st Sess., 1202 (1864)); Foner, *Free Soil*, 16; Foner, *Politics and Ideology*, 48.

were wary of the labor movement because they challenged the Radical tenet "that the triumph of the nation eradicated class."[59]

Freedom of contract in free labor raised some ambiguity and led to some contradictions. For example, there was arguably a tension between the freedom of contract and laws limiting work hours, which were the primary goal of the labor movement at the time.[60] The commitment to freedom of contract on the part of some Free Soilers proved to be a significant barrier to legislation limiting work hours. Some supported the formation of unions, but many antislavery men were also antiunion, arguably serving to justify "the emerging capitalist order of the North."[61] Eventually, the more radical goals of the labor movement foundered on the shoals of Republican commitment to capitalism. That is part of the story of Reconstruction. But the ideology of free labor that developed during the antebellum era influenced James Ashley and continued to inspire advocates for workers' rights throughout the nineteenth and twentieth centuries.

[59] Foner, *Free Soil*, 31–32, 18 (Jacksonian Democrats); VanderVelde, "Labor Vision," 471 (Thomas Shannon of California said that slavery "makes the many subject to the few, makes the laborer the mere tool of the capitalist, and centralizes the political power of the nation." Cong. Globe, 38th Cong., 1st Sess., 2948 (1864); Foner, *Politics and Ideology*, 57 (two movements criticized capital and labor relations in the antebellum United States: the labor movement and proslavery southerners); Montgomery, *Beyond Equality*, 232 (Radicals were wary of labor organizations because they challenged the Radical tenet that "the triumph of the nation eradicated class"); VanderVelde, "Labor Vision," 473 (repeated phrase "right to fruits of one's labor" was also a critique of the industrial state).

[60] Montgomery, *Beyond Equality*, 142, 179 (eight-hour workday movement goal was to make workers "masters of our own time"), 237 (Massachusetts bootmaker said that working only eight hours made him feel "full of life and enjoyment" because "the man is no longer a slave, but a man"; Mass Bureau of Labor Statistics, 1872, p. 278), 238 ("The struggle for shorter hours, in other words, was seen as a fight for the liberty of the worker"; Fincher's Trade Review masthead said, "Eight Hours: A Legal Day's Work for Freemen").

[61] Ibid., 246, 247 (the hardest hurdle to cross was "reluctance to interfere with freedom of contract"); Foner, *Politics and Ideology*, 24.

4

Ashley's Egalitarian Free Labor Vision

James Ashley first began to engage in politics as a young antislavery Democrat. In the early 1850s, disillusioned with the Democratic Party's proslavery stance, he left that party to help Salmon Chase and others found the new Republican Party. By 1853 a "broad-shouldered self-taught lawyer," Ashley was "a growing popular force" in Ohio. In speeches supporting his new political party, Ashley combined elements of antislavery constitutionalism, free labor ideology, and Jacksonian democracy. Ashley consistently adopted the most radical positions of the movements that influenced him. As an antislavery constitutionalist, Ashley was a strong supporter of racial equality and insisted that slavery was unconstitutional everywhere. On labor issues, Ashley argued that the interests of labor conflicted with capital, and he opposed all forms of unfree labor, including the Chinese "coolie" system. As a former Democrat, he championed public education and voting rights, and as early as 1856 he sought to extend those rights to free blacks.[1] As a new Republican, Ashley promoted an egalitarian free labor vision with roots in the economic populism of the Democratic Party.

Insights about Ashley's ideology must be gleaned primarily from the speeches that he gave on the campaign trail and in Congress. Most of his

---

[1] John Niven, *Salmon P. Chase: A Biography* (New York: Oxford University Press, 1995), 159. Ashley viewed Chase as a mentor and role model. He was a leading supporter of Chase in Chase's many political campaigns. Ibid. Ashley's views thus problematize the conventional view of northern Democrats as having a narrow view of the antislavery effort that did not extend to racial equality. See Pamela Brandwein, *Reconstructing Reconstruction: The Supreme Court and the Production of Historical Truth* (Durham: Duke University Press, 1999), 60.

papers were destroyed in a fire prior to Ashley's death. Fortunately, Ashley salvaged what he later called "speeches and fragments of speeches ... all old-fashioned anti-slavery appeals, such as in those days were everywhere made by our anti-slavery leaders against this crime of slavery." It is important to remember that each speech that Ashley gave had a historical context, audiences that he wished to reach, and policy goals that he wished to achieve. Nonetheless, his positions on most issues are remarkably consistent over time, as is the ideology that he expresses. Moreover, Ashley was particularly upfront about his views, even those that were unpopular at the time. As Ashley put it, "If I have one peculiarity which stands out more prominently than another, it is, that I define clearly and sharply my positions, and make my fight openly and squarely."[2]

Moreover, Ashley's speeches are useful for understanding contemporary public meaning. Private correspondence may indeed provide a more accurate source of what a person is thinking than his public announcement, but speeches are a matter of public record, putting the speaker on the spot, and fostering shared understanding. Whatever Ashley's inner thoughts may have been, his speeches were part of the public debate over slavery, in which he played a prominent role. He used his speeches to persuade his constituents and his colleagues and to explain what he hoped to accomplish with the measures that he supported. To that extent, they can aid our understanding of those measures, including the Thirteenth Amendment.

Until 1853, Ashley belonged to the Democratic Party. He considered himself a "Jefferson and Jackson" Democrat with a belief "in the wisdom and intelligence of the common man." As a Democrat, Ashley supported bank regulation, equitable tax policies, free labor, and free public schools. He was also an ardent populist, often condemning what he viewed as the privileged elite, including, but not limited to, slaveholders. Ashley thus argued that the true Democratic position was to be against slavery. Most Democrats disagreed with Ashley's interpretation of the party's principles. Southern Democrats supported slavery, and northern Democrats championed "popular sovereignty," which would allow individual states

---

[2] Letter from James Ashley to Benjamin Arnett, December 19, 1892, reprinted in *Duplicate Copy of the Souvenir from the Afro-American League of Tennessee to Hon. James M. Ashley of Ohio* (Benjamin Arnett, ed.) (Philadelphia: Publishing House of the AME Church, 1894) (hereafter referred to as *Souvenir*), 598; "The Ashley Banquet at the Oliver House," November 1864, *Toledo Commercial, Souvenir*, 309, 312.

then entering the Union to decide whether to adopt slavery. Ashley condemned the Democrats' version of "popular sovereignty," saying that we "cannot assent to the interpretation given by it to the so-called doctrine of popular sovereignty, which surrenders the rights of man to the unlicensed will of a majority." Ashley explained, "I believe in, and have always been an advocate of 'true' popular sovereignty, 'the right of a majority to rule (not enslave).' But I cannot recognize the principle as Republican or Democratic that would concede the right of the majority to enslave the minority, merely because they were poor, or because they were black, and without sufficient power to resist the wrong." Ashley also differed with his former party on the issue of states' rights. Most northern Democrats supported states' rights, opposed federal power to regulate slavery, and were openly and viciously racist.[3] By contrast, Ashley advocated broad federal power to end slavery and protect the rights of free blacks. During the Civil War, Ashley was a chief proponent of a territorial theory of Reconstruction, which would authorize complete federal control over rebel states. Ashley also became one of the staunchest supporters of racial equality measures in the Reconstruction Congress.

Ashley's story thus problematizes the conventional view of the role of the northern Democrats in antebellum and Civil War politics. While it is undeniable that northern Democrats who stayed in the party became a conservative force opposing broad Reconstruction measures, it also true that those who left the party became some of the most radical voices in the Reconstruction Congress. These former Democrats became an important faction in the Republican Party. They held many leadership positions, tended to ally themselves with the radical wing of the party, and "had considerable impact on the emergence of a distinctive Republican program and ideology." Moreover, Ashley continued to believe that his was the true Democratic voice. In 1864, Ashley wrote Salmon Chase suggesting that they form an alliance with the "war Democrats" to form a new "great National Party," and in 1874 he ran for Congress on the Democratic ticket.[4] From the beginning of his career Ashley championed voting

---

[3] Robert F. Horowitz, *The Great Impeacher: A Political Biography of James M. Ashley* (New York: Brooklyn College Press, 1979), 13; James Ashley, Address delivered at Charloe, Ohio (January 31, 1859), *Souvenir*, 22, 24–25; Brandwein, *Reconstructing*, 26, 38.

[4] Letter from James Ashley to Salmon P. Chase (August 5, 1864); Salmon P. Chase Papers, Manuscript Division, Library of Congress, Washington, DC). By "War Democrats," Ashley referred to the radical members of the Republican Party who, like himself, had roots in the Democratic Party; see Les Benedict, "James M. Ashley, Toledo Politics and the

rights and access to public schools for free blacks, and he supported universal suffrage. Ashley had seen how workers had used their political clout to transform the law of work during the Jacksonian era, and he wanted freed slaves to be able to do the same to improve their lives.

Ashley's disillusionment with the Democratic party began in 1844, when he attended the Democratic National Convention in Baltimore, Maryland. Ashley supported what he called the "anti-Calhoun" ticket, Martin Van Buren and Richard Johnson. By then, Ashley was already a seasoned political observer. He later recalled that he began "active systematic work as an abolitionist when but eighteen," when he claimed to have learned about every position of every public man of note or prominence in the South. Before the 1844 convention, Ashley stopped in Washington to "study the situation." (He later opined, "Imagine a boy of twenty studying the situation!") There, the Secretary of Treasury, George M. Bibb, introduced Ashley to John Tyler, then a candidate for president, and to "the great nullifier, John Calhoun."[5] Ashley found Calhoun charming and enjoyed his company. However, he hated what Calhoun had done to the Democratic Party, including masterminding the defeat of Van Buren by slaveholder John Tyler in the 1844 Democratic Convention. In his speeches, Ashley often claimed that proslavery interests had betrayed the Democratic Party.[6]

As the conflict over slavery continued to heat up, the prospects for a new, broader antislavery party improved. In 1850, Congress enacted a new Fugitive Slave Act, providing for the appointment of federal commissioners in counties where local officials refused to cooperate in returning fugitive slaves. During the debate over the act, Salmon Chase and New

---

Thirteenth Amendment," *University of Toledo Law Review* 38 (2007): 815, 821, 836. Ashley later returned to the Republican Party and ran for Congress as the Republican nominee in 1890 and 1892. Horowitz, *Great Impeacher*, 167.

[5] Address of Hon. J. M. Ashley at Memorial Hall, Toledo, Ohio, June 2, 1890, *Souvenir*, 714, 717–718. Ashley had met Van Buren at the Harrison inauguration. Ibid.

[6] See, e.g., Address of Hon. J. M. Ashley at Memorial Hall, Toledo, Ohio, June 2, 1890, *Souvenir*, 714, 718 ("Personally Mr. Calhoun was to me the most pleasing man I have ever met, and the memory of my interviews, and the letters which I afterwards received from him, will always be a source of pleasure"); "The Rebellion: Its Causes and Consequences," Address of Hon. James M. Ashley Delivered at College Hall in the City of Toledo, Thursday evening, Nov. 26, 1861, *Souvenir*, 171, 175, 182–183; Hon. James M. Ashley Unanimously Re-Nominated for Congress by the Republican Congressional Convention of the Tenth District at Napoleon, August 19, 1868, *Souvenir*, 505, 508, 511; Hon. James M. Ashley on Greeley and Grant, the Greeley Campaign of 1872, *Souvenir*, 560; Address of Hon. James M. Ashley before the "Ohio Society of New York," at the Fifth Annual Banquet, Wednesday evening, February 19, 1890, *Souvenir*, 692, 706.

York Senator William Seward emerged as Free Soil leaders. Nonetheless, the act was a crushing defeat for antislavery forces and strengthened their animosity to what they called the Slave Power, the union of southern slaveholders and northern business leaders who controlled the federal agenda.[7] The tension between pro- and antislavery forces in the Democratic and Whig Party reached the breaking point just as Ashley was gaining prominence in Ohio politics.

In 1853, Ashley left the Democratic Party to protest the party's support for slavery. The following year, the Kansas-Nebraska Act, which repealed the Missouri Compromise and allowed the residents of Kansas and Nebraska to vote to sanction slavery, prompted many other Democrats to join him. The act "united the radicals, divided the moderates, and fragmented the entire American political party structure." The passage of the Kansas-Nebraska Act prompted mass protest demonstrations throughout the country, with over 200 in the state of Ohio. Ashley participated in those meetings, where he met and befriended Salmon Chase, then a leading figure in both Ohio and national antislavery politics. In 1854, Ashley helped Chase to capitalize on the anti-Kansas-Nebraska Act rallies and form the Ohio Republican Party, and Ashley was elected one of the vice presidents of the Ohio state convention. Ashley represented Chase at the first convention of the national Republican Party in 1856, along with the legendary Ohio antislavery politician Joshua Giddings. George W. Julian of Indiana and Owen Lovejoy of Illinois also attended the convention and later became Ashley's allies in Congress. Thus Ashley "deserves credit for being one of the founders of the Republican Party" and formed important alliances during the party's formation.[8]

By 1856, Ashley was already considering a run for Congress. Some of Ashley's acquaintances urged him to run that year, but the thirty-two-year-old Ashley believed himself to be too young and inexperienced. Instead, Ashley campaigned for the Republican Party presidential candidate John Fremont, and his party's candidate for Congress, Richard Mott. During this campaign, Ashley gained political experience and established

---

[7] Fugitive Slave Act of 1850, ch. 60, 9 Stat. 462 (repealed 1864). The act responded to northern resistance to the 1793 Fugitive Slave Act, which required local officials to cooperate in returning fugitive slaves. Fugitive Slave Act of 1793, ch. 7, 1 Stat. 302 (repealed 1864); Hans L. Trefousse, *The Radical Republicans: Lincoln's Vanguard for Racial Justice* (New York: Alfred A. Knopf, 1968), 47; Eric Foner, *Free Soil, Free Labor, Free Men: The Ideology of the Republican Party before the Civil War* (New York: Oxford University Press, 1995), 92.

[8] Horowitz, *Great Impeacher*, 17, 18, 32; Niven, *Chase Biography*, 159.

his reputation in his northwest Ohio district. Campaigning for Mott, Ashley detailed his political and constitutional theories to his constituents and supporters. Ashley did this to persuade his audience, and also so that the voters would stand by him when he set out to implement his own agenda.[9] In these speeches, Ashley articulate an egalitarian free labor vision. In the following decade, Ashley would work to make that vision a reality.

Ashley's speeches echo the rhetoric and ideology of the antislavery constitutionalists who led the antislavery movement in his state of Ohio. Throughout his life, Ashley insisted that slavery was unconstitutional even before the Thirteenth Amendment. Thus, like others in the antislavery movement, Ashley engaged in the debate about the foundational principles of our nation, trying to determine our nation's essential identity. Ashley's constitutional arguments justified his abolitionist position against slavery throughout the United States. In addition, the Constitution provided a foundation for Ashley's theory of the rights of a free person, those rights that were infringed by the institution of slavery. Ashley was either unwilling or unable to imagine that the founding fathers, whom he so admired, had sanctioned slavery, which he so hated. Ashley insisted that James Madison and Thomas Jefferson opposed slavery even though they owned slaves. He claimed that the Founders, including Madison, would never have drafted a foundational document to protect that slavery.[10]

Ashley called the Northwest Ordinance, which prohibited slavery and involuntary servitude in the Northwest territories, the "Jeffersonian proviso" and insisted that "[i]n the days of Jefferson, [the Democratic Party] was for free States and free Territories." Ashley argued that slavery violated the natural rights of man that Jefferson had championed in those documents. He explained that "no consistent believer in that greatest and best charter of human freedom can do otherwise than acknowledge the justice of that principle which recognizes the natural right of every human being, which claims that they are entitled to the protection of life and

---

[9] Horowitz, *Great Impeacher*, 23, 33. Notable among his early speeches is that delivered in Montpelier, Ohio, in September 1856. See Closing Portion of Stump Speech Delivered in the Grove near Montpelier, Williams County, Ohio, September, 1856, by James M. Ashley, *Souvenir* at 601 (hereafter referred to as "Montpelier speech"). Frederick Douglass later referred to the speech as "the grand speech in Montpelier." Frederick Douglass, Introduction, *Souvenir*, 6.

[10] James Ashley, Speech in the House of Representatives, January 6, 1865, *Souvenir*, 333, 334–335.

liberty, by every law of man's enactment." Ashley claimed that those rights were enforceable via the Preamble to the Constitution. He explained, "If the government was organized for any purpose, it was to secure the blessings of liberty to ourselves and to our posterity, and not to enslave any man, nor to become the defenders of slavery."[11] This constitutional guarantee of freedom would apply anywhere in the country, including the existing states, and would also prohibit slavery in the territories.

The Constitution also provided a basis for Ashley's theory of rights of a free person. Ashley insisted, "The natural rights of the rich and the poor, the learned and the ignorant, the strong, and the feeble, of whatever country, caste or religious belief, should be held sacred and inviolable by Republicans." The first and foremost of those were the "right life to liberty," which he called "the birthright of the human race." Ashley argued that all people have a natural right to "the protection which the law of nature and the human race are entitled" and demanded "the equal protection of the law for every human soul within our gates, whether black or white, or of mixed blood."[12] Thus, Ashley linked the existence of natural rights to the government's duty to provide the equal protection of the law.

Like Chase, Ashley argued that the Due Process Clause of the Fifth Amendment prohibited slavery because slaves were deprived of life and liberty without due process of law. Ashley explained, "Neither the state, nor a corporation, must be recognized as having the right to deprive any person, however poor, whether white or black, of his life, or liberty, or property, except in punishment for a crime, of which he must be duly convicted in open court by a jury of his peers." Under the Supreme Court's ruling in *Barron v. Baltimore*, the Due Process Clause limited only the federal government – it did not apply to states.[13] This is one of the reasons why Ashley's Republican colleagues, including Salmon Chase, argued that slavery was illegal only in the territories. Notwithstanding

---

[11] Speech of Hon. James Ashley of Ohio Delivered in the US House or Representatives, January 17, 1861, *Souvenir*, 116, 127, 228; James Ashley, Address delivered at Charloe, Ohio (January 31, 1859), *Souvenir*, 24, 29 (hereafter referred to as "Charloe address").

[12] "Charloe address," *Souvenir*, 22, 24, 25; "Montpelier speech," *Souvenir*, 622 ("I demand for every human soul within our gates ... that they be protected in their right to life and liberty"). James Ashley, Draft memoir, John M. Morgan Papers relating to James M. Ashley, University of Toledo libraries, Ward M. Canaday Center Manuscript Collection, folder #3 at 13 (hereinafter referred to as "Draft memoir").

[13] Montpelier Speech, *Souvenir*, 622; See *Barron v. Mayor and City Council of Baltimore*, 32 U.S. (7 Pet.) 243 (1833).

Barron, however, Ashley argued that the Due Process Clause also prohibited slavery in the states.

In a draft memoir that he wrote at the end of his life, Ashley recalled that when campaigning for Congress in 1858, he did not ask Chase to speak on his behalf because Chase was "opposed to my views on constitutional interpretation." According to Ashley, Governor Chase "held to the Jefferson and Madison resolutions of 1798–99 while I did not. I held and in all my speeches affirmed, that the adoption of the national constitution by the citizens of nine states united us as one people and one nation: that in no line of the constitution did it recognize property in man, nor did it confer on Congress the power to enact a fugitive slave law of any kind, and that an honest interpretation of the constitution by the Supreme Court would destroy slavery everywhere beneath our flag. These propositions were affirmed by me in all of my public speeches. Gov. Chase and a majority of all public men affirmed the opposite of these propositions."[14] Ashley thus promoted the most radical version of antislavery constitutionalism, that slavery was unconstitutional everywhere, including the existing states.

Ashley's position that slavery was unconstitutional everywhere had been the position of some of the leaders of the Liberty Party, including Gerrit Smith and William Goodell. However, it was more radical than most of the new Republicans were willing to go. The Republican Party platform's position in favor of the denationalization of slavery was less confrontational than Ashley's, less threatening to the southern states. Ashley later recalled that he was disappointed that the party did not go farther in its opposition to slavery. He had introduced his own resolution, which would have provided "that a proper interpretation of the national Constitution, by the Supreme Court of the United States, would destroy slavery everywhere within the national jurisdiction as did the decision of Lord Mansfield, who declared 'that no slave could breathe on English soil.'" Other radicals were similarly disappointed with the party's decision and pushed the party to go further in its antislavery stance.[15]

---

[14] Ashley, "Draft memoir," 43. Here, Ashley referred to the Virginia Resolutions, in which Jefferson argued that state had the authority to resist federal law.

[15] See William Goodell, *Views of American Constitutional Law, in Its Bearing upon American Slavery* (Utica, NY: Jackson & Chaplain, 1844); Richard H. Sewell, *Ballots for Freedom: Antislavery Politics in the United States 1837–1860* (New York: Oxford University Press, 1976), 91; Ashley, "Draft memoir," 29. Here, Ashley is referring to the British case of *Somerset v. Stewart* (1772), which abolitionists viewed as a declaration that slavery was incompatible with natural law. See William M. Wiecek, *The Sources of*

Although many antislavery constitutionalists argued that slavery violated the Privileges and Immunities Clause of Article IV by depriving blacks of their citizenship rights, Ashley did not rely on this argument. This omission could be due to fact that citizenship was a touchy subject in Ohio politics in the mid-1850s. The anti-immigrant Know Nothing Party was prominent in Ohio, and Know Nothings played an influential role in Ohio politics. Moreover, supporters of the Know Nothings generally opposed slavery. As Chase, Ashley, and others worked to form an anti-slavery fusion party, they needed support from the antislavery Know Nothings. However, they also relied on the large population of German immigrants, who also opposed slavery. German immigrants constituted over 10 percent of Ohio's population, concentrated in Ashley's northwest Ohio district.[16] For a brief period of time, Ashley cooperated with all who opposed slavery, including the Know Nothings. He later regretted his decision. After that, German immigrants never trusted him, no matter how hard he tried to woo them. In stump speeches, Ashley repeatedly reminded his Republican audiences of the support from the Germans. As he said in an 1859 address in Charloe, Ohio, "Our success for the past two years is due in no small degree to the freedom-loving Germans." In part to win the German vote, Ashley "explicitly back[ed] civil and political rights regardless of ethnic origins."[17] Thus, it is not surprising that Ashley did not invoke the rights of citizenship in his constitutional arguments against slavery.

Like many of the antislavery constitutionalists, Ashley was from the start an outspoken proponent of racial equality. In an 1859 speech celebrating his first congressional victory, Ashley declared, "I cannot recognize the principle as Republican or Democratic that would concede the right of the majority to enslave the minority, merely because they were poor, or because they were black, and without sufficient power to resist

---

Antislavery Constitutionalism in America, 1760–1848 (Ithaca: Cornell University Press, 1977), 20; Foner, *Free Soil*, 128.

[16] See Chapter 2, supra. In this respect, Ashley differs notably from his Ohio colleague, Representative John Bingham. The rights of citizenship were a central theme in Bingham's antislavery constitutionalist philosophy. See Richard L. Aynes, "On Misreading John Bingham and the Fourteenth Amendment," *Yale Law Journal* 103 (1993); Rebecca E. Zietlow, "The Rights of Citizenship: Two Framers, Two Amendments," *University of Pennsylvania Journal of Constitutional Law* 11 (2009): 1269 (comparing Bingham's and Ashley's theories of citizenship); Niven, *Chase Biography*, 157–158; Benedict, "Toledo Politics," 823.

[17] Horowitz, *Great Impeacher*, 29; Benedict, "Toledo Politics," 823; "Charloe address," *Souvenir*, 29.

the wrong." Ashley supported civil rights measures for free northern blacks, and condemned the racism of southern slaveholders. In Ohio, Ashley opposed laws that restricted the rights of free blacks, which he called the "Black law of Ohio" and "barbarous enactments," enacted to appease "the slave barons." Ashley stated admiringly, "these accursed laws might have been on our statute books today but for the demand of the old antislavery guard for their repeal."[18] To Ashley, supporting the rights of free blacks was integral to the antislavery effort. Ashley argued that free people were entitled not only to be free from race discrimination, but also to the positive rights of workers that would empower them to assert their right to equal treatment.

Ashley's system of free labor would entail removing racial barriers to the exercise of free labor rights. Ashley understood the connection between the exploitation of black slave labor and racial subordination. He said, "I often wonder how your northern-born men can show such hostility to the black man. Singularly enough, I find here in the North, as in the South, that the hatred of the negro is not that he is black or of mixed blood, but because he is a slave. It is the hatred born of the spirit of caste, and not the hatred of color. Wherever the negro is free and is educated and owns property, you will find him respected and treated with consideration." Ashley pointed to the contradictory fact that while "nearly all the slave barons were, themselves, nursed and cared for while children by black slave mothers," those same slave barons felt threatened by the sight of free blacks. He implied that this was due to racism on the part of the slave owners.[19] To counter the effects of slavery, laws would also be needed to counter race discrimination. Here, Ashley makes the connection between racial oppression and the exploitation of slave labor. Racism provided an ideology to justify the degrading, inhumane treatment of slaves as no more than chattel property. The southern economy depended on the unpaid labor of slaves, and racism facilitated this exploitation.

When it came to racial equality, James Ashley's actions were consistent with his rhetoric. As a young man, he was active in the Underground Railroad, and he evidently made some friends and allies in the free black community. In Toledo, Ashley helped runaway slaves to found the

---

[18] Ashley, "Charloe address," *Souvenir*, 25; "Montpelier speech," *Souvenir*, 610–611.
[19] Ashley, "Montpelier speech," *Souvenir*, 606–608 (if the same slaves are free, then "that moment the odor arising from them congests the sensitive olfactories of every slave baron, and paralyzes his palpitating heart").

African Methodist Episcopal Church. During the Civil War, Ashley supported racial equality measures in the District of Columbia. He encouraged the inclusion of black soldiers in the Union forces and supported equal wages for their efforts.[20] Ashley was to be one of the foremost supporters of voting rights for blacks in the Reconstruction Congress.

In addition to his antislavery constitutionalism, Ashley also articulated a broad view of a positive right to free labor. Like the Free Soilers, Ashley condemned slavery's impact on free white workers as well as slaves. He argued that the institution of slavery harmed all workers and that the end of slavery would have a positive effect on the rights of all workers. Noted abolitionist Frederick Douglass explained that Ashley "puts the rights of humanity above every other right and, as inseparably connected with the rights of all races of men, he includes the rights of labor, and claims that humanity and labor have rights which are above and superior to the material interests of capital governments." Ashley viewed slavery as an inhumane, exploitative labor practice. But his interests in workers' rights went beyond ending slavery. Ashley linked the fight against slavery to the international struggle for worker's rights, and he opposed other exploitative labor practices in the United States, including the Chinese "coolie" system. Ashley later explained, "The opinions which I hold touching organizations of working-men and the relations of capital and labor, are the logical outgrowth of my early fight against the right of capital to legal ownership in man. An intelligent discussion of slave ownership involved of necessity the question of the proper relation between labor and capital."[21] Protecting the rights of workers was central to Ashley's ideology.

In his first speech to Congress in May 1860, Ashley extolled the virtues of a free labor society. Ashley explained, "The system of government adopted by [the states] in my judgment, is the best system known to man. It is the best, because it rests upon labor, and is created and controlled by the free and untrammeled will of the laborer ... experience has demonstrated that it is the only foundation upon which states and governments can safely and securely rest." Ashley described a free labor system as a system in which workers were entitled to certain rights, including citizenship, equality, the protection of the government, and the right to enjoy the fruits of their labor. "In such a government, the

---

[20] http://warren-ame.org/church-history.
[21] Douglass, Introduction, *Souvenir*, 3, 6; Ashley, "The Federation of Railroad Workers and All Wage Workers" – Gov. Ashley's Address, June 10th, 1891, to the International Train Dispatcher's Convention, on Co-operation and Strikes, *Souvenir*, 667.

laborers must not only be free, but they must be citizens; having rights which the government and all classes of citizens are bound to respect and defend – the poorest and humblest inhabitant being equal, before the law, with the richest and most powerful; sharing in its burdens, enjoying its protection." According to Ashley, a society based on free labor would include "the constitutional guarantee of the government to protect the rights of all and secure the liberty and equality of its people." In addition, Ashley argued that "every human soul within our gates" was entitled to "the secure possession of the fruits of their labor."[22] Ashley echoed the republican ideology of the labor movement when he spoke of the workers' right to the fruits of his labor.

Ashley contrasted the free labor society with that in which slavery was the norm, warning of the danger that it posed to all free labor. Ashley claimed that the men in the South had no religious or moral convictions against enslaving any race "and that, having no principles to deter them from the commission of such a wrong, all they want is the power, and they would reduce, without hesitation, the entire laboring population of whatever race or color, to bondage." Here, Ashley reached out to white northern workers to try to convince them that they had a stake in ending slavery. Ashley claimed that class antagonism in the South was "the real point of danger to the ruling class of the South."[23] He saw southern white workers as potential allies in the war against slavery and sought their support. Some of Ashley's speech on labor was standard Free Soil rhetoric, consistent with the middle-class championing artisans and small business owners. But Ashley went further than the Free Soilers, articulating a broader view of free labor that encompassed labor practices other than slavery. Moreover, Ashley made it clear that he viewed himself as participating in an international struggle to improve workers' rights.

In an 1856 Montpelier speech, Ashley spoke not only against slavery, but also against other labor practices that he viewed as similarly oppressive. He said, "I therefore repeat, that I am utterly opposed to the ownership of labor by capital, either as chattel slaves, or as apprentices for a term of years, as Chinamen are now being apprenticed in Cuba and in this country, ostensibly for seven years, but in reality for life."

[22] Speech of Hon. James Ashley of Ohio, Delivered in the US House of Representatives, May 29, 1860, *Souvenir*, 44, 45, 104; Ashley, "Montpelier speech," *Souvenir*, 622.
[23] Speech of Hon. James Ashley of Ohio, Delivered in the US House of Representatives, May 29, 1860, *Souvenir*, 44, 104; Cong. Globe, 36th Cong., 1st Sess., App. 364, cited in Foner, *Free Soil*, 120.

This passage is notable because Ashley here criticized apprenticeship, a common employment relationship in the colonies and the early days of the Republic that continued through the Reconstruction Era. Apprenticeship was arguably "voluntary" in the sense that apprentices initially agreed to enter the relationship. Here, Ashley points out that a labor practice that might at first appear voluntary can transform into an involuntary relationship, when the apprentice lacks the power to leave even exploitative conditions of labor. The Reconstruction Congress adopted this interpretation in the 1867 Anti-Peonage Act. In the 1850s, however, states differed in their interpretation of voluntariness.[24] Once again, Ashley expressed the stronger view.

In the same speech, Ashley condemned exploitative labor practices, including the "coolie" system in the West. "Coolies" was the term for Chinese immigrants who came to the United States to build the western railroads. Some came to the United States as free workers, others as contract workers. Many stayed to help build the transwestern railroads, and the railroads came to rely on their labor. These workers were treated poorly once they arrived, subjected to racial discrimination, relegated to shanty towns, and forced to work from sun up to sun down for low wages. Though the "coolie" system was most predominant after the Civil War, by 1856 James Ashley was already aware of it, and he repeatedly condemned it. In an 1859 speech, after he was elected to Congress, Ashley repeated his charges against the "coolie" system and maintained that the entire Republican Party was opposed to "coolie" labor. Ashley claimed that the Republican Party "favors ... more stringent laws to suppress not only the African slave trade but the enslavement of Chinese "coolies," or any other race of men, under whatever pretense the attempt may be made." Many of Ashley's Republican allies shared his views of the

---

[24] Ashley, "Montpelier speech," *Souvenir*, 622; Robert J. Steinfeld, *The Invention of Free Labor: The Employment Relation in English and American Law and Culture, 1350–1870* (Chapel Hill: University of North Carolina Press, 1991), 132. Apprenticeship was a deed between two parties with mutual consent, which usually lasted seven years. The apprentice was not paid wages but the master was legally obligated to provide for his needs (food, clothes, and teaching him a craft). The apprentice was legally obligated to obey his master. Ibid., 25. The law of apprenticeship began to conform with free labor only after the Civil War. In 1897, the US Supreme Court held that the involuntary servitude clause of the Thirteenth Amendment did not bar apprenticeship. *Robertson v. Baldwin*, 165 U.S. 275, 280 (1897). Id. at 175. On courts' interpretation of "involuntariness" in the antebellum era, see James Gray Pope, "Contract, Race, and Freedom of Labor in the Constitutional Law of 'Involuntary Servitude,'" *Yale Law Journal* 119 (2010): 1474.

"coolie" system. In 1860, Massachusetts Representative Thomas Eliot's Committee on Commerce issued an extensive report condemning the "coolie" trade. According to the Report, "From the moment of his capture the coolie is a slave. He is the subject, first, of the meanest deception, and then of a servitude in no respect practically different from that which the confessed African slave trade binds upon its victim."[25] Responding to the report, Congress passed the Prohibition of the Coolie Trade Act of 1862 banning the "coolie" trade.[26]

Ashley also spoke out against oppressive labor practices that fell short of slavery. "I am opposed to all forms of ownership of men, whether by the state, by corporations, or by individuals ... If I must be a slave, I would prefer to be the slave of one man, rather than a slave of a soulless corporation, or the slave of a state." Here, Ashley shares the labor movement's condemnation of "wage slavery," but his language goes beyond that ideology to question the fundamental principles of capitalism. Said Ashley, "I do not agree that capital shall own labor, North or South, nor in any country on God's green earth. I do not care whether that capital is in the hands of one man or in the hands of many men combined." What did Ashley mean by his reference to capital owning labor? Perhaps this was just the language of the day, representing nothing more than a middle-class vision of economics. But it is also possible that Ashley had been influenced by the early American socialist movement. In his influential paper, the *New York Tribune*, editor Horace Greeley advocated a doctrine of democratic socialism as he promoted ties between the antislavery and labor movements. Ashley often mentioned Greeley in his speeches, calling him part of the "old antislavery guard," and claimed to have been Greeley's friend since Ashley was twenty years old. It is also possible that Ashley was swayed by radical immigrants who had fled the failed 1848 socialist Revolution in Germany and settled in Ashley's district. If so, this passage reveals that Ashley's class consciousness went well goes beyond the middle-class Free Soil paradigm, placing him on the radical end of the spectrum in his advocacy for workers' rights.[27]

[25] H.R. Rep. 443, at 4 (1860).

[26] Cong. Globe, 37th Cong., 2nd Sess. (Feb. 19, 1862); 12 Stat. 340, 341. Although the act passed in 1862, provisions of the act were not extended to Japanese and other Asian "coolies" until February 9, 1869. Cong. Globe, 40th Cong., 3rd Sess. (Feb. 9, 1869). See Aarim-Heriot, *Chinese Immigrants*, 77.

[27] Ashley, "Montpelier speech," *Souvenir*, 621–622. See Adam Tuchinsky, *Horace Greeley's New York Tribune: Civil War Era Socialism and the Crisis of Free Labor* (Ithaca: Cornell University Press, 2009), 17. The *New York Tribune* was arguably "the

Ashley also viewed slavery from an international perspective. At Montpelier, he insisted, "In the eyes of all civilized peoples, we are, today, regarded as a nation of liars and hypocrites, professing devotion to the principles of liberty and justice, while pirating on the land and in the sea for men, women and children." After the Emancipation Proclamation, Ashley was happy to see a more positive connection to the worldwide struggle for free labor. "[T]he present will be a year ever memorable in the history of the republic and the world, a year in which the enfranchised millions of the United States can stretch forth their glad hands to the enfranchised millions of Russia, and thank God that the establishment of justice in the administration of these two great governments has made the chattelizing of men hereafter within all their borders forever impossible, and paved the way for breaking the bondage of men among all the nations of earth."[28] Thus, Ashley framed the end of slavery in the United States as part of a worldwide movement toward improving workers' rights.

Finally, though Ashley left the Democratic Party, he never turned his back on his Democratic roots. According to Ashley the Democratic Party "had shown a broader spirit in favor of human liberty than their opponents" until the party was taken over by Calhoun. Ashley's boyhood hero was the populist Democratic President Andrew Jackson. Though Jackson owned slaves and supported slavery, Ashley still believed that the principles of Jacksonian Democracy weighed against the peculiar institution. According to Ashley, Jackson had stood for the principle that "the government should be so administered as to secure the greatest good to

most important newspaper in antebellum America," with over 280,000 subscribers in New England and "areas of New England migration," such as the Ohio western reserve in which Ashley lived, in 1856. Ibid., 2; Hon. James M. Ashley on Greeley and Grant, the Greeley Campaign of 1872, Tuchinsky, *Horace Greeley's New York Tribune*, 560, 564. Speech of Honorable James M. Ashley of Ohio, in the House of Representatives, May 29, 1866 – Impartial Suffrage the Only Safe Basis of Reconstruction, *Souvenir*, 392, 411; Hon. James M. Ashley Unanimously Re-Nominated for Congress by the Republican Congressional Convention of the Tenth District at Napoleon, August 19, 1868, *Souvenir*, 505, 514; Ashley often thanked the German community for support, and they always remained an important constituency. See Ashley, "Charloe address," *Souvenir*, 22, 29 ("Our success for the past two years is due in no small degree to the freedom-loving Germans"); Ashley, Address Delivered October 14, 1860, *Souvenir*, 38, 42; Hon. James M. Ashley Unanimously Re-Nominated for Congress by the Republican Congressional Convention of the Tenth District at Napoleon, August 19, 1868, *Souvenir*, 505, 517; Niven, *Chase Biography* (10 percent of Ohio voters were German). Foner, *Free Soil*, 20 (most Republicans deplored the language of class conflict.).

[28] Ashley, "Montpelier speech," *Souvenir*, 613; James M. Ashley, Letter on President Lincoln's Emancipation Proclamation (Jan. 1, 1863), *Souvenir*, 240, 241–242.

the greatest number, protecting all, and granting special favors to none."
Ashley viewed the slave-holding elite as antidemocratic feudal barons,
intent on using the government to perpetuate their power at the expense
of the common man. Ashley repeatedly decried what he called "Congress
granting privileges to the few which are denied the many."[29]

Like the other former Democrats who made up a significant faction in
the new Republican Party, Ashley left his party "only after a prolonged
struggle against southern domination of the Democracy." In general,
former Democrats deeply resented the influence of slaveholders on their
party and were fiercely opposed to what they called the Slave Power. As a
former Democrat, Ashley claimed that destruction of economic privilege
would speed up economic advancement. He condemned the southern
elites who benefited from the institution of slavery. Condemning the Slave
Power was an article of faith for antislavery politicians of the time, an idea
that had its roots in Jacksonian Democracy. Ashley's mentor Salmon
Chase, also a former Democrat, relied on the Slave Power image to
support his antislavery arguments in his classic pamphlet "The Appeal
of the Independent Democrats," which outlined the slaveholder's conspiracy to overthrow the Missouri Compromise.[30] While Ashley rarely used
the term the "Slave Power," he often employed populist rhetoric against
the privileged elite, echoing the Slave Power theory.

The conventional view of northern Democrats is that they were
racially prejudiced and resistant to the broader implications of the
abolition of slavery.[31] While that was certainly true of many Democrats,
this view disregards the egalitarian nature of the Democratic vision in
the economic realm. In the antebellum era many Democrats had ties
to the labor movement, and the populists of Jacksonian democracy
condemned economic elites. Ashley seized on that populism to advocate
against slavery, which he saw as an oligarchic institution that was
antithetical to democratic norms. As we have seen, unlike many Democrats Ashley extended his egalitarian views to encompass advocacy for
racial equality.

---

[29] See Les Benedict, "Toledo Politics," 821 ("Throughout his career as a Republican, Ashley
stressed his Democratic roots"); Address of Hon. James M. Ashley before the "Ohio
Society of New York," at the Fifth Annual Banquet, Wednesday evening, February 19,
1890, *Souvenir*, 692, 706; Horowitz, *Great Impeacher*, 7; Ashley, "Charloe speech,"
Souvenir, 29; Ashley, Address Delivered in German Township, Fulton County, Ohio
(November 1, 1859), *Souvenir*, 30, 34.
[30] Foner, *Free Soil*, 150, 94, 18–19, 9.   [31] Brandwein, *Reconstructing*, 60.

Ashley did not condemn the privileged elite only because they owned slaves. He told his constituents that he was concerned about the concentration of power in general, and the use of that power against vulnerable people in society. He promised, "You believe, all of us believe, that a truly democratic government will see to it that the poor and defenseless are protected against the aggressions of the rich and powerful." Describing the ideal government, he said it would be one where "the poorest and humblest inhabitant [would be] equal, before the law, with the richest and most powerful." Ashley claimed that his new party, the Republican Party, was also opposed to the governing elite. Said Ashley, "The Republican Party is opposed to the proscription of any man, whatever his nationality or religion [and] opposed to a strong centralized government in the hands of an aristocratic privileged class."[32] The doctrine that required governing by a privileged elite "is now reversed, and a privileged class, who enslave the defenseless, are not only the special object and care of the government, but they control the government as absolutely as if they were the only citizens of the republic. To meet and assist the aggressions of this privileged class ... the Republican party was organized." Ashley promised that the Republican Party would deliver a "Plain and Simple Government, devoid of pomp, protecting all and granting special favors to none," and that "[l]ike the dews of heaven, its blessings shall fall upon the rich and poor, the north, the south alike."[33] Here, Ashley portrayed the Republican Party as a progressive version of the Democratic Party that he left, different because it was opposed to slavery.

Like the Jacksonians, Ashley proposed a concrete solution for empowering the common man (or woman) against the elite – expanding the electoral franchise. Ashley explained, "Both these governments, the State and Federal, derive all the power they possess directly from the people." Therefore, the people should have the right to vote. He referred to the right to vote as "a natural right, a divine right if you will, a right of which the government cannot justly deprive any citizen except as punishment for a crime." During the Reconstruction Era, Ashley was a stalwart champion of the right of freed slaves to vote. He explained that "the ballot is the only sure weapon of protection and defense for the poor man,

---

[32] Ashley, "Charloe speech," *Souvenir*, 28; Speech of Hon. James Ashley of Ohio, Delivered in the US House of Representatives, May 29, 1860, *Souvenir*, 44, 45; Address Delivered in German Township, Fulton County, Ohio (November 1, 1859), *Souvenir*, 31, 33.

[33] Ashley, "Charloe address," *Souvenir*, 22, 29; Address delivered in German Township, Fulton County, Ohio (November 1, 1859), *Souvenir*, 33, 34.

whether white or black. It is the sword and the buckler and shield before which all oppressions, aristocracies, and special privileges bow." At that time, many of his radical allies agreed. However, unlike most of them, Ashley had long been an advocate of suffrage rights. In early 1859, before he even went to Congress, Ashley started giving speeches advocating black suffrage. Ashley also supported women's right to vote. During Reconstruction, he proposed a constitutional amendment that would have established universal suffrage for all men and women alike.[34]

Finally, Ashley's Democratic roots are evident in his support of universal public education. Ashley believed that education was essential for an engaged citizenry to participate in the democratic process. He accused slave states of "den[ying] the masses of poor white children within its power the privilege of free schools." Ashley included public education as part of his proposed Reconstruction bills, and in 1867, he proposed a constitutional amendment that would have guaranteed free public education to all, including black children. As governor of Montana, Ashley gave a speech calling for public schools to be open to all races. Ashley made education a priority in his family as well, sending all of his children, including his daughter, Mary, to college.[35]

In 1858, Ashley was nominated as the Republican candidate for his congressional district in the first ballot. Ashley thanked the party for its support and said, "I feel pride in taking the place you have assigned me today in the great army of freedom." During his 1858 campaign, Ashley made over a hundred speeches. In his campaign speeches, Ashley traced his opposition to slavery to his childhood and claimed to have violated the Fugitive Slave laws as a young man. He later recalled, "My speeches on the slavery question and on fundamental propositions were as radical as the platform, which the Defiance convention declined to give me. But I determined if I was elected to have no misunderstanding with my

---

[34] James M. Ashley, "The Union of the States: The Majority Must Govern: It Is Treason to Secede," Speech to the House of Representatives, January 17, 1861, *Souvenir*, 116; Speech of Honorable James M. Ashley of Ohio, in the House of Representatives, May 29, 1866 – Impartial Suffrage the Only Safe Basis of Reconstruction, *Souvenir*, 392, 406. Horowitz, *Great Impeacher*, 43, 120 (describing Ashley's proposed suffrage amendment).

[35] James Ashley, Speech in the House of Representatives, "On the Constitutional Amendment for the Abolition of Slavery" (January 6, 1865), in *Souvenir*, 333, 337; 39th Cong., 1st Sess., 2879, cited in Horowitz, *Great Impeacher*, 151; Horowitz, *Great Impeacher*, 161, 166 (to include his daughter was "quite remarkable at the time, but not for a man who believed in women's suffrage").

constituents," and he felt obliged to "thoroughly educate the people on the slavery question."[36]

In a draft memoir written near the end of his life, Ashley recalled that his congressional district had historically been Democratic. He said that the Republican Party did not solidify its hold on the district "nor become free from pro-slavery influences until after the adoption of the Thirteenth Amendment." The Republican Party in his district was divided between former Whigs and Democrats. He recalled that while a majority of the Whigs who joined the Republican Party in 1856 had been disciples of Clay and Webster, "I had been brought up in the political schools of Jefferson" and was accustomed to antagonizing the Whigs. Ashley claimed that the Whigs in his district were "indifferent to the slavery question," defenders of the fugitive slave law, and bitterly hostile to his allies, Chase, Sumner, and Joshua Giddings. Ashley found himself handicapped in his campaigns "because of my radical antislavery opinions." As a result, his elections were always close.[37]

In the tense political atmosphere of 1858, Ashley sometimes faced the threat of violence while on the campaign trail. Early on in his campaign, he learned that there had been a failed attempt to gather a group of "reckless young men" to heckle him, so he gave as many speeches in the relatively safety of churches as possible. At one event, the group broke into a church and someone hit him over the head with a live goose. Ashley recalled keeping "perfectly cool" because he was young (only thirty-four), in good physical shape, and armed with a revolver. At another speech, in Leipsic, Ohio, an angry mob interrupted Ashley's speech. He charged the door and physically threw three men out. After that incident, he reported that he was never annoyed or hassled again on the campaign trail. Ashley won the 1858 election with 55 percent of the vote.[38] Thus, Ashley's size and commanding presence helped him to navigate the political waters in a highly contentious time.

Though elected to Congress in the fall of 1858, Ashley's first session did not convene until December 1859. He was an intrepid traveler, and voyaged all over the country to campaign for his political allies. In 1858, Ashley visited the state of Illinois to witness one of the legendary

[36] Horowitz, *Great Impeacher*, 29, 32; Ashley, "Montpelier speech," *Souvenir*, 621 ("Before I was twenty years of age, I had drawn up a plan to aid slaves to purchase their freedom, and to provide by statute law against a repetition of such villany as I have described").

[37] Ashley, "Draft memoir," 4, 1.   [38] Ibid., 34–35, 42, 45.

senatorial debates between Abraham Lincoln and Stephen Douglas. Inspired by Lincoln, Ashley accepted an invitation to remain in the state and, at the side of Salmon Chase, help with Lincoln's senatorial campaign. In the summer of 1859 Ashley attended rallies against the Fugitive Slave Act in Oberlin, Ohio, with Ohio Senator Benjamin Wade. In July and August, Ashley traveled the Midwest on Chase's behalf, trying to drum up support for his presidential candidacy. When the Chase campaign failed, Ashley switched to supporting Abraham Lincoln for president.[39] Ashley's campaigning brought him into contact with many allies, and he established a strong national reputation. By the time he arrived in Congress in 1859, he was one of the leaders of the Republican Party, poised to transform his egalitarian free labor ideology into law.

[39] Horowitz, *Great Impeacher*, 43, 44, 46; Address of Hon. J. M. Ashley at the Fourth Annual Banquet of the Ohio Republican League, Held at Memorial Hall, Toledo, Ohio, February 12, 1891, *Souvenir*, 747–748; Leonard L. Richards, *Who Freed the Slaves? The Fight over the Thirteenth Amendment* (Chicago: University of Chicago Press, 2015), 255, 14.

5

Ashley in Congress, 1859–1863

In November 1859, James Ashley traveled to Washington, DC, to begin his term in Congress. On the way there, Ashley stopped in Harper's Ferry to attend the execution of John Brown and meet with Brown's wife. Ashley wrote a letter to his Ohio constituents, saying, "Men may talk as they will, but I tell you there is a smoldering volcano burning beneath the crust, ready to burst forth at any moment; and an enemy to peace of almost every hearth-stone, is lurking in the heart of the apparently submissive lashed slave, and only those who have passed through an outbreak like this or the Southampton insurrection, can comprehend the danger and know for certainty that it exists." The Civil War was on the horizon, and Ashley was to be a central player in the Union Congress. When Ashley arrived in Washington, he enthusiastically jumped into the fray and used every opportunity he could find to further his antislavery mission. Ashley was already well known and well liked from his travels, and he had a prominent voice in Congress from the start. According to historian Robert Horowitz, "Aggressive and self-reliant, but good natured, Ashley was blessed with a radiant smile, which a Washington observer described as 'sunshine playing above a rock.' His good looks and jolly good humor made him a favorite of Washington hostesses." In February 1860, Ashley was appointed a member of the House Committee on the Territories.[1] From this important position, Ashley could directly

[1] Robert L. Stevens, ed., "John Brown's Execution – An Eye Witness Account," *NOQ*, 21 (autumn 1949): 140–148; *National Anti-Slavery Standard*, June 16, 1860, cited in Robert F. Horowitz, *The Great Impeacher: A Political Biography of James M. Ashley* (New York: Brooklyn College Press, 1979), 49–50.

attack slavery in the territories, one of the leading political issues in the fervor leading up to the Civil War. In his first years in Congress, Ashley used every means at his disposal to undermine slavery and promote his free labor vision.

As he entered Congress, Ashley and his allies faced two constitutional barriers to abolishing slavery. The first was the longstanding federal consensus that slavery was a matter of state law, so that the federal government could not abolish slavery in the states. Members of the Republican Party had adopted that consensus in their platform, which reflected fundamental principles of federalism. Northern Democrats, many of whom represented slave states, fought tooth and nail to protect state sovereignty over slavery. The second constitutional barrier was the Supreme Court's *Dred Scott* ruling that slaveholders had a constitutional right to own slaves and that any measure abolishing slavery would violate the Due Process Clause of the Fifth Amendment. *Dred Scott* seemed to preclude Congress from abolishing slavery anywhere. James Ashley insisted that slavery was unconstitutional everywhere and rejected both state sovereignty limitations and the Court's ruling in *Dred Scott*. Ashley's rejection of the federal consensus put him distinctly in the minority in his party. Most of his Republican colleagues agreed with Ashley that the Dred Scott decision was illegitimate, but they respected state sovereignty limits on congressional power to restrict slavery in the states. The Republican Party had been formed to combat slavery, but in 1859, it was unclear how that goal could be achieved without violating the Constitution.

The Civil War began early in Ashley's second year in Congress. The tumult of the early Civil War years disrupted the status quo. The federal consensus began to erode as Union troops entered rebel states and fugitive slaves crossed enemy lines. Members of Congress found that they could use their war powers to override state sovereignty concerns and "confiscate" and liberate fugitive slaves. Use of war powers also justified overriding the Court's ruling in *Dred Scott*. Ashley supported the use of war powers to liberate slaves, but he still wanted to abolish slavery everywhere. He argued that rebel states had reverted to territories under complete federal control. Ashley's territorial theory would have justified plenary federal power and eliminated state sovereignty barriers to abolition. In the early war years, Ashley's territorial approach proved too threatening to the nation's established system of federalism, and he never quite convinced his congressional colleagues. Ashley and his allies engaged in constitutional politics to achieve their goals.

When the Civil War broke out, Ashley immediately seized on the war's potential to bring about the end of slavery. To succeed, Ashley had to use his strategic skills and political connections. From the start, Ashley framed the war as "a contest that has for its motive power on the one side liberty, and on the other slavery."[2] As the war progressed, Ashley and his allies used congressional war powers and power over the territories to end slavery and protect the rights of the freed slaves. From the outset, Ashley supported the confiscation and liberation of slaves by the Union forces. Ashley led the effort to abolish slavery in the District of Columbia and the other US territories. He proposed early Reconstruction measures that would have liberated slaves in conquered territories and provided them with both land and civil rights. Ashley supported the Emancipation Proclamation and argued that the proclamation had established the Union as firmly on the side of liberty. With all of these efforts, Ashley laid the groundwork for the Thirteenth Amendment.

When he arrived in Congress, Ashley immediately allied himself with the radicals in the Republican Party. Historians vary in how they identify the radicals in the Civil War Congress, but under any definition, Ashley fits the bill.[3] He was a determined antislavery politician who championed equal rights for blacks and resisted any compromise with the southern rebel states. Sympathetic to labor, Ashley was also among the foremost champions of equal rights for blacks in Congress. Ashley counted other leading radical politicians among his best friends. Benjamin Wade, the Chair of the Committee on the Territories who in 1858 had presented

---

[2] "The Rebellion – Its Causes and Consequences," Address of Hon. James M. Ashley Delivered at College Hall in the City of Toledo, Thursday evening, Nov. 26, 1861, *Duplicate Copy of the Souvenir from the Afro-American League of Tennessee to Hon. James M. Ashley of Ohio* (Benjamin Arnett, ed.) (Philadelphia: Publishing House of the AME Church, 1894) (hereafter referred to as *Souvenir*), 171, 176.

[3] See Hans L. Trefousse, *The Radical Republicans: Lincoln's Vanguard for Racial Justice* (New York: Alfred A. Knopf, 1968), 4; Michael Les Benedict, *A Compromise of Principle* (New York: W. W. Norton, 1974), 22 (radicals were mostly free soil and "other determined antislavery politicians"; after the war began, radicals advocated complete emancipation and full civil rights for free men); Eric Foner, *Free Soil, Free Labor, Free Men: The Ideology of the Republican Party Before the Civil War* (New York: Oxford University Press, 1995), 104 (radicals are characterized by "a persistent refusal to compromise with the South on any question involving slavery"; lists Ashley as a radical); James Oakes, *Freedom National: The Destruction of Slavery in the United States, 1861–1865* (New York: W. W. Norton, 2013), 273 (referring to Ashley as a radical); Trefousse, *Radical Republicans*, 95 (Ashley was "the radical politician from Toledo"); Leonard L. Richards, *Who Freed the Slaves? The Fight over the Thirteenth Amendment* (Chicago: University of Chicago Press, 2015), 255, 14 ("from the beginning, Ashley was deemed a "wild eyed radical").

petitions for higher wages for workers, was one of Ashley's closest allies. Thaddeus Stevens, Chair of the House Ways and Means Committee, befriended Ashley as soon as he joined the House of Representatives. Ashley met Senator Charles Sumner soon after he arrived in Washington, and the depth of their friendship is evident in the fact that Ashley named his third son after Sumner. Sumner and Indiana Representative George Julian helped Ashley campaign for reelection during the difficult year of 1862.[4] The radicals had a strong impact on Civil War era policies. Ashley's friends and allies shared his passion for ending slavery by "confiscating" newly freed slaves, ending slavery in the District of Columbia and the territories, and formulating plans to reconstruct the conquered rebel states as a free labor society.

When Ashley entered Congress in the late fall of 1859, the political climate was extremely tense. The *Dred Scott* decision had heightened tensions between the pro- and antislavery forces, and the rise of the Republican Party threatened the hold that proslavery forces had enjoyed on national power for years. In 1858, New York Senator William Seward had given a widely publicized speech in which he argued that there was an "irrepressible conflict" between pro- and antislavery states, and "by 1860, the irrepressible conflict idea was firmly imbedded in the republican mind." In June 1858, the relatively moderate *New York Times* editorialized that slaveholders were like "feudal barons ... who [act] together always for the promotion of their common ends."[5] The specter of war hovered over the nation and antislavery sentiment was rising in the North.

On May 29, 1860, Ashley gave his first speech to Congress, in which he attacked the Supreme Court's *Dred Scott* decision and called for the immediate abolition of slavery. The address was warmly received and printed in a circular by the Republican National Committee. In this important speech, Ashley reaffirmed his antislavery constitutionalist views. He declared, "I do not believe that the Constitution of my country

---

[4] Trefousse, *Radical Republicans*, 27–28; Richards, *Who Freed the Slaves?*, 27; Address of Hon. James M. Ashley of Ohio, Delivered in the US House of Representatives December 17, 1868, on the death of Hon. Thaddeus Stevens of Pennsylvania, *Souvenir*, 640, 643 ("When I first entered this House, ten years ago, Mr. Stevens was one of the first to take me by the hand and welcome me"); Horowitz, *Great Impeacher*, 50–51, 80. Ashley's opponent in 1862 was the future Supreme Court Chief Justice Morrison Waite. Les Benedict, "James M. Ashley, Toledo Politics and the Thirteenth Amendment," *University of Toledo Law Review* 38 (2007): 815, 826.

[5] Foner, *Free Soil*, 69–70, 89 (citing *New York Times*, June 10, 1858).

recognizes property in man." Acknowledging that the Court had disagreed with him in the *Dred Scott* decision, Ashley questioned the authority of that Court. Ashley accused the slave-holding elite of using the federal courts to perpetuate slavery and choosing federal judges for their proslavery views. He insisted that "neither the executive, nor the judicial, nor law-making power is supreme. The Constitution is above them," and he exclaimed that the absolute power claimed for the Supreme Court "must be resisted." Ashley concluded, "Sir, when I took an oath to support the Constitution, I swore to support it as I understood it, and not as a majority of the Supreme Court may understand it, or any number of men, individually or collectively."[6] Thus, Ashley made it clear that he believed that constitutional meaning was not solely the province of the court, but also a subject of political debate. He was deeply engaged in constitutional politics.

Ashley described a country divided by the institution of slavery and contrasted the autocratic southern society with the northern culture of free labor. In the North, he said, the states had adopted "the best system known to man. It is the best, because it rests upon labor, and is created and controlled by the free and untrammeled will of the laborer ... they must be citizens; having rights which the government and all classes of citizens are bound to respect and defend." By contrast, in the southern states, "practically, the reverse of all this is true ... a class is dominant which fills all the offices, and controls the legislative, executive, and judicial departments of the government. They do not pretend to be loyal to the national Constitution." He continued, "The laborers upon whose toil these States exist are slaves, and have been declared not to be citizens, though born upon the soil, but simply persons, with no moral, social, or natural rights, that the dominant race are bound to respect."[7] Here, Ashley presented an idyllic view of life in the free states, and the rights that he believed free people should enjoy. He drew a sharp contrast between free states, which at least purported to respect those rights, and slave states, which openly violated them. Ashley had articulated a positive right to free labor, which poor whites, as well as slaves, were entitled to enjoy.

Ashley appealed to the poor whites in the southern states, whom he believed to be the natural allies of the antislavery effort. According to

---

[6] Speech of Hon. James Ashley of Ohio, Delivered in the US House of Representatives, May 29, 1860, *Souvenir*, 44 (hereafter referred to as "First House Speech"); Horowitz, *Great Impeacher*, 49, 51, 56, 79–80.

[7] Ashley, "First House Speech," *Souvenir*, 44, 45; Horowitz, *Great Impeacher*, 45.

Ashley, the privileged elite in the southern states were imposing a reign of terror, prohibiting anyone from even criticizing slavery and using racism to divide and weaken the working class. Ashley explained that in order for the slave-holding elites to maintain power, "The poor whites of the South, in whose hands, if united, resides the political power, must be kept divided, as they are today; and in order to keep them successfully divided, and fighting their supposed enemy, the free negro, and those who favor the prohibition of slavery in the Territories, they must be kept in ignorance." Lacking public education, poor whites would be unable or unwilling to discern their own economic interests. "[H]ere, sir, is disclosed the real point of danger to the ruling class of the South – the fear of rebellion on the part of the poor whites whom they now claim as loyal subjects." Ashley predicted a "violent revolution ... with all its attendant horrors," and made it clear that if that occurred, slavery would be its cause.[8] After the Civil War broke out, Ashley insisted that the only way to end it would be to eradicate its cause – slavery – and replace it with a regime of free labor described in his first speech to Congress.

Republican Abraham Lincoln was elected president in November 1860. Lincoln was relatively moderate, but his election was a clear threat to the future of slavery. In December 1860, the state of South Carolina seceded from the Union. In the House, members voted 145–38 to create a committee to solve the secession crisis. Ashley was one of the thirty-eight to vote no. President Lincoln and many congressional leaders sought a compromise to defuse the crisis, even proposing a constitutional amendment that would prevent the federal government from ending slavery. Ashley opposed all compromise measures. In a speech on January 17, 1861, Ashley argued that the people of the United States were tired of "compromises" with slavery. "[T]he truth is, slavery is gasping for breath; it is struggling for a new lease on life ... What the people of this country want, what they expect and demand at our hands, is not new truces with slavery, but a permanent settlement of this question the only way it can ever be settled to give peace and contentment to the country, and that is, wherever the national jurisdiction extends, by the just rule of right and liberty."[9] According to Ashley, compromise with slavery would

---

[8] See Horowitz, *Great Impeacher*, 56, 47; Ashley, "First House Speech," *Souvenir*, 99, 107. Ashley insisted that slavery would end if freedom of speech and the press were available in southern states. Ibid., 112.

[9] Richard H. Sewell, *Ballots for Freedom: Antislavery Politics in the United States 1837–1860* (New York: Oxford University Press, 1976), 359; Oakes, *Freedom National*, xx; Trefousse, *Radical Republicans*, 144; Richards, *Who Freed the Slaves?*, 15, 20; Foner,

only perpetuate the conflict. As Steward had argued in his influential speech, Ashley believed the conflict between slavery and freedom was inevitable and unavoidable while slavery endured.

Ashley claimed that the federal government had the power to stop southern states from seceding. He called the southern state's alleged right to secede a "heresy," "denounced by the leading men of the Revolution." He claimed that the Guaranty Clause empowered the national government to protect "the whole people in all the States against the violation of their personal rights and liberties, even though committed by legislative majorities," and authorized the government to intervene to protect loyal people in the seceding states. "It is [the general government's] duty to protect and secure [the loyal minority] in the enjoyment of all their constitutional rights, and by FORCE if necessary." If the conflict ended in violence, he warned, it would be the fault not of the federal government but of the seceding states. "May God in his mercy avert the catastrophe of civil and servile war. But if it must come, I pray that the doom of slavery, which will be inevitable, may not also prove the doom of the slave masters." If civil war is forced on the nation "for the purpose of extending and making slavery perpetual, he must indeed be blind who does not see that the system will go out in blood."[10] Even before the war began, Ashley characterized it as a battle to end slavery.

When the Civil War began in April 1861, the war's impact on slavery was far from a foregone conclusion. Ashley's Republican allies immediately advised Lincoln to use martial law to free the slaves. However, many of the northern Democrats came from the border states where slavery was still legal.[11] They insisted that the only purpose of the war was to save the Union, and not to end slavery. Nonetheless, the war was already making inroads into slavery. Prior to the Thirteenth Amendment, and as early as May 1861, military emancipation began to free thousands of slaves. Ashley strongly supported this development, embracing military emancipation from the start of the war.

After the firing on Fort Sumter, Ashley traveled to Ohio, Indiana, and Illinois, where he rallied recruits for the Union Army. During those travels, Ashley became convinced that antislavery sentiment had grown

---

Free Soil, 224; Speech of Hon. James Ashley of Ohio Delivered in the US House or Representatives, January 17, 1861 (hereafter referred to as "House speech"), *Souvenir*, 116, 118.

[10] Ashley, "House speech," *Souvenir*, 131, 135, 138, 157.

[11] Oakes, *Freedom National*, 80–81, 145–146.

significantly. Ashley also visited Generals Benjamin Butler and Ulysses S. Grant at the front. There, he learned that soldiers were involved in early efforts to free slaves. On May 23, 1861, three slaves ran to freedom and joined the General Butler's Union forces at Ft. Monroe, Virginia. Butler was a Democrat from Lowell, Massachusetts, a lawyer who defended workers' rights against local mill owners.[12] Prior to the war Butler was a fusion Democrat and had never been strongly antislavery. Nonetheless, Butler was to become a hero to antislavery forces and a strong ally of James Ashley, because he kept the fleeing slaves in his camp and refused to send them back. The general argued that the Fugitive Slave Clause did not apply to foreign countries, which, he pointed out, Virginia claimed to be. Butler notified President Lincoln, asking for approval and setting off a debate over what Union forces should do with fugitive slaves.[13]

The slaves who fled over enemy lines raised some complicated constitutional questions related to federalism and the separation of powers. Since the beginning of the Republic, the "federal consensus" had barred Congress from banning slavery in existing states, and not even the Republican Party had claimed authority to do so. Ashley argued that the Confederate states had ceased to be states when they rebelled and reverted to the status of territories, within Congress's plenary authority. However, few members of Congress agreed with Ashley's territorial theory. Thus, they had to grapple with the question of where Congress would get the power to end slavery. Military emancipation enabled members of Congress to rely on their war powers. Some members of Congress argued that slaves could be emancipated as a criminal punishment for their rebel masters, but it was not clear what power Congress could use to impose that punishment. The alternative was for the president to use his power as Commander in Chief to free the slaves as a military measure. President Lincoln eventually took this approach when he issued the Emancipation Proclamation. However, Ashley and his congressional allies wanted Congress to take the lead.

[12] Richards, *Who Freed the Slaves?*, 24; Oakes, *Freedom National*, 95. According to historian James Oakes, "Butler presented himself to voters as the enemy of corporations and the friend of working people." Ibid., 91.

[13] Oakes, *Freedom National*, 95–97. Butler had endorsed the proslavery Lecompton constitution for Kansas, voted fifty times for Jefferson Davis at the 1860 Democratic convention, "and appealed to white workers with racial demagoguery." In the state legislature he supported Charles Sumner for senator, but then campaigned for Buchanan in the 1856 presidential election. Ibid., 91, 95.

At the beginning of the war military commanders were divided about what to do when slaves escaped to their lines. General Butler confiscated and freed the fugitive slaves in Maryland, but in western Virginia, General George McClellan assured the Virginia residents that their "property" in slaves would be safe. In Washington, the president and members of Congress were compelled to decide what military officials should do with the fugitive slaves. Ashley supported Butler's approach. He visited Butler at Fort Monroe just two days after the General liberated the first fugitive slaves. The day before he left to visit Fort Monroe, Ashley wrote an open letter to criticize McClellan (without using his name) and argue Butler's cause.[14]

Ashley began his letter by describing the historical significance of the controversy. "One of the most important of all political questions ever presented for the consideration of any administration in this country, is about to be forced upon this administration, and I rejoice that it must come now ... I allude to the disposition of the slaves, who, as our army penetrates into the South will desert from the camps and plantations of the rebels and join our ranks." Ashley insisted that the fugitive slaves could be "confiscated" as property, and then emancipated. He pointed out, "If we send them back we strengthen the enemy. If we permit them to come, we destroy the enemy ... Shall the government use its military power to weaken itself and strengthen its enemies? Would any nation engaged in a war with another nation thus act?" Ashley predicted that the end of slavery was inevitable because "the people of the United States will never consent to fight against the slave barons and at the same time fight to make slavery perpetual. You cannot make a free people fight for and against a great crime at the same time." He argued that if the slaves were property, the Union troops could hold them "just as they would any property," to prevent the rebels from using their labor for their military effort. Ashley insisted that the war was not "for the enslavement of any people, but a war for their liberation."[15] Ashley had considerable evidence to support his view. The Confederate Constitution established a constitutional right to own slaves and contained numerous provisions protecting the rights of slaveholders. Nonetheless, the question of whether

---

[14] Oakes, *Freedom National*, 104; Horowitz, *Great Impeacher*, 65; Important Letter from Hon. J. M. Ashley, Washington, May 24, 1861, *Souvenir*, 165.

[15] Important Letter from Hon. J. M. Ashley, Washington, May 24, 1861, *Souvenir*, 169, 166.

slavery caused the war, and the impact that the war should have on slavery, was contested throughout the conflict.

In the summer of 1861, a new party formed in the North – the Union Party. Ashley attended the Union convention and was appalled to find that the party's platform declared that the sole purpose of the war was to preserve the Union. The Union Party did well in Ohio and the unionist effort gained momentum. In July, Congress easily passed the Crittenden resolution, which attempted to limit the Union effort to suppressing the rebel insurrection. Ashley voted for the Crittenden resolution in the interest of party unity, a vote that he later regretted.[16] He then set out to change public opinion on the issue. Ashley knew that convincing the public that slavery had caused the war was the first step toward convincing them to abolish it.

In July and August, Ashley went on a speaking tour to contradict the Unionists. He repeated his charge that slavery caused the Civil War, and claimed that ending slavery would be the only way to end the war. He insisted, "This is a war about slavery and you and I know it." The argument that slavery had caused the war provided an additional, powerful justification to end the peculiar institution. He explained, "You and I know that the overthrow of slavery will not only end the war, but, beyond all doubt, save the Union and preserve constitutional liberty." Throughout the war, Ashley continued to argue that slavery had caused the war, and the war could be won only by ending slavery. In the summer of 1861, there was already evidence that Ashley would be proven correct. "In the states that had seceded from the Union, slavery was already losing the protection it had under the Constitution." The "federal consensus" was being undermined by the facts on the ground.[17]

In July 1861, Senator Lyman Trumbull introduced a bill authorizing Union troops to confiscate slaves from rebel owners. Consistent with the "universal Republican conviction ... that slaves were not recognized as property under the Constitution," Trumbull's bill used language from the Fugitive Slave Clause. The bill provided that any person claiming to be entitled to the labor of any other person, and using that labor to support the rebel cause, shall forfeit the right to such service or labor and the

---

[16] Richards, *Who Freed the Slaves?*, 36, 381; Horowitz, *Great Impeacher*, 68; Address of Hon. James M. Ashley before the "Ohio Society of New York," at the Fifth Annual Banquet, Wednesday evening, February 19, 1890, *Souvenir*, 692, 697 (referring to his vote on the Crittenden resolution as the only time that he faltered in the antislavery effort, and expressing shame at the memory).

[17] Richards, *Who Freed the Slaves?*, 38, 201, 208; Oakes, *Freedom National*, 102, 104.

"person" (i.e., slave) shall be discharged from service – that is, emancipated.[18] Ashley was only too happy to support this bill and argued that it fell within Congress's war powers. In a speech in Congress citing John Quincy Adams, he said, "More than a year ago, I proclaimed to the constituency which I have the honor to represent, my purpose to destroy the institution of slavery ... I then declared, as I now declare, that 'justice, no less than our own self-preservation as a nation, required that we should confiscate and emancipate, and thus secure indemnity for the past and security for the future.'" Thaddeus Stevens agreed, arguing that emancipating an enemy's slaves was a classic use of war powers "giving freedom to the oppressed." The vote in favor of this Confiscation Act, the first federal law in US history to emancipate slaves in states where slavery was legal, was almost unanimous. Within a year of its passage, tens of thousands of slaves were freed by the act, which made military emancipation official Union policy.[19]

The first Confiscation Act applied only to slaves who had been used in the war effort. In December 1861, Lyman Trumbull introduced a bill to confiscate the property of all rebels and free their slaves, regardless of whether they were working for the rebel effort. Some members of Congress thought the Second Act was unconstitutional, too much like punishment for a crime rather than a war measure. Thus, it seemed to go beyond Congress's power to enact war measures. Ashley and his allies offered a different justification for this far-reaching statute. Ashley argued that rebel states reverted to the status of territories subject to plenary control by Congress and to the jurisdiction of his Committee on the Territories. According to Ashley, when the people of the rebel states violated the national Constitution and confederated into a hostile government, "there can be no constitutional State governments in such States." Thus, he claimed, the US Congress had full sovereignty over those territories, and all concerns of state sovereignty were eliminated. On May 20, 1862, Massachusetts Representative Thomas Eliot relied on the territorial theory when he sponsored a radical emancipation bill that would have freed all slaves of rebels, as a criminal punishment, based on the theory that the Constitution no longer applies to seceded states. The territorial bill failed by a close margin, but the war powers theory eventually prevailed.[20]

---

[18] Oakes, *Freedom National*, 118, 120.

[19] Cong Globe, 37th Cong., 2nd Sess., App. 225–227, cited in Horowitz, *Great Impeacher*, 78; Oakes, *Freedom National*, 135, 110, 142, 143.

[20] Oakes, *Freedom National*, 228; Horowitz, *Great Impeacher*, 72; General Ashley's Speech at San Francisco, California, September 17th, 1865, *Souvenir*, 370, 375; Cong. Globe, 37th Cong., 2nd Sess., 1797; Oakes, *Freedom National*, 231.

The Second Confiscation Act freed all slaves of disloyal masters in rebel territories. The far-reaching act distinguished between confiscation of property, limited by the constitution's restrictions on Bills of Attainder, and emancipation of slaves, not limited because, as antislavery activists had argued, the Constitution did not recognize property in man. With this act, Congress authorized Benjamin Butler and other military leaders to continue confiscating all of the freed slaves who they encountered. Section 6 of the act called for a presidential proclamation that persons still aiding and abetting the rebellion would have their property seized (including slaves). Democrats and border state members of Congress "were scandalized by the vast implications of the Second Confiscation Act." Republicans passed the bill over their protestations.[21] The Second Confiscation Act had a huge symbolic importance, officially aligning the Union forces with the antislavery mission.

Another category of military emancipation measures focused on repealing the Fugitive Slave laws. In July 1861, Owen Lovejoy introduced a resolution declaring that the soldiers should not capture or return fugitive slaves. While that measure failed, in March 1862 Congress approved a bill that prohibited the US military from enforcing the Fugitive Slave Clause. That act had enormous symbolic significance. Conflicts over fugitive slaves had plagued the country in the years leading up to the Civil War and antislavery activists despised the federal Fugitive Slave laws. Ashley later proposed a bill to rescind the 1850 Fugitive Slave Act, which died in committee in 1863.[22] By then, confiscation and the Thirteenth Amendment were set to supersede the hated measure.

Ashley argued that his territorial theory provided a basis to reconstruct the rebel states based on his free labor vision. In late 1861 and early 1862, the Union's military position was precarious, and victory was far from certain. Nonetheless, Ashley had already begun to envision what the country would be like after the Union prevailed. On December 11, 1861, Ashley and Benjamin Wade, the Chair of the Senate Committee on the Territories, met with Secretary of Treasury Salmon Chase to discuss a strategy for reframing the relationship between the rebel states and the federal government. Chase suggested that rebel states had reverted to territories, and the two committee chairs agreed. They came

---

[21] US Statutes at Large, 37th Cong., 2nd Sess., 589–592; Oakes, *Freedom National*, 232, 240.

[22] Cong. Globe, 37th Cong., 2nd Sess., 130, 956, 358–359; Paul Finkelman, *Slavery and the Founders: Race and Liberty in the Age of Jefferson* (Armonk, NY: M.E. Sharp, 1996); Horowitz, *Great Impeacher*, 91.

up with a plan to use the territorial theory to undermine the institution of
slavery. Using his position on the Committee on the Territories, Ashley
introduced the first proposed Reconstruction Act. Ashley's Reconstruction Act would have not only freed the slaves, but also confiscated rebel
lands in areas where Union forces had prevailed.[23] The act would have
established temporary governments in rebel territories based on Ashley's
egalitarian free labor vision.

Ashley First Reconstruction Act would have authorized the president
to take possession of states and establish a temporary civil government
with three branches, legislative, judicial and executive. The act would
have ended slavery in those territories and authorized the confiscation of
land from "abandoned, forfeited or confiscated estates." The act provided
for this land to be leased in lots no more than 160 acres to "loyal
occupants," including freed slaves. The act reflected Ashley's Democratic
roots and interest in racial equality. It would have mandated the creation
of public schools, which would be open to all children, white and black.
All adult males, white and black, would be allowed to vote and sit on
juries.[24] The bill would have gone a long way toward establishing the free
labor society that Ashley envisioned.

On February 11, 1862, Charles Sumner introduced a Reconstruction
bill similar to Ashley's in the Senate. Nonetheless, their bills had little
chance of passage in 1862. President Lincoln disliked Ashley's territorial
theory of Reconstruction, termed the "state suicide" theory. Lincoln
always insisted that the southern states had remained states throughout
the conflict. Indeed, Ashley later recalled, "On no one subject did we
disagree with Mr. Lincoln so radically as that of reconstruction." Moreover, as the subsequent debate over the abolition of slavery in the District
of Columbia revealed, Ashley's colleagues were not yet ready to consider
uncompensated emancipation. After the war was over, the Reconstruction Congress adopted many of the other provisions of Ashley's proposed
act, but notably never embarked on the land redistribution that Ashley
had advocated in 1862.[25]

---

[23] Horowitz, *Great Impeacher*, 71–72; see Copy of the First Reconstruction Bill Introduced
in Congress by Mr. Ashley, *Souvenir*, 363. According to Ashley, the bill was prepared in
June 1861, only two months into the war. Letter from James Ashley to Benjamin Arnett,
Souvenir, 360.

[24] Copy of the First Reconstruction Bill Introduced in Congress by Mr. Ashley, *Souvenir*,
363–365.

[25] Horowitz, *Great Impeacher*, 73–74; Ashley was also unsuccessful at his attempt to repeal
the Fugitive Slave Act. Ibid., 91; Address of Hon. J. M. Ashley at Memorial Hall, Toledo,
Ohio, June 2, 1890, *Souvenir*, 714, 757; Eric Foner, *Politics and Ideology in the Age of*

Of his first Reconstruction bill Ashley later recalled, "I soon learned that not one of my Republican colleagues on the committee were then prepared to say that they would vote for my bill." With the help of then Chase, Sumner, and Wade, Ashley set out to persuade his colleagues. Eventually, all but one Republican on the committee voted for the bill, but he could not get the bill through the House. Ashley recalled that the minority of the Territorial Committee denounced the bill, saying that "the bill was intended to emancipate at once, and forever, all slaves, and to seize all public lands belonging to the rebel States, and lease or give such lands, and forfeited or confiscated estates, to slaves so emancipated." He admitted, "That was undoubtedly my purpose, and there are today, thousands of thinking men, who now believe it failed to do this act of prudence and justice." Ashley's bill was tabled, with his fellow Ohioan John Bingham voting against the motion. Eventually, Congress enacted Reconstruction measures similar to Ashley's bill, but without the land reform measure. Ashley later opined that "experience has taught us, that the reconstruction measures finally enacted by Congress, were not as safe, or as desirable, as my original bill which provided for putting the rebel States in territorial condition, until Congress should provide by law for their reorganization." He voted for the bill that eventually passed because it was the best they could get, but later mused, "I thought then, and think now, that we fell short of our duty to the black man."[26]

In the spring of 1862, Ashley was elected chair of the Committee on the Territories. Ashley was most proud of the Committee's role in abolishing slavery in the District of Columbia and in other federal territories. Since Theodore Dwight Weld's classic treatise, antislavery activists longed to end slavery in the nation's capital. Weld's pamphlet was widely revered by the antislavery constitutionalists who helped to inform the Republican Party. Prior to the war, however, there had not been the political will in Congress to act. In 1862, the time was ripe. The Union was fighting a war against the forces of slavery, yet slavery still reigned in the nation's capital. Ashley proposed the first bill to abolish slavery in the District of Columbia, and he played a leading role in ushering the bill through the House of Representatives.[27] This time, he met a receptive audience.

---

the *Civil War* (New York: Oxford University Press, 1980), 131 (describing Thaddeus Stevens's efforts at land reform during the Reconstruction Era). Notably, after the war, Ashley prioritized voting rights over land redistribution. Ibid., 133.

[26] James Ashley Letter to Benjamin Arnett, December 22, 1892, *Souvenir*, 360–362, 368.

[27] Theodore Dwight Weld, "The Power of Congress over the District of Columbia," *The Antislavery Examiner No. 6*, reprinted from the *New York Evening Post*, with additions by the author, published by the *American Antislavery Society*, no. 5 (New York, 1838).

*the 15th k
language is
re enslaved
but
then*

Ashley's bill tracked the language of the Northwest Ordinance: "That from or after the passage of this act, neither slavery nor involuntary servitude, except as punishment for crime, whereof the party shall have been duly convicted, shall exist in the District of Columbia; and thereafter it shall not be lawful for any person in said District to own or to hold a human being as a slave." Ashley's bill would have ordered emancipation without compensation, but uncompensated emancipation was "too radical for its time." With their eyes on the loyal border states, Lincoln and then-Treasury Secretary Chase wanted slave owners to be compensated, and emancipation gradual. In his March 3, 1862, Cooper Union Speech, Lincoln proposed compensated emancipation of slaves in the border states. In the Senate, Henry Wilson's bill followed Lincoln's lead and provided compensation for the slaveholders in the District of Columbia.[28]

Ashley objected to both aspects of Lincoln's and Chase's approach to abolition of slavery in the territories. However, he followed Wilson's lead and accepted compensation to get the bill passed. Ashley explained, "I intend to vote for this bill as a national duty ... I am a practical man, and shall support this bill as the best we can get at the time." He grudgingly conceded that "if it be necessary to employ gold to [achieve emancipation], let gold be employed." Ashley insisted that emancipation be immediate, overriding the will of his president, and here he had the support of his party. Every Republican in Congress voted for the measure, which the president signed on April 16, 1862. Ashley counted that bill as one of his greatest political achievements.[29]

During the debate over the emancipation of slaves in the District of Columbia, Ashley responded to his colleagues' concern that freed slaves would cause an increase in crime and disorder.[30] Ashley pointed out that there was already a well-developed black culture in the District. He noted

See Oakes, *Freedom National*, 270; Richards, *Who Freed the Slaves?*, 55. Senator Henry Wilson also introduced a bill that would abolish slavery in the District of Columbia. Lea S. VanderVelde, "Henry Wilson, Cobbler of the Frayed Constitution, Strategist of the Thirteenth Amendment," *Georgetown Journal of Law and Politics* 15 (2017): 173.

[28] Horowitz, *Great Impeacher*, 75–76; Richards, *Who Freed the Slaves?*, 57–58; Trefousse, *Radical Republicans*, 211.

[29] Speech of Hon. James M. Ashley of Ohio in the House of Representatives on the Bill for the Release of Certain Persons Held to Service or Labor in the District of Columbia, April 11, 1862, *Souvenir*, 213, 214–215; Richards, *Who Freed the Slaves?*, 58; Trefousse, *Radical Republicans*, 213; Letter from James Ashley to Benjamin Arnett, December 22, 1892, *Souvenir*, 329, 331.

[30] Richards, *Who Freed the Slaves?*, 58; Speech of Hon. James M. Ashley of Ohio in the House of Representatives, April 11, 1862, *Souvenir*, 220, 221.

that free blacks owned property, attended church, and sent their children to schools. "They are taxed for the support of schools from which their children are excluded, and maintain separate schools of their own. They have societies for the support of their sick and disabled, and never permit one of their number to be buried at public expense. In thirty years not one of their number has been convicted of a capital offense. As a body, they are industrious, frugal, orderly, trustworthy and religious. Instead of an increase, I venture to predict, as one of the results of this great measure, a decrease in disorder, theft, idleness and crime." To bolster his argument, Ashley read a proclamation from a meeting of black ministers in the city, declaring April 13, 1862, a day of thanks and prayer for their coming freedom. "Need I say to this House and the country that the men who could draft and adopt such a preamble and resolution will receive their freedom with heartfelt joy, and not with riotous and offensive demonstrations?" Ashley also supported a bill that provided public education for black children who lived in the District.[31] Here, Ashley showed his true commitment to racial equality and revealed his connections with the black community in the city where he then lived.

Later that summer, with Ashley as Chair of the Committee on the Territories, Congress passed a bill to end slavery in all federal territories. This bill, and the one emancipating slaves in the District of Columbia, conflicted with the Court's ruling in *Dred Scott* that slaveholders had a constitutional right to own slaves. The second bill was especially suspect given the lack of compensation for the slaveholders. If the slaveholders had a property right in their slaves, the second bill was arguably a taking without just compensation, violating the Takings Clause of the Fifth Amendment. However, for decades antislavery activists had maintained that there was no constitutional right to property in man, a bedrock principle of the Republican Party.[32] Ashley addressed the question by attacking the authority of the Supreme Court. He said, "Sir, neither the executive, nor the judicial, nor law-making power is supreme. The Constitution is above them," and insisted that the absolute power claimed for the Supreme Court "must be resisted." Many of his colleagues agreed.

---

[31] Speech of Hon. James M. Ashley of Ohio in the House of Representatives, April 11, 1862, *Souvenir*, 221–222; Trefousse, *Radical Republicans*, 214.

[32] Horowitz, *Great Impeacher*, 77; The DC bill arguably did not amount to a taking of property since it provided compensation for the freed slaves; see Oakes, *Freedom National*, 8.

"The *Dred Scott* decision was dead" to them,[33] undermined by political resistance and events on the battlefield.

As Chair of Committee on the Territories, Ashley also presided over the creation of new, antislavery states. These states would help to form a tightening noose around slavery, and ensure more antislavery sentiment in Congress. The first such state was the state of West Virginia, formed not from a territory but out of the state of Virginia. When Virginia seceded, the western counties of the state voted against secession. They held a referendum in 1862 and applied for statehood. West Virginia originally wanted to be a slave state, but Republicans required the state to abolish slavery in order to enter the Union. Benjamin Wade, chair of the Senate Committee on Territories, prepared a bill to organize West Virginia as a free state. Ashley presided over the bill in the House. Lincoln signed the bill on December 31, 1862, and issued the Emancipation Proclamation the next day.[34]

In May 1862, Ashley introduced a bill to create another state out of the Territory of Arizona. Ashley argued that the people of Arizona wanted to become a state so that they could be protected against Indians and violent secessionists. "The band of secessionists now having control of this Territory must be driven out of it, and there is no way by which this can be done so easily, and the territory so effectually secured to the Union, as by giving it a territorial organization." Of course, the bill included the "Jefferson proviso" that barred slavery in the new state. Ashley argued that the passage of the bill would place the federal government on the side of freedom. However, the House voted to postpone his motion, and Arizona did not become a state until 1912. In 1864, Ashley helped facilitate the admission of the neighbor state of Nevada just in time to ensure one more state's vote for the Thirteenth Amendment.[35]

Finally, Ashley and his allies used wartime measures to promote the rights of free blacks. In the summer of 1862, the war was not going well for the Union effort. Radicals blamed General McClellan for being

---

[33] Ashley, "First House Speech," *Souvenir*, 44, 53; Trefousse, *Radical Republicans*, 213.

[34] Oakes, *Freedom National*, 294–295, 299; Trefousse, *Radical Republicans*, 271; Horowitz, *Great Impeacher*, 83.

[35] Speech of Hon. James M. Ashley, of Ohio, in the House of Representatives, May 8, 1862, on the Government of the Territory of Arizona, *Souvenir*, 226, 231, 228, 239, 237; Horowitz, *Great Impeacher*, 102. Ashley also introduced the enabling acts for the Territories of Nebraska and Colorado, drew up bills creating the Territories of Montana and Wyoming, and played a role in organizing the Idaho and Dakota Territories. Ashley Obituary, *New York Times*, September 17, 1896.

too indecisive, and too conservative on the slavery issue. They also began to argue that freed slaves should be allowed to serve in the Union Army. But at the time US law restricted military service to free white citizens. On July 17, 1862, Congress enacted a Militia Act, which removed the words "free" and "white" from the qualifications for military service. This begged the question of whether freed slaves were US citizens and thus eligible for military service. Attorney General Edward Bates issued a thirty-page document repudiating everything that Chief Justice Taney had said about citizenship in his *Dred Scott* opinion. According to Bates, the Constitution made no distinction between blacks and whites; there was no such thing as partial citizenship; and national citizenship takes precedence over state citizenship. Abolitionists widely celebrated the Bates ruling. It paved the way for the Emancipation Proclamation, which Lincoln said was a military measure to enable more blacks to serve in the army. Ashley was happy to see blacks serving in the military and argued that service justified the extension of rights to free blacks.[36]

The fall 1862 election was a tough election for Ohio Republicans, and Ashley was no exception. Frank Waggoner, the conservative editor of *The Toledo Blade*, launched an editorial campaign to defeat Ashley by accusing him of corruption. Ashley was later exonerated of the charges, but they took their toll on his support. Meanwhile, Ashley focused his campaign on his opposition to slavery. Lincoln had issued his preliminary emancipation proclamation that fall, and Ashley claimed credit for it. Antislavery newspapers "rallied to Ashley's defense during the campaign." For example, the *New York Independent* stated that the nation could not afford to lose the services of such a "brave, bold man, who always fights on the side of humanity and justice," and asserted that "the President is desirous of Mr. Ashley's re-election." Noted antislavery politicians Charles Sumner and George Julian traveled to Ohio to campaign for Ashley. The vote was close, but Ashley squeezed out a victory. In a three-man race, he won by 1100 votes.[37]

In his draft memoir, Ashley recalled that he was the only Republican from Ohio who was elected in 1862, and claimed that "I would have been

[36] Horowitz, *Great Impeacher*, 79; Oakes, *Freedom National*, 357, 359–361; Richards, *Who Freed the Slaves?*, 83, 102; see Speech of Honorable James M. Ashley of Ohio, in the House of Representatives, May 29, 1866 – Impartial Suffrage the Only Safe Basis of Reconstruction, *Souvenir*, 392, 401.

[37] Horowitz, *Great Impeacher*, 80–82 (citing *New York Independent*, October 2, 1862); Richards, *Who Freed the Slaves?*, 162.

defeated, but for the heroic and manly fight of solid anti-slavery me."
Other notable members of the Reconstruction Congress were defeated
that year, including John Bingham (chief author of Section 1 of the
Fourteenth Amendment) and Samuel Shellabarger (chief proponent of
the 1870 Enforcement Act), were defeated "by the same class of men
who organized the 'bolting movement' in the northern Ohio district,
against [Ashley]." The year 1862 was a bad one for Republicans nationally. Democrats gained twenty-eight seats in Congress and purged dissi-
dents from the party.[38]

However, the tough campaign in the fall of 1862 seems to have only
strengthened Ashley's resolve. On January 31, 1863, Ashley wrote a letter
to his constituents to celebrate the Emancipation Proclamation. Said
Ashley, "Today the Rubicon was crossed, and the nation, thanks to the
persistent demands of her earnest sons, is at last irrevocably committed to
the policy of universal emancipation." He continued, "I may be over
sanguine in my hopes of the future, but it seems to me as if the hour has
struck when the Union contemplated by our fathers is about to be realized." Ashley's dream that the war would bring about the end of slavery
seemed to be coming true. "I have believed from the first, as my constituents well know, that slavery must die before the rebellion could end."[39]

Yet the Emancipation Proclamation was actually fairly conservative. It
did not apply to border states or territory already conquered, which
meant that over 800,000 slaves would remain in bondage. According to
historian Michael Vorenberg, "Americans understood that the proclamation was but an early step in putting black freedom on secure legal
footing." Moreover, critics argued that the proclamation was unconstitutional, that the president lacked the power to make such a proclamation. According to historian Leonard Richards, it was "beyond
question" that "the Taney Court would strike down emancipation."
The Emancipation Proclamation had created a paradox. "The problem,
simply put, was that unionists were now supposed to fight two seemingly
incompatible wars: one against slavery, and one for a constitution that
supported slavery." Ashley had been making this argument from the

[38] James Ashley, Draft Memoir, John M. Morgan papers relating to James M. Ashley,
University of Toledo libraries, Ward M. Canaday Center Manuscript Collection, box, 1,
folder 2, p. 5; Richards, *Who Freed the Slaves?*, 163.

[39] Mr. Ashley's Letter on President Lincoln's Emancipation Proclamation from *The Toledo
Commercial*, January 1, 1863, *Souvenir*, 240, 241–243.

beginning of the war, but the Emancipation Proclamation brought the paradox to the fore. In September 1863, Ashley declared, "I tell you that the government is irrevocably committed to the policy of emancipation, and no power on this earth can turn it back."[40] The following year, he led the effort to irrevocably commit his country to the abolition of slavery by amending the Constitution.

---

[40] See Richards, *Who Freed the Slaves?*, 78, 71; Michael Vorenberg, *Final Freedom: The Civil War, the Abolition of Slavery, and the Thirteenth Amendment* (New York: Cambridge University Press, 2001), 1, 34; Eloquent Speech of Gen. Ashley at Bowling Green, September, 1863, at the Wood County Union Convention, *Souvenir*, 257, 261.

6

The Thirteenth Amendment and a New Republic

In the fall of 1863, James Ashley came to Washington to begin the thirty-eighth session of Congress. After a bruising 1862 reelection fight against future Supreme Court Justice Morrison Waite, "he had won a national reputation as an unswerving foe of slavery, a defender of the oppressed, and a man of intelligence, enthusiasm, and conviction."[1] In December, Ashley was the first member of Congress to propose an amendment to the Constitution that would end slavery. Ashley and his allies had gone as far as they could with the existing Constitution. Although members of Congress mostly ignored *Dred Scott*, it loomed as a proslavery precedent. Lincoln's Emancipation Proclamation was an incomplete, temporary war measure, liable to be overturned by the Supreme Court or a future president. The war measures adopted by Congress, including the Confiscation Acts, were also temporary by nature, arguably limited to the duration of the war. State sovereignty still limited the extent to which Congress could regulate slavery, especially in the loyal border states. State sovereignty also limited Congress's power to reconstruct the rebel states. In Ashley's view, only a permanent and national solution would be sufficient to end slavery and ensure that Congress could protect the rights of freed slaves. Therefore, he proposed an amendment to the Constitution

<hr>

[1] Robert F. Horowitz, *The Great Impeacher: A Political Biography of James M. Ashley* (New York: Brooklyn College Press, 1979), 89 (1978). For an excellent account of Ashley's 1862 election campaign against Morrison Waite, see Les Benedict, "James M. Ashley, Toledo Politics and the Thirteenth Amendment," *University of Toledo Law Review* 38 (2007): 815.

that would abolish slavery and empower Congress to define and protect the fundamental rights of free people.

Amending the Constitution to abolish slavery was a revolutionary concept. Along with the Bill of Rights (adopted almost simultaneously with the ratification of the original Constitution), the Constitution had been amended only twice before, and the document "had become sacred in American culture." Most members of Congress believed that the Thirteenth Amendment would fundamentally alter the system of federalism established by the original Constitution by overturning the "federal consensus" that states regulated slavery.[2] Opponents thus claimed that the amendment itself was unconstitutional. However, Lincoln's Emancipation Proclamation had made it clear that freeing slaves were essential to the war effort. As free blacks entered the Union Army, their sacrifices showed that they were able and willing soldiers, loyal to the Union. The tide of northern public opinion was turning, even in the border states. Abolition was an increasingly popular cause. Ashley was ready to seize the moment, but he and his allies had to engage in constitutional politics to succeed.

On December 14, 1863, Ashley proposed a series of measures to further the abolition of slavery and protect the rights of free blacks. First, Ashley presented bills to admit Colorado and Nebraska to statehood and to create the Montana Territory. These measures would expand the number of free states and territories and establish the right of free blacks to vote in the Montana Territory. Second, Ashley proposed a join resolution calling for blacks in rebellious districts to be enlisted in the Union Army, with pay and rations equal to that of white Union soldiers. Along with aiding the war effort, this bill would provide free blacks an opportunity to prove their loyalty to the Union and strengthen the argument that they deserved equal rights. Third, Ashley offered a bill to repeal the 1850 Fugitive Slave Act, as well as "all acts and parts of the acts for the rendition of fugitive slaves," and to remove qualifying language from the Second Confiscation Act. Those bills would have expanded the wartime measures that were already eroding the institution of slavery, but they died in committee. Finally, and most importantly, Ashley proposed a constitutional amendment and a Reconstruction Act implementing that

---

[2] Michael Vorenberg, *Final Freedom: The Civil War, the Abolition of Slavery, and the Thirteenth Amendment* (New York: Cambridge University Press, 2001), 107. Ashley did not share this view because he already believed that the federal government had the power to regulate slavery in the existing states. However, his own Republican Party had rejected that view and only the most radical members of Congress agreed with Ashley on this point. See Chapter 2, supra.

amendment.[3] All of these measures together laid out Ashley's free labor vision. In his speeches supporting these measures, Ashley articulated the same antislavery vision that he had throughout his earlier career. However, he also adopted an additional argument from the antislavery constitutionalist ideology – that freed slaves would be citizens, entitled to the protection of the federal government.

Ashley's proposed Thirteenth Amendment differed from that of the amendment that was eventually adopted. The language of his amendment, like that which was adopted, tracked the language of the Northwest Ordinance: "Article. Slavery or involuntary servitude, except in punishment of crime, whereof the party shall have been duly convicted, is hereby forever prohibited in all the States of this Union, and in all Territories now owned or which may be hereafter be acquired by the United States." The language that Congress eventually adopted simplified the final clause, replacing it with "any place subject to its jurisdiction." Ashley chose not to propose his friend Charles Sumner's version of the amendment, which would have declared all persons "equal before the law."[4] Although Ashley agreed with Sumner's goal, he realized that Sumner's version was unlikely to succeed, and he did not want to "hazard the passage" of *any* antislavery amendment. Along with Senator Lyman Trumbull, Ashley used the language of the "Northwest Proviso," which had been revered by antislavery activists for decades, and could appeal to northern Democrats. Later debates over the 1866 Civil Rights Act revealed that many Republicans in the Thirty-Ninth Congress believed that the Thirteenth Amendment empowered them to legislate racial equality. However, because the debates over the Thirteenth Amendment took place during a politically sensitive time, many Republicans chose not to articulate the broader meaning of the amendment for the rights of freed slaves.[5] Ashley was not so reticent. From the outset he made it clear that

---

[3] Cong. Globe, 38th Cong., 1st Sess., 19–20; 38th Cong., H.R. 11, 12, 13, 14½, 15; H.R. Joint Resolution 6.

[4] Cong. Globe, 38th Cong., 1st Sess., 19. Compare with Section 1 of the Thirteenth Amendment: "Neither slavery nor involuntary servitude, except as punishment for crime whereof the party shall have been duly convicted, shall exist within the United States, or any place subject to its jurisdiction." According to Ashley, that change "materially improved" the Amendment. Letter from James Ashley to Benjamin Arnett, December 22, 1892, *Duplicate Copy of the Souvenir from The Afro-American League of Tennessee to Hon. James M. Ashley of Ohio* (Benjamin Arnett, ed.) (Publishing House of the AME Church, Philadelphia, 1894) (hereafter referred to as *Souvenir*), 329, 331; Vorenberg, *Final Freedom*, 51.

[5] Cong. Globe, 38th Cong., 2nd Sess., 531 (January 31, 1865); Vorenberg, *Final Freedom*, 55–56, 105–108.

he believed that the abolition of slavery would empower Congress to establish equal rights for blacks.

A week after he proposed his version of the amendment, Ashley proposed a Reconstruction bill that would enforce the amendment and lay out a blueprint for a free labor society.[6] The bill was similar to the Reconstruction bill that he proposed in 1862. While no longer authorizing the seizure of rebel lands, this bill contained the same broad protections for the rights of freed slaves. Ashley's bill would have guaranteed "equality of civil rights before the law ... to all persons in said states." The bill also would have recognized freed slaves as citizens, with the right to vote and to serve on juries. Ashley hoped that freed slaves themselves would play a prominent role in restructuring the rebellious states. He was one of the first members of Congress to condition Reconstruction on the voting rights of freed slaves,[7] and remained adamant on this issue throughout the Reconstruction Era. To Ashley, the abolition of slavery would facilitate the formation of a new republic based on the principals of liberty and equality.

Speaking to concerns that his amendment itself was unconstitutional, Ashley now articulated a new theory to justify both the amendment and his Reconstruction Act. He claimed that Congress's authority to enforce the Guarantee Clause authorized it to establish a republican form of government in the conquered states. Ashley had long argued that slavery violated the Guaranty Clause. Moreover, unlike Ashley's territorial theory, the Guaranty Clause theory acknowledged that the rebellious states continued to exist, albeit in violation of the Constitution. The preamble of Ashley's new Reconstruction bill explained that the rebellious states had "renounced their allegiance to the Constitution of the United States and abrogated the Republican form of Government therein established." According to Ashley, it was the duty of Congress "to establish state governments under the Constitution, to provide by law for eliciting the will of the loyal people of said states." Although Ashley

---

[6] Although Ashley's version of the Thirteenth Amendment lacked an enforcement provision, he evidently believed that an enforcement clause was not necessary. This was a widely held view at the time, given the Court's ruling in *Prigg v. Pennsylvania* upholding Congress's power to end the Fugitive Slave Act notwithstanding the lack of an enforcement provision in the Fugitive Slave Clause. *Prigg v. Pennsylvania*, 41 U.S. 539 (1842). See Rebecca E. Zietlow, *Enforcing Equality: Congress, the Constitution, and the Protection of Individual Rights* (New York: NYU Press, 2006), 45–46.
[7] Ashley added the equality of rights language in a January 7, 1864, amendment to the bill. Horowitz, *Great Impeacher*, 92, 107, 94; H.R. 48, sec. 4, 5.

never fully abandoned his territorial theory, his Guaranty Clause strategy was significantly more palatable to President Lincoln and congressional moderates. Ashley was appointed to a select committee, headed by radical Representative Winter Davis, to formulate a plan for reconstructing the rebellious states.[8]

On March 30, 1864, Ashley gave a major speech presenting his reconstruction bill to his colleagues, a speech that was later endorsed by his friend Charles Sumner. Though it was not at all clear which side was going to win the war at the time, Ashley insisted that "[t]hanks to our heroic army, the rebellion is now so far suppressed, that the question of reconstruction is forced upon and demands our immediate consideration." In this speech, Ashley began to refer to freed slaves as "loyal citizens." He explained, "The question before us, how shall the States whose governments have been usurped or overthrown, be re-established and their loyal citizens be re-invested with all the rights, privileges and immunities of citizens of the free States in the American Union." Ashley continued to advocate his territorial theory of reconstruction. Nonetheless, he conceded that the committee members could not agree whether the rebel "usurpation has destroyed the constitutional governments of the seceded states," justifying congressional intervention to enforce the Guaranty Clause, or whether "the States thus in rebellion have committed State suicide." Whatever the theory behind the act, it would restore the rebel states to the Union, with "freedom as their fundamental law" by enabling "loyal citizens" (including freed slaves) to vote and thus empower them to recreate their own governments.[9]

Ashley argued that Congress, and not the President, should play the leading role in the Reconstruction effort. He insisted, "The only alternative left to the Government of the United States ... is for Congress, representing the supreme sovereignty of the nation, to provide by law for the protection of the lives and property of its citizens."[10] Ashley's bill went well beyond what had so far been suggested by President Lincoln,

---

[8] H.R. 48, *Toledo Commercial*, December 28, 1863; Horowitz, *Great Impeacher*, 92–93.

[9] Speech in the House of Representatives, March 30, 1864: "The Liberation and Restoration of the South" (hereafter referred to as "Reconstruction speech"), *Souvenir*, 264–266, 272, 278, 281; Letter from Charles Sumner (Boston, November 8, 1864), *Souvenir*, 310 ("His various indefatigable labors and his elaborate speech on 'Reconstruction,' shows that he sees well what is to be done in order to place peace and liberty under irresistible safeguards").

[10] Ashley, "Reconstruction speech," *Souvenir*, 277.

who had called for only loyal white men to have the right to vote.[11] Ashley also would have imposed more restrictions than Lincoln on the voting rights of former rebels. Ashley's bill languished in committee, as the committee put forward a more moderate bill sponsored by Henry Winter Davis, eventually known as the Wade-Davis Act. Davis's bill was more radical than Lincoln's and would have declared all slaves in rebellious states forever free. Unlike Ashley's, however, the Wade-Davis Act would not have extended the right to vote to freed slaves.[12] Davis saw his bill as an alternative to the amendment, in case the amendment failed. Ashley, on the other hand, had seen his bill as enforcing the Thirteenth Amendment, a supplementary measure. Moreover, Congress had just considered the issue of black suffrage in their March 17 debate over Ashley's proposal to admit Montana Territory. The Senate supported suffrage, but the House rejected it. The House vote over Montana squelched the chance that black suffrage would be included in the Wade-Davis bill or any other Reconstruction effort at the time. The Wade-Davis Act, not Ashley's bill, was eventually approved by Congress, but Lincoln stopped even that with a pocket veto. Ashley later noted of himself and his radical allies that "at the outset [of the Reconstruction effort] our differences with Mr. Lincoln [were] marked and pronounced on some of the most important questions which confronted us."[13]

Meanwhile, the week before Ashley's Reconstruction speech, Senator Lyman Trumbull had proposed his own version of the Thirteenth Amendment to the Senate. The Senate took up Trumbull's amendment almost immediately, and Trumbull's version was eventually adopted. During the congressional debate over the amendment, members of Congress debated matters of principle and articulated ideological doctrines. However, it is important to remember that those members of Congress were also engaged in political struggles and implementing political strategies. The Civil War was in full swing, and its conclusion was far from certain. The year 1864 was also a presidential election year, so partisan politics were particularly divisive. During the April Senate debate, Republicans saw the amendment as a winning issue in the upcoming elections, and sought to link it to their presidential candidate, Abraham Lincoln.

[11] See Horowitz, *Great Impeacher*, 94.

[12] Ashley, "Reconstruction speech," *Souvenir*, 277; Horowitz, *Great Impeacher*, 94; Benedict, *Compromise*, 70–83.

[13] Benedict, *Compromise*, 78–79, 83; Address of Hon. J. M. Ashley at the Fourth Annual Banquet of the Ohio Republican League, Held at Memorial Hall, Toledo, Ohio, February 12, 1891, *Souvenir*, 747, 753.

Thus, most supporters of the amendment in the Senate were deliberately vague about its scope and meaning beyond the obvious abolition of slavery. The Senators saw the amendment as a means to unite Republicans, and sought to avoid the divisive issue of racial equality.[14]

In the Senate opponents argued that the Thirteenth Amendment was unconstitutional because it would abolish an institution that the Framers supported and upend the country's system of federalism. For example, Kentucky Senator Garrett Davis claimed that "[t]he power of amendment as now proposed ... would invest the amending power with a faculty of destroying and revolutionizing the whole government." Complicating the matter was the fact that antislavery constitutionalists had always claimed that slavery was already unconstitutional. Trumbull responded to this critique by insisting that the Framers would have approved of the amendment. "Our fathers who made the Constitution regarded it as evil, and looked forward to its early extinction. They felt the inconsistency of their position, while proclaiming the equal rights of all to life, liberty and happiness, that denied liberty, happiness and life itself to a whole race." Charles Sumner also pointed out the inconsistency between the Constitution and the language of liberty and equality in other foundational documents, claiming that the amendment simply "brought the Constitution into avowed harmony with the Declaration of Independence."[15] Antislavery constitutionalists had long revered the Declaration, and supporters of the amendment invoked it to show that it would create a new Republic based in the Declaration's promise.

The issue that predominated in the Senate debate was the ongoing question of whether slavery was the cause of the war. Proponents argued that the Slave Power had caused the war, a war that could be won only by abolishing slavery. Opponents argued that moralizing New England Puritans had started the war by attempting to legislate morality, and the amendment would only compound that mistake. Northern Democrats appealed to racism, claiming that freed slaves would be unable to live on their own and raising the specter of "miscegenation."[16] Republicans

---

[14] Vorenberg, *Final Freedom*, 59, 90–91, 93. Trumbull used the language from Thomas Jefferson's Northwest Ordinance to appeal to War Democrats. Ibid., 59. Henry Wilson also introduced his own version of the Thirteenth Amendment. See Lea S. VanderVelde, "Henry Wilson, Cobbler of the Frayed Constitution, Strategist of the Thirteenth Amendment," *Georgetown Journal of Law and Politics* 15 (2017): 173.

[15] Cong. Globe, 38th Cong., 1st Sess., 1313, 1482 (March 29, 1864).

[16] See Cong. Globe, 38th Cong., 1st Sess., App. 104 (March 31, 1864). New Hampshire Senator Daniel Clark claimed that the Slave Power "has set armies in the field, and she now seeks the nation's life and the destruction of the Government." Cong. Globe, 38th

countered that slaveholders who ravaged their female slaves were the real culprits, condoned by proslavery northern Democrats. By and large, however, Republicans tried to avoid discussing issues of race during their debate over the Thirteenth Amendment. They did not wish to alienate the northern Democrats whose votes they needed to approve the amendment. Republicans pointed to the sacrifices that African American soldiers was already making for the Union, to justify emancipation and argue that free blacks would be able to fend for themselves after slavery was ended. Moreover, at that time, many Republicans seemed to take it for granted that blacks would generally receive equality before the laws.[17] Nonetheless, in the debate over the Thirteenth Amendment few senators were as outspoken about the rights of freed slaves as Ashley had been with his Reconstruction bill.

The crucial factor in the Senate debate was Democratic Senator Reverdy Johnson of Maryland, who delivered the most persuasive, nonpartisan speech in support of the amendment. Echoing Lincoln's "House Divided" speech of six years before, Johnson insisted that "a prosperous and permanent peace can never be secured if [slavery] is permitted to survive." Senator Johnson opined that the only thing more dangerous than slavery was the view that states' rights trumped federal power. Johnson's speech sent a shock wave through national politics, but it also reflected a growing opposition to slavery in the loyal border states. The day after Johnson's speech, the Maryland state legislature began to draft a new antislavery constitution. The tide of public opinion was turning toward abolition. On April 8, 1864, the Thirteenth Amendment passed the Senate by a 38–6 vote.[18]

By the time the amendment made it to the House of Representatives that summer, however, the political winds had changed. The Union Army had not been doing well on the battlefield, and the mood was especially partisan, with Republicans favoring, and Democrats opposing, the amendment. Thus, proponents of the amendment faced an uphill battle.

Cong., 1st Sess., 1369 (1864); Delaware Senator Willard Saulsbury claimed that slavery was the will of God, and "His providence is inequality and diversity." Cong. Globe, 38th Cong., 1st Sess., 1442 (April 6, 1864); California Senator James McDougall argued that the abolition of slavery would lead to cross-breeding and eventually extinguish the white race. Cong. Globe, 38th Cong., 1st Sess., 1490 (April 8, 1864). See Vorenberg, *Final Freedom*, 100–101.

[17] Cong. Globe, 38th Cong., 1st Sess., 1438 (April 6, 1864); Vorenberg, *Final Freedom*, 104–115 (arguing that Senators Harlan, Henry Wilson, and others took this position).

[18] See Vorenberg, *Final Freedom*, 96–97; *New York Times*, April 6, 1864, p. 1; Cong. Globe, 38th Cong., 1st Sess., 1490 (April 8, 1864).

As in the Senate, Republicans framed the amendment as important war measure. California Republican Thomas Shannon claimed that abolishing slavery would help the war effort because slavery was the "root of the accursed tree" and the cause of the war. Democrats countered that the amendment would prolong the war and "throw away every hope of reconciliation." As in the Senate, Democrats also attacked the amendment on constitutional grounds. They argued that the amendment would undermine the very foundation of the original Constitution.[19] They predicted that the amendment's enforcement clause would undermine the existing system of federalism.

Ashley's proposed Reconstruction bill influenced the House debate over the Thirteenth Amendment because it presented a concrete model of equality rights for freed slaves. Democrats thus had grounds to accuse the Republicans of having "radical, ulterior motives," including the expansion of voting rights. They accused Republicans of supporting racial equality and hurled the same racist accusations that they had in the Senate. For example, Indiana Representative William Holman predicted that Republicans would use the clause to "invade the states" to effect the "elevation of the African to the August heights of citizenship." Many Republicans chose to stay silent on the meaning of enforcement, to avoid alienating conservative Republicans and War Democrats. It was undeniable that as one of the amendment's chief proponents, Ashley had proposed doing exactly what Holman predicted with his Reconstruction bill. However, the House Republicans were far from united over voting rights or any other measures that Ashley had proposed.[20]

Nonetheless, House Republicans were more forthcoming than their colleagues in the Senate about the amendment's broader implications. Ashley had made his position clear and laid his prosuffrage cards on the table. Representative Isaac Arnold proclaimed that the amendment would be a sign of a "new nation" with liberty and equality before the law as its cornerstone. Illinois Republican Ebon Ingersoll said that the amendment would bestow upon freed slaves "a right to till the soil, to earn his bread

---

[19] Vorenberg, *Final Freedom*, 136–137. In Grant's campaign in the wilderness, 45,000 Union soldiers had died, with 7000 killed or injured in one day at Cold Harbor. Ibid. Cong. Globe, 38th Cong., 1st Sess., 2949 (June 14, 1864) (Shannon); Rep. Martin Kalbfleisch declared that the amendment would "cause other and more radical changes, until in the end, of the now solid and perfect structure which has stood the test of years, scarce a vestige will remain." Cong. Globe, 38th Cong., 1st Sess., 2945–2946.

[20] Vorenberg, *Final Freedom*, 128, 130, 132; Cong. Globe, 38th Cong., 1st Sess., 2962 (June 14, 1864) (remarks of Rep. William S. Holman); ibid., 2962 (June 15, 1864).

by the sweat of his brow, and enjoy the rewards of his own labor ... and a right to the endearment and enjoyment of family ties." During the House debate over the Amendment, Republicans praised African American soldiers and revealed a growing sense of egalitarianism. On June 14, 1864, the day before the vote on the Amendment, Congress passed Ashley's bill authorizing equal pay for black soldiers. This is evidence that while the Republicans at the time read equal rights through the lens of labor, their free labor ideology "assumed that blacks and whites would generally receive equal treatment before the laws."[21]

The presidential election loomed over the first House vote on the Thirteenth Amendment. New York Democrat Fernando Wood bitterly opposed the amendment, and he enforced party unity. Only one Democrat, Ezra Wheeler of Wisconsin, spoke in support of the amendment, and as a first-term congressman he lacked the influence that Reverdy Johnson had in the Senate. The House voted along partisan lines, and the amendment failed. Ashley switched his vote to "no" so he could bring up the amendment again. Two weeks later, when asked by his colleagues when he would bring up the amendment again, Ashley declared, "The record is made up, and we must go to the country on the issue thus presented. When the verdict of the people is rendered next November I trust this Congress will return determined to ingraft that verdict into the national Constitution." He vowed to bring up the amendment in December, after the election.[22]

The fate of the Thirteenth Amendment was now linked to the reelection campaigns of President Lincoln, Ashley, and his Republican colleagues. In the spring, it had become a defining issue for both parties. In the fall, Republicans were more reluctant to raise the issue, and some of those in close races downplayed the issue of black freedom.[23] Despite the fact that

---

[21] Cong. Globe, 38th Cong., 1st Sess., 2989 (June 15, 1864) (Arnold); ibid., 2990 (Ebersoll); Vorenberg, *Final Freedom*, 104, 131–132; Leonard L. Richards, *Who Freed the Slaves? The Fight over the Thirteenth Amendment* (Chicago: University of Chicago Press, 2015), 255, 105.

[22] Vorenberg, *Final Freedom*, 137, 140. Revealing the intense partisanship of the time, the Wisconsin Democratic Party punished Wheeler for his vote by denying him the nomination for reelection. Christopher Dell, *Lincoln and the War Democrats: The Grand Erosion of Conservative Tradition* (1975), 305, cited in Vorenberg, *Final Freedom*, 137; Address of Hon. James M. Ashley before the "Ohio Society of New York," at the Fifth Annual Banquet, Wednesday evening, February 19, 1890, *Souvenir*, 692, 705; Horowitz, *Great Impeacher*, 97, 100; Cong. Globe, 38th Cong., 1st Sess., 3357, *Souvenir*, 707.

[23] Vorenberg, *Final Freedom*, 116, 142, 171.

he was also in a close race, Ashley made the Thirteenth Amendment a central issue in his campaign and as he campaigned for Lincoln. He believed that "if we could force the issue of the Thirteenth Amendment into the pending presidential contest, and Mr. Lincoln should be elected in November, that the requisite number of liberal Democrats and border state Union men who had voted against the defeated amendment in June might be prevailed upon to vote with us after Mr. Lincoln had been re-elected on that issue." In his campaign speeches, Ashley "repeatedly affirmed man's equality before the law" and claimed to have written the antislavery amendment.[24]

The Republicans received a huge boost in September 1864, when Atlanta fell to General William Tecumseh Sherman. Lincoln won the election with 55 percent of the vote and declared that the election was a popular mandate for the amendment. Ashley's vote was much closer. He was campaigning against a Democratic war hero who was supported by Clark Waggoner, the owner of *The Toledo Commercial* and Ashley's political nemesis.[25] Ashley lost the local vote, but he prevailed due to the absentee vote from the soldiers on the battlefield. In a letter to Charles Sumner, Ashley expressed relief at his victory. He said, "I have had a terrible fight" against "Colonel Rice – the McClellan nominee." Fortunately, "[t]he soldiers in the army saved me – I acknowledge it." Ashley issued a notice thanking the troops for their support: "For your generous support I can only promise Fidelity to your cause, and in the future, as in the past, continuous devotion to your interests." The Republicans generally did well in the fall 1864 election, and things were looking up for Ashley's amendment.[26]

In mid-November 1864, Ashley's supporters held a victory banquet for Ashley in his home town of Toledo. Ashley invited Sumner to attend or write a letter to the attendees. Sumner complied with Ashley's request, as

---

[24] Ibid., 171; Richards, *Who Freed the Slaves?*, 193; Address of Hon. James M. Ashley before the "Ohio Society of New York," at the Fifth Annual Banquet, Wednesday evening, February 19, 1890, *Souvenir*, 692, 706. Hon J. M. Ashley, by the Republican Congressional Convention at Toledo, May 24th, 1864, *Souvenir*, 298, 300 ("with unfaltering faith, I have maintained the great democratic idea of man's equality before the law").

[25] Horowitz, *Great Impeacher*, 101; Vorenberg, *Final Freedom*, 174; Richards, *Who Freed the Slaves?*, 196.

[26] Letter from Ashley to Charles Sumner, November 15, 1864, Charles Sumner Papers, Houghton Library, Harvard University; James Ashley, To the Officers and Soldiers of the Union Army from the Congressional Tenth District, *Souvenir*, 305, 307; Richards, *Who Freed the Slaves?*, 192.

did then-Treasury Secretary Salmon Chase. In his letter, Chase told the crowd, "It has been my privilege for many years to rank him among my true and faithful friends; but it is not alone, or chiefly as a friend, that I rejoice in his re-election." Sumner's letter agreed: "I know Mr. Ashley well and honor him much. He has been firm where others have hesitated, and from an early day saw the secret of war, and I may add also, the secret of victory." Sumner continued, "There is also an amendment to the Constitution, prohibiting slavery throughout the United States. Nobody has done more for it, practically, than your Representative." The letters having been read, Ashley triumphantly took the podium and celebrated his victory. He reminded his audience that from the first time he ran for Congress, he had always argued that "slavery was the crime of all crimes" and "the sum of villanies." Ashley insisted that his opposition to slavery, and support of the amendment, had been the key to his victory.[27] Thus, he claimed his reelection as a mandate for the amendment.

Back in Congress, Ashley's fellow Republicans also claimed that the election represented a "popular verdict ... in unmistakable language" in favor of the amendment. Opponents of the amendment protested that it had not really been important in the election. However, the tide of public opinion had turned toward abolishing slavery. All over the country, "not only slavery but legal inequality was everywhere under attack." Northern states were repealing state black laws that had barred black immigration, limited the rights of free blacks, and mandated segregation.[28] Ashley had gambled on the fall elections, and he had won. But to succeed in the final push, he needed a good strategy and the help of the newly reelected president.

Ashley became the sponsor of the Thirteenth Amendment in the House. Fresh from his own victory, he came up with a strategy to convince his colleagues who had voted against the amendment in June. To succeed, Ashley had to draw on his years of studying political

---

[27] See the Ashley Banquet at the Oliver House, November 1864. From the *Toledo Commercial, Souvenir,* 309; Letter from Salmon P. Chase (Cincinnati, November 14, 1864) expressing his regrets at being unable to attend the banquet, *Souvenir,* 310; Letter from Ashley to Charles Sumner, November 15, 1864, Charles Sumner Papers, Houghton Library, Harvard University. Ashley asked Sumner to "please write a letter to be read on the occasion and publish with the proceedings and if you have no objections would like to have you refer to my congressional record, my speech on Reconstruction and my hanging up the constitutional amendment to be voted on at this session." Ibid.

[28] Godlove Orth, Cong. Globe, 38th Cong., 2nd Sess., 142. See also ibid., 155 (Higby), 189 (Kasson), 220 (Broomall), 244 (Woodbridge), 258 (Rollins); Vorenberg, *Final Freedom,* 187–188.

dynamics and courting political allies, and to ask for help from President Lincoln. That fall, Lincoln had once again been at loggerheads with the Ashley and his radical allies, this time over the issue of readmitting Louisiana into the Union. Lincoln insisted that he would not sign any Reconstruction bill unless Congress recognized Louisiana with his strong allies in the government. However, Ashley and the other radicals did not want to recognize Louisiana without a guarantee of black suffrage.[29] Nonetheless, with the Thirteenth Amendment, Ashley and Lincoln shared the same goal. This time, much of Ashely's advocacy took place behind closed doors, off the public record. The final push for the Thirteenth Amendment tested all of Ashley's political skills, and he prevailed.

To get the votes needed to approve the amendment, Ashley analyzed the list of his colleagues who had voted against it in June. Ashley later recalled that he gave special attention to the "characters and antecedents" of the thirty-six House members who had not voted for the amendment the first time around. Ashley had to crack the partisan solidarity and convince some Democrats to vote for the amendment. He began a systematic study of the men whose cooperation and votes were needed for success, and drew up a plan to convince them.[30] He had to win some Democratic votes.

Ashley put together a list of border Democrats whom he thought he could persuade and sought out the aid of two prominent border state colleagues, Missouri's Frank Blair and Maryland Representative Winter Davis, to persuade them. Ashley asked Blair and Davis for a list of names of people from border states who could be counted on or persuaded to vote for the amendment. Ashley also looked for a list of northern Democrats who might vote for the amendment. In this effort, he sought help from two New York radicals, Reuben Fenton and Augustus Frank. With their help, Ashley targeted seventeen Democrats and set out to change their votes.[31] Some of them were lame ducks with nothing to lose, others had a record of voting with Ashley. Of the seventeen men, twelve ultimately voted for it, two missed the vote, and three voted against it. Ashley later gave credit to these men for the success of the amendment. He recalled, "As I look back now on their manly acts and votes in favor of

---

[29] Vorenberg, *Final Freedom*, 179; Benedict, *Compromise*, 91.
[30] Address of Hon. James M. Ashley before the "Ohio Society of New York," at the Fifth Annual Banquet, Wednesday evening, February 19, 1890, *Souvenir*, 692, 706; Horowitz, *Great Impeacher*, 118.
[31] Horowitz, *Great Impeacher*, 101; Richards, *Who Freed the Slaves?*, 148, 157, 185.

the constitutional abolition and prohibition of slavery everywhere beneath our flag, their self-sacrificing heroism rises into the sublime." Ashley explained, "Of the twenty-four border-State and Northern men who made up this majority which enabled us to win this victory, all had defied their party discipline, and had deliberately and with unfaltering faith marched to their political death. These are the men whom our future historians will honor, and to whom this nation owes a debt of eternal gratitude."[32] Without Ashley to pressure them, however, they might not have taken that "manly" and "heroic" vote.

Ashley also had to ensure that his Republican colleagues would stand behind him and support the amendment. He wrote more than a hundred letters urging his fellow Republicans to promote the amendment in their home states. In a December 25, 1864, circular, Ashley urged his colleagues to attend the vote on the amendment, then scheduled for January 9, 1865. He cautioned, "Fifty-six members are regarded as sure to vote against us, if they are present." He continued, "However, of the Opposition, nineteen are set down as doubtful. Eight or ten of this number we hope will vote for the proposition, and the others may voluntarily absent themselves." Finally, he asked that "[i]f from any cause you are uncertain as to whether you can be present or not, please telegraph some member of the Opposition at once, and secure a pair, and as soon as you secure one, telegraph the fact to me, and have whoever you pair with telegraph me also, so that I may know Saturday night exactly how the vote will stand." Despite his plans, January 9 arrived and Ashley realized that he did not have enough votes. He postponed the vote until the end of the month, and asked the president for help.[33]

After his election, Lincoln had taken/took two actions to further black freedom. First, he appointed Salmon Chase to replace Supreme Court Chief Justice Roger Taney, the author of the *Dred Scott* decision who had died in October. Second, Lincoln urged Congress to adopt the Thirteenth Amendment. Lincoln wanted the amendment to be approved as soon as

---

[32] Richards, *Who Freed the Slaves?*, 185; Letter from James Ashley to Benjamin Arnett, *Souvenir*, 332; Address of Hon. James M. Ashley before the "Ohio Society of New York," at the Fifth Annual Banquet, Wednesday evening, February 19, 1890, *Souvenir*, 692, 713.

[33] James Oakes, *Freedom National: The Destruction of Slavery in the United States, 1861–1865* (New York: W. W. Norton, 2013), 478–479; James M. Ashley, Circular Letter, December 25, 1864, Abraham Lincoln Papers at the Library of Congress, Transcribed and Annotated by the Lincoln Studies Center, Knox College, Galesburg, IL; Vorenberg, *Final Freedom*, 198.

possible. Once called upon, the president and his administration worked closely with Ashley to achieve this goal. As president, Lincoln had control over a great deal of federal resources and could dole out patronage. Lincoln did not make any promises himself, but he "let his lieutenants make the bargains and use his name to seal the agreement." Ashley served as one of those lieutenants. Opponents accused Ashley of resorting to bribery to get votes for the Thirteenth Amendment.[34] It is true that Lincoln gave Ashley the power to negotiate on his behalf. For example, Ashley apparently promised New Yorker Anson Herrick that his brother would be nominated as a federal revenue assessor. Secretary of State William Henry Seward also campaigned for the amendment and used "questionable, even corrupt methods" to influence people. For example, the Lincoln administration helped Democrat Andrew J. Rogers, an anti-emancipationist, to preserve his railroad monopoly. Rogers then missed the vote on the amendment. There was also a rumor that Lincoln was involved in a deal to get rid of Sumner's antimonopoly legislation to get a vote from a member of Congress from New Jersey. There was no paper trail of money, and it is not clear whether bribes were paid or, if so, whether the bribes influenced the process.[35] However, it does appear that Ashley was willing to use any means necessary to accomplish his lifetime goal.

Did Ashley and Lincoln go beyond the customary logrolling and methods of persuasion in order to achieve a positive vote on the Thirteenth Amendment? While there is evidence that they did, we may never know for sure. What is known is that Ashley prepared a careful strategy to achieve the vote and that he executed it successfully. Years later, Ashley could recall exactly whom he had targeted with his efforts and how each member of the House had voted. Moreover, despite his many differences with Lincoln over Reconstruction measures, Ashley developed a close relationship with the president during the months spent working toward passage of the Thirteenth Amendment. Ashley later recalled Lincoln fondly and claimed to have met with the president and conversed with him often. After Lincoln's assassination, Ashley served as a pallbearer when Lincoln's funeral train passed through Cleveland. Ashley's grief at

---

[34] Vorenberg, *Final Freedom*, 176, 198; Horowitz, *Great Impeacher*, 102; Richards, *Who Freed the Slaves?*, 203.

[35] Richards, *Who Freed the Slaves?*, 206–207, 212; Vorenberg, *Final Freedom*, 182, 200; Oakes, *Freedom National*, 479 ("There is little question that money for bribes was made available, but no hard evidence that it was ever paid for").

the president's death may have influenced his disastrous attempt to impeach President Andrew Johnson, whom he evidently believed to be partially responsible for Lincoln's death.[36]

Ashley reintroduced the amendment on January 6, 1865. In his speech introducing the amendment, Ashley reiterated the themes that he had voiced since his stump speech days in Ohio. He began his speech by quoting Abraham Lincoln, saying, "Mr. Speaker, if Slavery is not wrong, nothing is wrong." Ashley then listed all of the reasons that slavery had to be abolished. First, "No observer of our history, or of the political parties which have been organized and disbanded, now hesitates to declare that slavery is the cause of this terrible civil war." Moreover, Ashley claimed that Union soldiers were in favor of the amendment. He claimed, "Almost every letter I receive from the brave men who are in the Army from my district contains the anxious inquiry, 'What of the constitutional amendment: will it pass?'" Union soldiers had been engaged in the earliest confiscation efforts. Now Ashley invoked the soldiers to add legitimacy to his claim. Ashley also claimed a popular mandate, insisting that "constituents at home and soldiers in the field of four fifths of representatives this floor" supported the amendment.[37]

Like Trumbull, Ashley had to respond to the critique that the amendment itself was unconstitutional. Like Trumbull, Ashley insisted that slavery was contrary to the intent of the Framers. He explained, "Our fathers were men of ideas, and they believed that with the adoption of the Constitution slavery would cease to exist ... they were not guilty of the infamy of making a Constitution which, by any fair rules of construction, can be interpreted into a denial of liberty, happiness and justice to an entire race." Ashley also spoke to his antislavery constitutionalist friends, maintaining that, correctly interpreted, the Constitution was an antislavery document. Nonetheless, he explained, it was necessary to amend the Constitution. The proslavery forces had usurped the federal government and "persistently violated ... the fundamental principles of government," and the Constitution had been "grossly perverted by the Courts." Finally, Ashley argued that slavery had corrupted the government and harmed poor whites as well as the enslaved blacks. "It has denied the masses of

[36] Address of Hon. James M. Ashley before the "Ohio Society of New York," at the Fifth Annual Banquet, Wednesday evening, February 19, 1890, *Souvenir*, 692, 708; Horowitz, *Great Impeacher*, 111, 115; Benedict, "Toledo Politics," 815.

[37] Ashley, Speech in the House of Representatives, January 6, 1865, Cong. Globe, 38th Cong., 2nd Sess., 138, 141 (January 5, 1865), *Souvenir*, 333, 334–335.

poor white children within its power the privilege of free schools, and
made free speech and free press impossible within its domain; while
ignorance, poverty and vice are almost universal wherever it domin-
ates."[38] Here, Ashley emphasized the negative impact of slavery on the
southern white working class. While slavery persisted, poor whites would
continue to suffer.

Addressing the Democrats' claim that the amendment would violate
state sovereignty, Ashley insisted instead that Congress had jurisdiction
over the matter because slavery violated federal rights. Once again, he
claimed that the Guaranty Clause of Article IV obliged Congress to ensure
that states had a republican form of government. "The provision of the
national Constitution which imposes upon Congress the duty of guaranteeing to the several States of the Union a republican form of government,
is one which impresses me as forcibly as any other with the idea of the
utter indefensibility of the State sovereignty dogma."[39] Ashley had never
given much credence to state sovereignty claims. Now, he emphasized the
importance of a federal remedy for the evils of slavery.

Ashley argued, "If we adopt a theory that a State once a State is always
a State we have no safety from factions and revolutions." He insisted that
"we must keep steadily in view the fact that ... the national Constitution
is the supreme law of the land, and that the Government organized under
it is clothed with the sovereignty of the whole people. The first and highest
allegiance is due from the citizen to the national Government." According
to Ashley, the national government had a corresponding duty to protect
US citizens, including freed slaves. "The Constitution guarantees that the
citizens of each State shall enjoy all the rights and privileges of citizens of
the several States. It is a universal franchise which cannot be confined to
States, but belongs to citizens of the republic."[40] By amending the Constitution, Congress could recognize newly freed slaves as citizens and protect
their rights. Prior to the war, antislavery constitutionalists had often made
this citizenship-based argument against slavery. By 1866, a supermajority
of Congress agreed, establishing freed slaves as citizens with the
1866 Civil Rights Act.

---

[38] Ashley, Speech in the House of Representatives, January 6, 1865, *Souvenir*, 335 ("If the
national constitution had been rightfully interpreted, and the government organized
under it properly administered, slavery would not have legally existed in this country
for a single hour"), 336–337.

[39] Ibid., 344.

[40] Cong. Globe, 38th Cong., 2nd Sess., 140 (January 6, 1865); *Souvenir*, 344.

Ashley used his speech to articulate a rosy vision of a country governed by the principles of free labor. According to Ashley, once slavery was abolished, the United States would become "the most powerful and populous, the most enterprising and wealthy nation in the world." Here, Ashley echoed the Free Soil argument that slavery was holding back the nation's economy and industrial development. Ashley argued that the Thirteenth Amendment would guarantee "our system of free labor ... with free schools and colleges, and a free press" and would establish "a constitutional guarantee of the government to protect the rights of all and secure the liberty and equality of its people."[41] Once again, Ashley linked freedom to liberty, equality, and protection of the government and articulated a broad theory of the rights that would be enjoyed by freed slaves.

Ashley concluded his speech by once more linking the end of slavery in the United States to the worldwide movement toward free labor. "The eyes of the wise and good in all civilized nations are upon us. The men who embrace and defend the democratic idea in Europe are patiently and anxiously waiting to have us authoritatively proclaim to the world that liberty is the sign in which we conquer; that henceforth freedom is to be the animating principle of our government and the life of our Constitution."[42] He called on every "loyal man" to vote to end "the despotism of American slavery in the Republic." Thus, Ashley laid out his theory of the Thirteenth Amendment and set the stage for the dramatic vote.

While Ashley had articulated the most comprehensive case for the amendment, some of his colleagues elaborated on his case. Indiana Representative Godlove Orth agreed with Ashley that Congress had a duty to restore a republican form of government, which would be accomplished by the amendment. Orth cited the Declaration of Independence, claiming that "the effect of such amendment will be ... a practical application of that self-evident truth, 'that all men are created equal, endowed by their creator with certain unalienable rights; that among these are life, liberty and the pursuit of happiness.'" Similarly, New York Republican Thomas Davis said that the amendment would "make every race free and equal before the law, ... securing to each the fruits of its own progression." Pennsylvania Republican Glenni Scofield agreed that it was Congress's

---

[41] Ibid., 353; see Eric Foner, *Free Soil, Free Labor, Free Men: The Ideology of the Republican Party before the Civil War* (New York: Oxford University Press, 1995), 40 ("The most cherished values of the free labor outlook – economic development, social mobility, and political democracy – all appeared to be violated in the south").

[42] Ashley, Speech in the House of Representatives, January 6, 1865, *Souvenir*, 355.

duty to "restore to the deluded and betrayed masses the blessings of a free Republic" and that the amendment would do just that.[43]

However, some Republican supporters of the amendment did not agree with Ashley that freedom would entail the right to vote. When opponents argued that the amendment would lead to voting rights for black men, Oregon Republican John McBride responded that "a recognition of natural rights is one thing, a grant of political franchises is quite another." Moreover, even the stalwart radical Thaddeus Stevens demurred when Democrat Sunset Cox asked him how he stood on the doctrine of "negro equality." Later, Stevens would stand with Ashley as one of the fiercest proponents of suffrage rights, but for now, he deliberately kept his interpretation of equality vague. Thus, Ashley's Republican allies were reluctant to spell out exactly what rights the freed slaves would enjoy after the amendment was approved. Ashley's Reconstruction bill and other measures promoted far-reaching measures for the freed slaves. Many of his allies believed that to ensure that the amendment would be approved, they "had to keep this legislation detached from the first constitutional amendment dealing exclusively with African American freedom."[44] Only after the amendment became law did the Republicans engage in earnest with the project of enforcing the law of freedom.

To ensure that he had the votes to approve the amendment, Ashley postponed the final vote to January 31, 1865. On that day, the gallery was packed with spectators, including members of the Supreme Court, women who had organized a massive petition campaign in favor of the amendment, and Frederick Douglass's son, Charles. Ashley took the floor and the gavel. Ashley later recalled, "Never before, and certain I am that never again, will I be seized with so strong a desire to give utterance to the thoughts and emotions which throbbed my heart and brain ... I knew that the hour was at hand when the world would witness the complete triumph of a cause, which at the beginning of my political life I had not hoped to live long enough to see." Ashley began the proceedings by allowing the newly converted Democrats to state their case.[45] In a message

---

[43] Cong. Globe, 38th Cong., 2nd Sess., 143 (January 6, 1865) (Orth), 142 (Davis), 145 (Scofield).

[44] Cong. Globe, 38th Cong., 2nd Sess., 202 (McBride); Stevens said unconvincingly, "I have never held to that doctrine of negro equality ... not equality in all things – simply before the laws, nothing else." Cong. Globe, 38th Cong., 2nd Sess. 125. See Vorenberg, *Final Freedom*, 191.

[45] Vorenberg, *Final Freedom*, 205–206; Oakes, *Freedom National*, 479; "Ohio Society speech," *Souvenir*, 692, 709.

read by the clerk, Democrat Archibald McAllister of Pennsylvania explained that although he had voted against the amendment in June, he had changed his mind and was now convinced that it would be impossible to negotiate peace with the Confederates. McAllister declared his intention to vote "against the cornerstone of the Southern Confederacy, and declare eternal war against the enemies of my country." Three other "converted Democrats" also testified about their change of mind. Having demonstrated the break in Democratic party unity, Ashley called for the vote on the amendment. Twenty-five years later, Ashley could still remember, and describe in detail, how the vote proceeded and the suspenseful excitement as one former opponent of the amendment after another rose to speak in its favor.[46] It was a triumphant moment for Ashley. His strategy had succeeded.

When the vote had been recorded, the gallery audience exploded into cheers. Charles Douglass was surprised at the emotion expressed by the crowd, "Republicans went wild. Some threw their hats to the roof. Others smashed them against their desks. Many cheered. Many wept. Many embraced." Hugs and kisses and cheering went on for five minutes. Then the crowd "poured out into the streets to continue the celebration." Thirty years later, Ashley's friend George Julian remembered, "It seemed to me I had been born into a new life, and that world was overflowing with beauty and joy." Ashley wired *The Toledo Commercial*, "Glory to God in the highest! Our country is free!" The *National Anti-Slavery Standard* wrote: "The credit belongs principally to Mr. Ashley of Ohio. He has been at work the whole session, and it is his management that secured passage of the Joint Resolution."[47]

In April 1865, President Abraham Lincoln was assassinated, and Andrew Johnson took his place. Although Johnson was from the slave state of Tennessee, the radicals initially hoped that he would be tougher on the rebels than Lincoln had been. Ashley and his radical allies tried to convince the new president to support suffrage rights for the newly freed slaves, without success. During the summer of 1865, as states considered the question of whether to ratify the Thirteenth Amendment, popular support for black suffrage grew. According to historian Michael Les

---

[46] Cong. Globe, 38th Cong., 2nd Sess., 523 (January 31, 1865). The three other Democrats were Pennsylvania Representatives Alexander Coffroth and William Miller and New York's Anson Herrick. Oakes, *Final Freedom*, 479; *Souvenir*, 692, 711.

[47] Richards, *Who Freed the Slaves?*, 215; Vorenberg, *Final Freedom*, 208; Horowitz, *Great Impeacher*, 104, 106.

Benedict, "The movement had spread nationwide." In Ohio, conservative
Republican John Sherman argued simply, "If we can put Negro regiments
there [in the South] and give them bayonets, why can't we give them
votes? Both are weapons of offence and defense. Votes are cheaper and
better." On July 4, 1865, members of Congress throughout the nation
give speeches supporting black suffrage.[48] Ashley enthusiastically joined
the effort.

In the summer and early fall of 1865, Ashley traveled to California in
order to drum up support for radical Reconstruction measures, inviting
Charles Sumner to join him. In his letter, Ashley reported that before his
travels, he had campaigned with George Julian and John Bingham in the
Western Reserve. He predicted, "We shall carry the state without fail for
Bingham and the union." Though Sumner declined, Ashley was still
warmly greeted as he articulated his broad vision of Reconstruction,
which included suffrage rights for all free inhabitants.[49] In a September
1865 speech in San Francisco, Ashley laid out what he called the radical
plan for Reconstruction. At the time, Ashley was still chair of Committee
on the Territories, and he was introduced as "having done more than any
other man to carry through Congress the constitutional amendment
forever prohibiting slavery in the United States." Ashley explained his
territorial theory of Reconstruction, still claiming that the United States
had full sovereignty over the conquered rebel states. Ashley then insisted
that all "loyal" men, "without distinction of race or color," must be
allowed to vote for delegates to the proposed constitutional conventions.
He declared, "All I demand in the reorganization of State governments in
the rebel States, is justice – justice alike to loyal white and loyal black –
justice to the rebels also – justice tempered with mercy." He insisted that
this justice could be secured only by the ballot. In a speech in Sacramento
ten days later, Ashley reiterated that he believed that the primary goal of
Reconstruction was to secure impartial suffrage for loyal men.[50]

In the meantime, caught up in the emancipatory spirit, some northern
states, including Illinois, Rhode Island, Michigan, Maryland, and West

[48] Benedict, *Compromise*, 101, 103–105, 110; *New York Tribune*, June 14, 1965, p. 1,
cited in Benedict, *Compromise*, 110.
[49] Letter of James Ashley to Charles Sumner, August 5 and September 18, 1865, Charles
Sumner Papers, Houghton Library, Harvard University; Horowitz, *Great Impeacher*,
112–113.
[50] General Ashley's Speech at San Francisco, California, September 17th, 1865, *Souvenir*,
370, 371, 375–376, 378; Speech of Hon. J. M. Ashley of Ohio, Delivered at Sacramento,
California, Friday evening, September 29, 1865, *Souvenir*, 385.

Virginia, seized the opportunity and ratified the amendment within a week of its passage in Congress. Twenty-three states ratified the amendment quickly and without controversy. However, if the seceded states were included in the tally, Article V of the Constitution required twenty-seven states to meet the requisite three-fourths of states ratifying the amendment. Some radicals, including Charles Sumner, argued that the rebellious states should not count in determining the number of states needed for ratification. Ashley disagreed, along with his colleagues Senators Lyman Trumbull and Jacob Howard.[51] The Thirty-Eighth Congress adjourned without an official pronouncement on the number of rebellious states needed for ratification. This left the oversight to President Lincoln and, after his assassination, to President Johnson. Both presidents saw the amendment as a tool for sectional reconciliation and thus included the rebellious states in the count. Johnson followed Lincoln's lead and urged southern states to ratify. The new president made ratification of the Thirteenth Amendment a condition of readmission for the rebellious states.[52] The final states needed to ratify – New Hampshire, Oregon, and Georgia – voted early in December 1865. On December 18, 1865, Secretary of State Seward certified the Thirteenth Amendment as part of the Constitution. The Reconstruction Congress immediately sought to shape the meaning of the Thirteenth Amendment's promise of freedom.

---

[51] Vorenberg, *Final Freedom*, 225–226, 233; Oakes, *Freedom National*, 481.
[52] Vorenberg, *Final Freedom*, 226, 228, 233; Richards, *Who Freed the Slaves?*, 229. Only the border states of Delaware and Kentucky, as well as the state of New Jersey, voted not to ratify. Oakes, *Freedom National*, 485; Vorenberg, *Final Freedom*, 233.

7

Enforcing the Thirteenth Amendment

Reconstruction and a Positive Right to Free Labor

Even before Secretary of State William Seward certified the Thirteenth Amendment as part of the Constitution, James Ashley and his congressional allies began to debate the concrete meaning of freedom. By the fall of 1865, evidence of southern resistance to Reconstruction measures was mounting. Southern states enacted racially discriminatory laws, known as "Black Codes," and southern officials bristled as newly freed slaves attempted to assert their independence. In Congress, even the moderates and conservatives began to realize that "freedom must mean not simply the absence of bondage but other legal disabilities as well." Enforcing the Thirteenth Amendment, Congress sought to establish freed slaves as citizens who could exercise fundamental human rights, and engaged in fierce debates over the content of those rights. Ashley argued that the right to suffrage preceded all other rights, but he also demanded measures ensuring racial equality. His colleagues were equivocal about suffrage rights, but they adopted measures prohibiting race discrimination, including the 1866 Civil Rights Act and the Equal Protection Clause of the Fourteenth Amendment. Members of the Reconstruction Congress also debated the meaning of freedom of contract, which had been so central to antislavery ideology.[1] Conservative members of Congress insisted that the

---

[1] Michael Les Benedict, *A Compromise of Principle* (New York: W. W. Norton, 1974), 22, 121; Michael Vorenberg, *Final Freedom: The Civil War, the Abolition of Slavery, and the Thirteenth Amendment* (New York: Cambridge University Press, 2001), 236 (2001). The majority of radicals agreed with Ashley about the need for measures protecting racial equality. Hans L. Trefousse, *The Radical Republicans: Lincoln's Vanguard for Racial Justice* (New York: Alfred A. Knopf, 1968), 310. Slaves had been denied the right to contract with their employers or to engage in most other commercial transactions. Most Americans thought

right to contract precluded government interference with the market, but the Black Codes belied that claim. Instead, Congress adopted substantive measures to empower freed slaves and other workers to exercise their right to contract effectively. With the 1866 Civil Rights Act, the 1867 Anti-Peonage Act, and the 1868 Eight Hour Act, Congress established a positive right to free labor, including the right to work for a fair wage, free of undue coercion, and without discrimination based on race, and made it enforceable throughout the nation.

The Reconstruction Era was central to the transformation of workers' rights in the nineteenth century. James Ashley had long anticipated the broader implications of the end of slavery on workers' rights. In 1860, Ashley had outlined his vision of a society based on free labor, in which "the laborers must not only be free, but they must be citizens; having rights which the government and all classes of citizens are bound to respect and defend – the poorest and humblest inhabitant being equal, before the law, with the richest and most powerful." Ashley and his allies enacted measures consistent with his race- and class-based vision, including the Second Freedman's Bureau Act, the 1866 Civil Rights Act, the 1867 Anti-Peonage Act, and the 1868 Eight Hour Act. Ashley later explained, "Beginning with our early anti-slavery struggle, you will find that I uniformly made my appeals for the rights of all labor, black and white, and demanded for each an equitable share in the property which his toil created."[2] However, Ashley failed in his effort to reinforce those rights with his proposals for universal suffrage. Moreover, Ashley's failed attempt to impeach President Johnson reduced his prominence as a congressional leader and brought about the end of his congressional career.

Congress enacted the first comprehensive Reconstruction bill, the first Freedman's Bureau Act, before the end of the Civil War. It became law in March 1864, signed by President Abraham Lincoln. The Freedman's

abolishing slavery ensured the ascendance of contract and contract freedom. Amy Dru Stanley, *From Bondage to Contract: Wage Labor, Marriage, and the Market in the Age of Slave Emancipation* (New York: Cambridge University Press, 1998), 4.

[2] Speech of Hon. James Ashley of Ohio, Delivered in the US House of Representatives, May 29, 1860, *Duplicate Copy of the Souvenir from the Afro-American League of Tennessee to Hon. James M. Ashley of Ohio* (Benjamin Arnett, ed.) (Philadelphia: Publishing House of the AME Church, 1894) (hereafter referred to as *Souvenir*), 44, 45; James Ashley, Centennial Oration, Wood County Centennial Celebration, July 4, 1876, *Souvenir*, 578, 599.

Bureau Act created a federal agency and empowered it to assist freed
slaves and create a system of free labor. Its relatively vague provisions
authorized the Bureau to divide abandoned property into forty-acre tracts
of land and sell them to freed slaves and white refugees. The Bureau was
also authorized to provide emergency food, clothes, and shelter for freedmen. Southern states resisted the Freedman's Bureau's efforts. Bureau
officials found it necessary to protect freed slaves from unscrupulous
employers, discriminatory state laws, and racially motivated violence.[3]
It was an arduous task, necessitating the active involvement of the US
military. General O. O. Howard, the head of the Freedman's Bureau, was
optimistic at the outset, but President Johnson refused to support the
Bureau. Howard petitioned Congress to give the Bureau more authority,
including the power to enforce federal law and thus protect newly freed
slaves. Congress responded with the Second Freedman's Bureau Act
and the 1866 Civil Rights Act. The Civil Rights Act authorized Bureau
officials to sue to enforce the federal rights of the newly freed slaves and
created federal jurisdiction to hear those cases. The Freedman's Bureau
Act would have given the US military enforcement power as well. The two
measures thus enhanced federal protections of newly freed slaves and
protected their right to free labor.

During the summer of 1865, southern states reluctantly ratified the
Thirteenth Amendment but resisted its effect. With the Black Codes,
southern states openly reinstated the law of master/servant for blacks
and imposed indentured servitude on freed slaves. The Black Codes
required black workers to form year-long contracts with their employers
by mid-January each year. The codes imposed restrictions on free movement, which often forced freed slaves to contract with their former
masters, and applied the doctrine of specific performance to all black
residents. Artisans (independent workers) were required to seek annual
licenses from district courts, and all were subject to criminal penalties if
they quit their jobs. Black Codes also authorized state courts to bind out
orphans, or any children under the age of eighteen if the court determined that their parents lacked the means to care for them, to work for
employers chosen by the courts. Vagrancy laws, apprenticeship systems,
and criminal penalties for breach of contract were all designed to control
the black labor force. Thus, southern states introduced a system of

---

[3] Benedict, *Compromise*, 37; Donald G. Nieman, *To Set the Law in Motion: The Freedman's Bureau and the Legal Rights of Blacks* (Millwood, NY: KTO Press, 1979), xv–xvi;
Trefousse, *Radical Republicans*, 304.

legally compelled labor to address concerns about labor shortage and perpetuate slavery in all but name.[4]

Not surprisingly, the newly freed slaves were outraged by the Black Codes. They chafed at the restrictions on their movement and choice of employer and type of work. Freed slaves resisted the legal requirements that they work for their own masters and took to the roads, traveling to look for family members and better employment. According to historian Eric Foner, "[M]any former slaves saw freedom as an end to the separation of families, the abolition of punishment by the lash, and the opportunity to educate their children. Others stressed that freedom meant the enjoyment of 'our rights in common with other men.'" Freedom certainly did *not* mean returning to the same plantations, working for the same masters, and being subjected to their legally sanctioned control once again. As a black soldier in South Carolina wrote in 1866, "I am opposed myself to working under a contract. I am as much at liberty to hire a White man to work as he to hire me, I expect to stay in the South after I am out of service, but not to muster myself to a planter."[5] Freed people wanted to escape economic dependency on their former masters, as well as the "racial enmity" associated with "legal slave relations." Many former slaves sought to own their own land, viewing land ownership as the natural outcome of emancipation. They believed that by fighting for the Union they had earned the right to reap "the fruits of their own labor." Many freed slaves feared that if they entered into contracts with their masters, they would be dragged back into slavery. The deep history of racial antagonism made it difficult for former slaves to transition to wage contracts because the former slaves and their former masters did not

---

[4] David Montgomery, *Citizen Worker: The Experience of Workers in the United States with Democracy and the Free Market during the Nineteenth Century* (New York: Cambridge University Press, 1993), 120; David Montgomery, *Beyond Equality: Labor and the Radical Republicans 1862–1872* (Urbana and Chicago: University of Illinois Press, 1967), 73, 85; Eric Foner, *Politics and Ideology in the Age of the Civil War* (New York: Oxford University Press, 1980), 104; Robert J. Steinfeld, *The Invention of Free Labor: The Employment Relation in English and American Law and Culture, 1350–1870* (Chapel Hill: University of North Carolina Press, 1991), 171.

[5] See Eric Foner, *Reconstruction: American's Unfinished Revolution, 1863–1877* (New York: Harper Collins, 1988), 78, 80 ("With emancipation, it seemed that half of the South's black population took to the roads ... The ability to come and go as they pleased would long remain a source of pride and excitement for former slaves") (citing Letter of Melton Linton to South Carolina Leader, March 31, 1866, quoted in Gerald D. Jaynes, *Branches without Roots: Genesis of the Black Working Class in the American South, 1862–1882* (New York, 1886), 75).

trust each other.[6] The freed slaves sought federal protection for all of their civil rights, including the right to control over their working conditions.

In November 1865, the Colored People's Convention of the State of South Carolina convened in Charleston to "deliberate upon the best plans calculated to advance the interests of our people." The South Carolina Conference enacted a resolution rejecting "a negro code, or any other class legislation by the State, considering as we do the same to be unjust and anti-republican." The Conference called for "a code of laws for the government of *all*, regardless of color," and demanded "the establishment of good schools for the thorough education of our children." They accused the South Carolina state legislature of denying them the right to vote and serve on juries, which they referred to as rights of citizenship. The Conference pointed out that the Black Codes deprived them of "the right to engage in any legitimate business" and charged that the legislature had "given us no encouragement to pursue agricultural pursuits, by refusing to sell us lands" and adopting laws that would "thrust us out or reduce us to serfdom." They asked to be treated the same as white men. Northern blacks also called for federal protection. Speaking for the Pennsylvania State Equal Rights League in November 1865, William Nesbit, Joseph C. Bustill, and William D. Forten celebrated the end of slavery and demanded that "every vestige of this foul, barbarous and unscrupulous enemy of man and his inalienable rights, shall be forever swept from this land." The Pennsylvania group demanded the right to travel around the country and "to be politically and legally equal with our white fellow citizens." They asked for Congress to prevent any legislation based on race and demanded the right to vote. Speaking before the Hall of Representatives in St. Louis, Missouri, on January 27, 1886, J. Mercer Langston of Oberlin, Ohio, urged lawmakers to establish "Equality under law" for free blacks.[7] He urged lawmakers to erase the word "white" from the state laws, and thus make manhood, not color, the basis of suffrage. In Congress, Ashley and his allies responded to their pleas.

---

[6] Stanley, *Bondage to Contract*, 40–41.

[7] Proceedings of the Colored People of the State of South Carolina (Charleston, South Carolina), November, 1985, in Philip Foner and George E. Walker, eds. *Proceedings of the Black State Conventions, 1840–1865* (Philadelphia: Temple University Press, 1980), 283; Congressional Address: William Nesbit, Joseph C. Bustill, William D. Forten, on behalf of the Pennsylvania State Equal Rights League (Nov. 1865); J. Mercer Langston, A Speech on "Equality before the Law" in the Hall of Representatives, in the Capitol, Missouri.

Immediately after the Thirteenth Amendment became law, Illinois Senator Lyman Trumbull introduced legislation to enforce the amendment and protect the rights of the newly freed slaves. Trumbull's first bill, which eventually became known as the 1866 Civil Rights Act, was based primarily in Congress's power to enforce the Thirteenth Amendment. Trumbull's second bill was an amendment to the Freedman's Bureau Act, adding a declaration of civil rights to the act and giving federal officials enforcement power to protect those rights. The Freedman's Bureau Amendment was intended to be temporary in effect and was based on Congress's war powers. Nonetheless, members of Congress saw the two measures as connected, a joint effort to protect the rights of freed slaves and expand civil rights throughout the country. Trumbull's Freedman's Bureau Amendment and the Civil Rights Act contained identical "lists of the civil rights of men to be guaranteed by the national government." According to noted legal scholar Jacobus tenBroek, together the bills were "the practical application of the idea of equality as an essential principle of liberty."[8]

Constitutional scholars tend to view the 1866 Civil Rights Act in isolation and argue that it applies to a relatively narrow set of common law "civil rights."[9] Many scholars analyze the act to better understand the Fourteenth Amendment, which Congress adopted virtually simultaneously.[10] These scholars largely overlook the Civil Rights Act's role in a comprehensive scheme to protect the labor rights of the freed slaves. Together, the 1866 Civil Rights Act and the Freedman's Bureau Amendment expanded federal jurisdiction to protect a positive right to free labor. The Second Freedman's Bureau and Civil Rights Acts employed virtually identical language to define the rights of the freed slaves that the Bureau was assigned to protect. Massachusetts Representative Thomas Eliot explained that the Freedman's Bureau Act was "novel legislation . . . rendered necessary by the . . . liberation from slavery of four million

---

[8] Robert F. Horowitz, *The Great Impeacher: A Political Biography of James M. Ashley* (New York: Brooklyn College Press, 1979), 117; Benedict, *Compromise*, 148; Jacobus tenBroek, "Thirteenth Amendment to the Constitution of the United States: Consummation to Abolition and Key to the Fourteenth Amendment," *California Law Review* 39 (1951): 171, 186–187.

[9] See Mark Graber, The Second Freedman's Bureau Bill's Constitution, Texas Law Review 94 (2016): 1361, 1362 (poimting out that legal historians tend to overlook the significance of the Second Freedman's Bureau Act and only focus on the 1866 Civil Rights Act).

[10] See George Rutherglen, *Civil Rights in the Shadow of Slavery: The Constitution, Common Law, and the Civil Rights Act of 1866* (New York: Oxford University Press, 2013), 4.

persons whose unpaid labor had enriched the lands and impoverished the hearts of their relentless masters." According to Eliot, freedmen were being denied their right to enter into fair contracts and the Bureau was making every effort to ascertain a fair wage. Trumbull's bill would have given the Bureau meaningful enforcement power. According to Senator Lott Merrill of Maine, the Freedman's Bureau Act was "designed to protect [the freedman] from his old master, to open up opportunities to him, to reach out the hand of the nation and stand between him and absolute want." President Johnson vetoed the act, but Congress pushed forward with the Civil Rights Act that had been intended to supplement it.[11]

The 1866 Civil Rights Act provided that all persons born within the United States, including freed slaves, are citizens of the United States. The act's Citizenship Clause is the most "revolutionary aspect" of the act, since it purported to overturn the Supreme Court's *Dred Scott* decision holding that persons of African descent could not be citizens. The act further provided that those persons "shall have the same right, in every State and Territory in the United States, to make and enforce contracts, to sue, be parties, and give evidence, to inherit, purchase, lease, sell, hold, and convey real and personal property, and to full and equal benefit of all laws and proceedings for the security of person and property, as is enjoyed by white citizens." The 1866 Civil Rights Act is well known to constitutional scholars as the predecessor to the Fourteenth Amendment, upheld by the Supreme Court as an exercise of Congress's power to address the "badges and incidents" of slavery.[12] But the 1866 act did not solely address the badges and incidents of slavery – it was directed at ending slavery itself. The racially discriminatory contracts that most concerned the Thirty-Ninth Congress were the labor contracts that imposed indentured servitude on the newly freed slaves. The principle goal of the 1866 Civil Rights Act was protecting the rights of those workers.

Throughout the debates over the act, its supporters said repeatedly that they wanted to prevent the southern states from reinstituting slavery.

[11] 39th Cong., 1st Sess., 513, 514 (Jan. 30, 1866); ibid., 156 (Merrill). Rep. Eliot also complained that land was not being confiscated and redistributed. Ibid., 514. Nieman, *To Set the Law in Motion*, 109.

[12] 1866 Civil Rights Act, 14 Stat. 27–30, April 9, 1866; Vorenberg, *Final Freedom*, 235. A century after the law was enacted, the US Supreme Court upheld a provision of the act that prohibited race discrimination in contracts, as applied to a real estate transaction. The Court held that Congress could reasonably have believed that race discrimination in real estate contracts was a "badge or incident of slavery." See *Jones v. Alfred Mayer Co.*, 392 U.S. 409 (1968).

Introducing his own measure in December 1865, Senator Henry Wilson argued that legislation was necessary to overturn the Black Codes because they were "wholly inconsistent with the freedom of the freedmen." To support his point, Wilson cited a South Carolina law that he said would make freed men into servants, a Georgia statute regulating contracts between master and servant, and a similar law from Mississippi.[13] Wilson also argued that "the vagrant laws of that States were used to make slaves of men whom we have made free." In the House, Massachusetts Republican Thomas Eliot agreed: "In Mississippi houses have been burned and negroes have been murdered. In Alabama a new code, a slave code in fact, has been attempted to be passed." Of the South Carolina vagrancy law, Illinois Republican Burton Cook concluded, "it is apparent that under other names and in other forms a system of involuntary servitude might be perpetuated over this unfortunate race."[14]

Senator Trumbull based the civil rights bill on the congressional power to enforce the Thirteenth Amendment. Trumbull explained, "The second clause of that amendment was inserted for ... the purpose ... of preventing State Legislatures from enslaving, under any pretense, those whom the first clause declared should be free." Introducing the bill, Trumbull made it clear that he believed that the Thirteenth Amendment imposed on Congress an "affirmative duty to protect Negroes against individual invasions of their new found freedom and civil rights when the inaction of the state or its failure to supply protection made such invasions possible." His colleague, Pennsylvania Representative Martin Thayer, agreed that Congress's enforcement power extended to "abolish[ing] and destroy[ing] forever ... all features of slavery which are oppressive in their character, which extinguish the rights of free citizens, and which unlawfully control their liberty."[15] Supporters of the act argued that slavery meant not only treating blacks as second-class citizens and racially inferior, but also treating them as a submissive and easily exploited source of labor. The 1866 act was to address and remedy both facets of the institution.

---

[13] The Georgia statute authorized employers to discharge employees for drunkenness, disobedience, immorality, or want of respect, and making leaving employment or enticing servants away illegal. The Mississippi law also forbade the leasing of lands or houses outside of the cities, "making freed slaves landless and homeless." Cong. Globe, 39th Cong., S. 39 (Dec. 13, 1865).

[14] Cong. Globe, 39th Cong., S. 39 (Dec. 13, 1865) (Wilson); 39th Cong., 1st Sess., 603 (Feb. 2, 1866) (Wilson), 517 (Jan. 30, 1866) (Eliot), 1124 (March 1, 1866) (Cook).

[15] Cong. Globe, 39th Cong., 43 (Trumbull); tenBroek, "Thirteenth Amendment," citing 39th Cong., 1st Sess., 472; 39th Cong., 1st Sess., 1152 (March 1, 1866) (Thayer).

The Civil Rights Act would protect the freed slaves' right to freedom of contract so that they could benefit from their own labor. Trumbull explained that the bill "declares that all persons in the United States shall be entitled to the same civil rights, the right to the fruit of their own labor, [and] the right to make contracts." Ohio Senator John Sherman agreed that, as citizens, newly freed slaves were entitled to earn "the fruits of their own labor" and to be "protected in their homes and family." Sherman insisted that it would be a "mockery" to "yet deny [to freedmen] the right to make a contract and secure the privileges and the rewards of labor." Leaders in the labor movement had often used the phrase "fruits of one's labor " to criticize the wage-based industrial system and argue that workers were entitled to more than mere wages.[16] To these members of the Reconstruction Congress, the "fruits of their labor " included the right to enter into contracts with employers, free of race discrimination and undue coercion – in other words, a positive right to free labor.

Opponents of the bill argued that the act did not fall within Congress's power to enforce the Thirteenth Amendment, which was limited to ending chattel slavery. For example, Senator Edgar Cowan insisted that the Thirteenth Amendment enforcement power "was not intended to over-turn this government and to revolutionize all the laws of the various states everywhere." Senator Willard Saulsbury agreed that the attempt "to confer civil rights which are wholly distinct and unconnected with the status or condition of slavery, is an attempt unwarranted by any method of process or sound reasoning." To that argument, Senator Jacob Howard replied, "We are told that the amendment simply relieves the slave from obligation to render service to his master . . . If theirs is the true construction, then state can pass laws denying Negroes the right to purchase property, have a home and shelter, have a wife and family, to reduce him to a condition infinitely worse than actual slavery." Howard rejected Cowan's cramped view of the amendment, and his colleagues overwhelmingly agreed.[17]

Opponents of the bill also insisted that the amendment could not have a broader meaning, because that would upset existing labor laws. According to Kentucky Senator Garrett Davis, the bill originated in a

---

[16] Cong. Globe, 39th Cong., 1st Sess., 599 (Feb. 2, 1866) (Trumbull); Mr. Sherman, 39th Cong., 1st Sess., 42, cited in Stanley, *Bondage to Contract*, 56; Lea S. VanderVelde, "The Labor Vision of the Thirteenth Amendment," *University of Pennsylvania Law Review* 138 (1989): 437, 474.

[17] Cong. Globe, 39th Cong., 1st Sess., 499, 476, 504.

mistaken policy and would not result in peace or reconcile the different races. Davis explained, "There are in all the old Slave states men whose business and whose ownership of lands will require them to employ the negroes who were lately slaves as laborer; but much the larger white population will have no such demand for such labor."[18] He continued, "The passage of such as bill as this is calculated to produce interference between, and a disturbance of, the relations of the black laborer and his white employer ... If the bill is passed, it will promote feud and enmity between the white employer and the black laborer." Davis insisted that such a feud could be avoided only by allowing states, which are most interested in "harmonizing" the relationship between employers and workers, to regulate that relationship. The act would upset the balance by giving too much power to black workers.

In his veto message, President Andrew Johnson shared Davis's concern about the bill's impact on labor practices. The president said, "To me the details of the bill seem fraught with evil." He explained, "This bill ... intervenes between capital and labor, and attempts to settle questions of political economy through the agency of numerous officials, which interest it will be to foment discord between the two races." Johnson continued, "The white race and the black race of the South have hitherto lived together under the relationship of master and slave – capital owning labor. Now, suddenly, the relationship is changed, and as to the ownership, capital and labor are divorced." Johnson's veto message condemned the bill's impact on state sovereignty. The president proclaimed, "In all our history, in all our experience as people living under the Federal and State law, no such system as that contemplated by the details of the bill has ever before been proposed or adopted." But why did the president care about state sovereignty? His veto message makes clear that he wanted states to be able to regulate labor relations in a way that greatly favored the employer over the employee, maintaining the common law that had been supplanted by the Thirteenth Amendment. Congress disagreed with the president, voting not only to approve the act, but also, by more than a two-thirds' margin in both houses, to override the presidential veto.[19]

---

[18] Cong. Globe, 39th Cong., 1st Sess., 1416 (March 15, 1866).

[19] Message from President Andrew Johnson to the Senate of the United States, Cong. Globe, 39th Cong., 1st Sess., 1681 (March 27, 1866); James D. Richardson, ed. *Messages and Papers of the Presidents of the United States*, 1789–1897 (Washington: Government Printing Office, 1896–99), 6: 405–416; Benedict, *Compromise*, 156, 164–165 (noting that the Republican Party was united in its opposition to the president); Horowitz, *Great*

Thus, the debate over the 1866 Civil Rights Act reveals a consensus on both sides of the aisle that the act would alter the balance of power between employers and employees, at least in the southern states. Former slaveholders would no longer be allowed to use race discrimination as a means of subordinating black workers. By a supermajority vote, members of the Thirty-Ninth Congress sided with the workers and established their right to work free of undue coercion and race discrimination. Most members of Congress avoided discussing the act's impact in the northern states where laws were not facially racially discriminatory. However, prominent members of Congress made it clear that the Thirteenth Amendment would have a national impact. On July 4, 1865, Henry Wilson declared that he wanted the former rebels to understand "that Slavery is destroyed, and with its death, the compromises of the Federal Constitution, the laws of Congress, the black laws of the late slave States, and of the free States, and all the political dogmas and ideas upon which this system of slavery depended, must be numbered among the things of the past." During the debate over his Freedman's Bureau Act, Lyman Trumbull agreed that "out of deference to slavery, which was tolerated by the Constitution of the United States, even some of the non-slaveholding States passed laws abridging the rights of the colored man which were restraints upon liberty. When slavery goes, all this system of legislation, devised in the interest of slavery and for the purpose of degrading the colored race ... goes with it."[20] The 1866 Act's antidiscrimination provisions applied in the entire country, including the northern states.

More problematic was the fact that the act did not protect the right to contract per se, but only racially discriminatory violations of the right to contract. The bill was directed at the early Black Codes, which expressly discriminated on the basis of race. After the harsh reaction to the facially discriminatory Mississippi and South Carolina Black Codes, other southern legislatures enacted laws that were mostly nondiscriminatory on their face, understanding that officials would administer them in a discriminatory fashion. Facially neutral laws enabled those states to get away with enforcing vagrancy laws and specific performance laws against freed

Impeacher, 118; Senate votes to override the veto, 35–15, Cong. Globe, 39th Cong., 1st Sess., 1809 (April 6, 1866). House override 122–41, Cong. Globe, 39th Cong., 1st Sess., 1861 (April 9, 1866).

[20] Celebration by the Colored People's Educational Monument Association in Memory of Abraham Lincoln, on the Fourth of July, 1865, reprinted in Foner, *Reconstruction*, 5, 23–24 (quoting the *New York Herald*, July 3, 1865); Cong. Globe, 1st Sess., 322 (1866) (Sen. Trumbull).

slaves. The act simply did not give federal officials clear authority to protect freedmen against covert discrimination.[21] Thus, the 1866 Civil Rights Act was an imperfect, and incomplete, measure to establish a positive right to free labor. Nonetheless, the act was a landmark. It was the first civil rights legislation ever enacted by Congress, and the first attempt to make the promise of freedom concrete and effective.

James Ashley supported the 1866 Civil Rights Act and the Freedman's Bureau Act. In a May 1866 speech, Ashley condemned the Black Codes, insisting that "[i]f I were a black man I would rather go into rebellion and revolution than submit to such an intolerable wrong." Citing a long list of leaders in the abolitionist movement, including William Lloyd Garrison, Wendell Phillips, Horace Greeley, and Gerrit Smith, Ashley claimed that they would have demanded justice and equal rights for black men and loyal men of the South. "Make the community of interest one by guaranteeing the equal rights of all men before the law, and the fidelity of every inhabitant of such a commonwealth becomes a necessity not only from interest but from a love of justice."[22] As a "foremost advocate of racial equality," Ashley supported the act's prohibition against race discrimination and protection of labor rights. However, he was disappointed that neither bill included the right to vote among the federal rights protected by the measures. Senator Trumbull justified this omission by arguing that he wanted to protect blacks with national action so that black suffrage and leaders in southern government would matter less. Radicals agreed to omit suffrage rights from the 1866 act in a futile attempt to appease the recalcitrant President Johnson.[23] However, the discriminatory Black Codes had revealed how southern state legislatures would act if blacks were not allowed to vote. Invoking his roots as a Jacksonian Democrat, Ashley insisted that former slaves could only truly be free if they had some say in self-government.

In the spring of 1866, Ashley once again used his position as Chair of Committee on the Territories to advocate for suffrage for freed slaves. Ashley now called for "impartial" suffrage, including voting rights for women. In March 1866 Ashley proposed a new constitutional amendment "to prepare a definite program of Reconstruction," which would

---

[21] Nieman, *To Set the Law in Motion*, 98, 110 113.
[22] Speech of Honorable James M. Ashley of Ohio, in the House of Representatives, May 29, 1866 – Impartial Suffrage the Only Safe Basis of Reconstruction (hereafter referred to as "Suffrage speech"), *Souvenir*, 392, 411, 413.
[23] Trefousse, *Radical Republicans*, 28; Benedict, *Compromise*, 147, 157.

have given blacks and women the right to vote. His proposed amendment would have provided that "No state shall deny the elective franchise to any of its inhabitants, being citizens of the United States, above the age of twenty-one years because of race or color; but suffrage shall be impartial." Ashley argued that large numbers of loyal men in the rebel states wanted to strengthen their hands by giving blacks the ballot, and explained, "Sir, it is the cause of the loyal white and black men that I plead; it is their cause which this Congress is fighting." Ashley insisted that the only way to reconstruct the South was to make sure that all loyal citizens could vote. He called the right to vote "a natural right, a divine right if you will, a right of which the government cannot justly deprive any citizen except as punishment for a crime," and confirmed that he expected that all blacks, including northern blacks, would have the right to vote.[24]

Ashely thus pleaded with his colleagues that citizenship rights included the right to vote. The parlance of the day distinguished between "civil" rights, which were linked to citizenship, and "political rights," which were not. For example, white women were considered citizens but they lacked the right to vote. Ashley's call for universal suffrage would have upended the traditional dichotomy. To reinforce his argument, Ashley asked his audience to consider the perspective of the black man whose "ancestors had been in bondage for two hundred years." He reminded them that freed slaves had fought for the Union Army and sacrificed their lives for their country. Ashley explained, "The ballot is the only sure weapon of protection and defense for the poor man, whether white or black. It is the sword and buckler and shield before which all oppressions, aristocracies and special privileges bow."[25] Only universal suffrage would ensure that blacks could be equal citizens in Ashley's free labor society.

On April 30, 1866, the Joint Committee on Reconstruction proposed its version of the Fourteenth Amendment. Section 2 of that amendment was similar to Ashley's proposal, except that it expressly limited voting rights to men. Ashley supported the amendment, but in a speech to Congress on May 29, 1866, he spoke out against the limitation of the franchise to men. Ashley commented, "It will be noticed that in

[24] Cong. Globe, 39th Cong., 1st Sess., 2879; Ashley, "Suffrage speech," *Souvenir*, 402, 406, 408.
[25] Rogers Smith, *Civic Ideals: Conflicting Visions of Citizenship in U.S. History* (New Haven: Yale University Press, 1997), 306; Ashley, "Suffrage speech," *Souvenir*, 407–409.

prescribing the qualifications of electors, in one of the amendments suggested by me, I omit the word 'male' and use the words 'all citizens of the United States above the age of twenty-one years.' I did this purposely, as I am unwilling to prohibit any State from enfranchising its women if they desire to do so."[26] In his support for women's suffrage, Ashley went beyond even the most radical of his colleagues. Women had been active in the abolitionist movement. Women had led the national petition effort for abolition, and had filled the galleries on the January 31 House vote. Prominent abolitionists including Susan B. Anthony and Elizabeth Cady Stanton argued that women should also benefit from the expansion of fundamental rights during the Reconstruction Era. Ashley evidently agreed with them, but his colleagues rejected his pleas for women's suffrage. They approved Section 2 of the Fourteenth Amendment, the only constitutional provision that expressly limited suffrage rights to "male inhabitants" of any state.[27]

Ashley's support for suffrage rights for the newly freed slaves grew out of his roots as a Jacksonian Democrat but also reflected political expediency. Ashley and his colleagues knew that blacks were likely to vote Republican and that without their votes the newly readmitted states could tip the balance for the Democrats in local offices and in Congress. As Ashley pointed out, the Thirteenth Amendment had repealed the hated Three-Fifths Clause (under which slaves were counted as only three-fifths of a person for purposes of representation), ironically increasing the influence of the former slave states in Congress and the Electoral College.[28] In Sections 2 through 4 of the Fourteenth Amendment, Congress gave southern states an incentive to allow blacks to vote. However, that proved to be insufficient. It was not until 1869, with the oncoming Democratic majority staring them in the face, that Congress approved the Fifteenth Amendment to prohibit the denial of the franchise based on race.

---

[26] Horowitz, *Great Impeacher*, 118; Ashley, "Suffrage speech," *Souvenir*, 392, 394, 397.

[27] See, e.g., Declaration of Sentiments, adopted at the Seneca Halls Convention in Seneca Falls, in Jean W. Matthews, *Women's Struggle for Equality: The First Phase, 1828–1876* (Chicago: Ivan V. Dee, 1997), 199; Elizabeth Cady Stanton, Address to the Legislature of the State of New York, in Gertrude Stein, *Three Lives* (Boston: Bedford St. Martin's, 2000), 223; Sara M. Evans, *Born for Liberty: A History of Women in American* (New York: Free Press, 1989), 81; US Constitution, Amendment XIV, Section 2.

[28] Speech in the House of Representatives, March 30, 1864, "The Liberation and Restoration of the South," *Souvenir*, 278 ("Since the emancipation of the slaves, the three-fifths representation clause in the Constitution is practically abolished, and each emancipated slave will hereafter be enumerated as an inhabitant").

In addition to recalcitrance on the issue of suffrage, the Reconstruction Congress never adopted an effective land reform program. Many of Ashley's allies, including Stevens, Sumner, George Julian, Wendell Phillips, and Benjamin Butler, advocated for confiscation of property. Thaddeus Stevens explained that confiscation and redistribution of property would help to create a black middle class, and insisted that land reform was more important than suffrage rights for newly freed slaves. Ashley had provided for the confiscation and redistribution of land in his proposed Reconstruction bills but was unable to convince his colleagues to enact them during the war. After the war, Ashley insisted that the right to vote was more important than the acquisition of property. Ashley argued, "If I were a Black man with chains just stricken from my limbs, without home to shelter me or mine, and you should offer me the ballot, or a cabin and forty acres of cotton land, I should take the ballot." The 1866 Civil Rights Act prohibited race discrimination in land contracts as well as labor contracts, but southerners fiercely resisted any attempts to provide freed slaves with their own land. The Freedman's Bureau, under General O. O. Howard, returned almost all of the land to its original owners. Eventually, enthusiasm for land reform faded, and the former slaves were forced once again to work on the property of the very planters who had enslaved them. Ashley later lamented the lack of Reconstruction Era land reform measures, stating, "I thought then, and think now, that we fell short of our duty to the black man."[29]

In the fall of 1866, President Johnson actively campaigned against Reconstruction and the radical members of Congress who supported it. Moderate Republicans emphasized their conservative side, distancing themselves from the radicals. They denied charges that they intend to impose suffrage and claimed that the Fourteenth Amendment was an offer of settlement to the South. However, the radicals did well in the elections, increasing their number and their influence in Congress. Moreover, Ashley did not try to hide his radical tendencies from his constituency. According to historian Hans Trefousse, in his last term in Congress Ashley was an "ultra" radical, allied with Stevens and Sumner. The ultras called for "complete and immediate racial equality," even though "championship of racial equality in the North was not popular at the time." Despite their divisions, Republicans were united about one thing. They ran against the President and in favor of Reconstruction. Republicans

---

[29] Foner, *Politics and Ideology*, 134, 138, 144; Ashley, "Suffrage speech," *Souvenir*, 407–408; Letter from Ashley to Benjamin Arnett (December 22, 1892), *Souvenir*, 362.

won a majority of over three-fourths of each branch of Congress, and returned ready to ramp up their Reconstruction effort in the face of presidential opposition.[30]

In the spring of 1867 Ashley proposed yet one more Reconstruction Act based on the territorial theory. His proposal would have established free public education and required the states to "secure to all citizens of the United States within said State, irrespective of race or color, the equal protection of the laws, including the right of elective franchise." Moderate and conservative Republicans, led by John Bingham and Henry Raymond, attacked Ashley's bill and Stevens's land reform proposals. At Stevens's request Ashley withdrew his bill but gave a speech reaffirming his commitment to Reconstruction. Ashley's speech was constantly interrupted with questions and comments from the opposition, but his statement on the franchise was "greeted with ringing applause." Bingham moved to refer the bill to the Joint Committee on Reconstruction, and on January 28 the House approved Bingham's motion. By early February, Ashley and Stevens realized that their bills would never pass and agreed to a plan of military reconstruction.[31] Meanwhile, Ashley and his allies continued their project to enforce a positive right to free labor. This time they focused on northern workers, courting an alliance between radicals and northern labor.

From 1867 to 1890, "democracy hastened the destruction of onerous forms of personal subordination to masters, landlords and creditors." During Reconstruction, the same development was repeated for black workers as the free market enshrined its rules in the legal definition of the wage contract. Ashley's friend and ally George Julian called the labor question "the logical sequence of the slavery question." In November 1865, veteran abolitionist Wendell Phillips said that, after twenty-eight years of fighting slavery, "we fitly commence a struggle to define and arrange the true relations of capital."[32] Ashley agreed, later explaining that "[t]he opinions which I hold touching organizations of working-men and the relations of capital and labor, are the logical outgrowth of my

---

[30] Benedict, *Compromise*, 197–198, 208; Montgomery, *Beyond Equality*, 261–262; Trefousse, *Radical Republicans*, 339, 344.

[31] Cong. Globe, 39th Cong., 2nd Sess., 781, 782, 816, 1096; Horowitz, *Great Impeacher*, 147.

[32] Montgomery, *Citizen Worker*, 50–51; Stanley, *Bondage to Contract*, 61 (citing Speech of George Julian in the US House of Representatives,*Workingman's Advocate*, April 1, 1871; and "Wendell Phillips on the Eight Hour Question," *National AntiSlavery Standard*, November 18, 1865 (speech at Faneuil Hall).

early fight against the right of capital to legal ownership in man."[33] He saw measures to protect freed slaves and northern workers as part of an international movement for workers' rights. Along with the 1866 act, other Reconstruction measures reveal that the labor questions in the postbellum North and South were interconnected.

Northern workers had a mixed reaction to the Civil War. During the war, only working-class people were subject to the draft because they could not pay the $300 fee to avoid it. This inequity gave rise to some antidraft riots. Most notably, in 1863, the city of New York exploded into a full-blown race riot, with the draft lottery igniting the protest. Nonetheless, northern workers largely supported the Civil War, which they saw as devoted to preserving "the world's only political democracy." Northern workers were among the staunchest supporters of the Union effort.[34] Workers enlisted heavily in the army and supported Lincoln's reelection to president. Trade unionists flocked to the Union Army and remained supporters of President Lincoln. Labor leaders praised the sacrifices of working men in saving the Union and fighting slavery, and urged workers to continue to fight the battle for universal freedom. Meanwhile, those who remained at home did not abandon their struggle for an eight-hour workday. In New York alone, for example, there were over ninety trade-wide strikes during the war.[35]

Labor advocates formed an alliance with congressional radicals and influenced early Reconstruction measures. During the long military occupation of New Orleans, workers provided the loyal 10 percent of white votes that Lincoln needed to justify his presidential Reconstruction effort. Ashley's friend General Benjamin Butler, who had initiated the "confiscation" of slaves who escaped over Union lines, presided over that occupation. Butler had strong ties to the Massachusetts labor movement and also courted worker's sympathies in New Orleans. In 1864 the New Orleans labor organizations supported the Free State Party, called for abolishing slavery and "the power of the aristocrat," to shift the power

---

[33] The Federation of Railroad Workers and All Wage Workers – Gov. Ashley's Address, June 10th, 1891, to the International Train Dispatcher's Convention, on Co-operation and Strikes, *Souvenir*, 667.

[34] Montgomery, *Beyond Equality*, 91–92, 96, 103–105; William H. Lofton, "Appeal of the Abolitionists to the Northern Working Classes," *The Journal of Negro History* 33, no. 3 (July 1948): 249, 283.

[35] Montgomery, *Beyond Equality*, 93–95, 98–101; Sean Wilentz, *Chants Democratic: New York City and the Rise of the American Working Class, 1788–1850* (New York: Oxford University Press, 1984), 395.

from planters to the city. After the election, they adopted a new state constitution that abolished slavery and empowered the state legislature to grant Negro suffrage. Their new organic law established a progressive income tax, opened public schools to blacks and whites, and proclaimed a nine-hour workday and a minimum wage. These progressive reforms were repealed soon after, when the returning Confederate soldiers elected a Democratic "Redeemer" government, but they served as a model of what labor could achieve with political clout. General Butler returned to Massachusetts, ran for Congress, and continued to court the working-man's vote.[36]

Nationally, the Thirteenth Amendment was a catalyst that brought about the new paradigm of free labor. As Lea VanderVelde points out, many members of Congress saw the amendment as a charter of labor freedom. During debates over the 1866 Civil Rights Act, Senator Henry Wilson connected the oppression of the poor white man to that of the newly freed slaves, explaining, "[W]e have advocated the rights of the black man because the black man was the most oppressed type of the toiling men of this country."[37] Ashley often drew a connection between slavery and workers' rights throughout the country. He hoped that the end of slavery would bring about the improvement of conditions for working people throughout the country, and he worked with his colleagues in the Reconstruction Congress to bring this about.

In 1867, Congress enforced the "involuntary servitude " clause of the Thirteenth Amendment with the 1867 Anti-Peonage Act. The act had its genesis in disputes over slavery in the territories during the Civil War. In 1860, the House passed a bill that would have repealed all acts of the New Mexico legislature authorizing slavery and involuntary servitude, but the bill did not get through the Senate. In 1865 US Attorney General James Speed returned to the matter, saying that he feared that the New Mexico law could reestablish "a grinding and odious form of slavery." In January 1867, the Senate ordered the Committee on Military Affairs to investigate the practice of peonage in New Mexico "to consider if any further legislation is needed to prevent the enslavement of Indians in New Mexico or any system of peonage there."

---

[36] Montgomery, *Beyond Equality*, 115–117.

[37] Ibid. ("For these members, free labor was not just the absence of slavery and its vestiges; it was the guarantee of an affirmative state of labor autonomy"). Lea VanderVelde argues that "in the Republican ideology, the degradation of one worker was the degradation of all working people." VanderVelde, "Labor Vision," 445; Cong. Globe, 39th Cong., 1st Sess., 343 (1866).

The commission found that the army was assisting with the capture of runaway peons and suggested legislation to stop it.[38]

The Anti-Peonage Act prohibited "the holding of any person to service or labor under the system known as peonage" in any place in the United States or the Territory of New Mexico. The act described peonage as "establish[ing], maintain[ing] or enforc[ing], directly or indirectly, the voluntary or involuntary service or labor of any persons as peons, in liquidation of any debt or obligation, or otherwise." The act went beyond the language of the Thirteenth Amendment, prohibiting "voluntary" as well as "involuntary" servitude.[39] That language was added in the Senate "so that there could be absolutely no question about the scope of the practices outlawed." In the Senate, opponents argued that peonage was voluntary if the peon voluntarily entered into the relationship with his creditor. Many peons and indentured people wished to leave working relationships into which they originally entered voluntarily, because they were being paid or treated poorly by their employers. In his early speeches, Ashley attacked such arrangements and declared himself "utterly opposed to the ownership of labor by capital, either as chattel slaves, or as apprentices for a term of years."[40] With the 1867 Anti-Peonage Act, members of the Reconstruction Congress adopted Ashley's approach.

During debate over the act, its supporters claimed that it did not matter whether a worker chose servitude; what mattered was "whether the resulting condition was degrading to workers and employers." The sponsor of the bill, Senator Henry Wilson, explained that the bill would elevate the status of all low wage workers because where peonage had been eliminated, "peons who once worked for two or three dollars a month are now able to command respectable wages." Pennsylvania Senator Charles Buckalew explained that the terms of debt service were "always exceedingly unfavorable" to the laborer and argued that the

[38] Robert J. Steinfeld, *The Invention of Free Labor: The Employment Relation in English and American Law and Culture, 1350–1870* (Chapel Hill: University of North Carolina Press, 1991), 173, 180, 183–184; Cong. Globe, 3 January 1867, 239–241.
[39] Anti-Peonage Act, Mar. 2, 1867, ch. 187, 14 Stat. 546, now codified as amended at 18 U.S.C. §1581 et seq. and 42 U.S.C. §1994; Cong. Globe, 39th Cong., 2nd Sess., ch. 187, March 2, 1867; 39th Cong., 2nd Sess., ch. 187, March 2, 1867; Avi Soifer, "Federal Protection, Paternalism, and the Virtually Forgotten Prohibition of Voluntary Peonage," *Columbia Law Review* 112 (2012): 1607.
[40] Steinfeld, *Invention of Free Labor*, 184; See Cong. Globe, 39th Cong., 2d Sess. 1571 (Sen. Davis); Closing Portion of Stump Speech Delivered in the Grove near Montpelier, Williams County, Ohio, September, 1856, by James M. Ashley, *Souvenir*, 601, 622.

system "degraded both the laborer and the owner himself."[41] In the House, there was little debate over the Anti-Peonage Act. Iowa Representative John Kasson explained that he believed that peonage was "very much like slavery," and his colleagues evidently agreed. James Ashley voted in favor of the measure. Thus, the members of the Thirty-Ninth Congress, including James Ashley, showed that they believed that the Thirteenth Amendment gave them the power to prevent exploitative employment practices well beyond the institution of chattel slavery. The 1867 Anti-Peonage Act outlawed indentured servitude throughout the country. This act thus "marked the triumph in law of free labor ideas, denying to state the authority to enact legislation that might criminally punish breaches of labor contracts or specifically compel their performance."[42]

Ashley also supported a measure that was directly addressed to northern labor practices, the 1868 Eight Hour Act. Members of the Reconstruction Congress had cited the sacrifices of the freed slaves for the Union effort to justify measures to protect their rights. Now, labor leaders used the war to cultivate "their own mythology of the war and emancipation."[43] At this crucial juncture in the evolving law of labor, labor advocates drew on the free labor ideology that had animated the antislavery and labor movements prior to the Civil War. Labor cultivated alliances with many of the same members of Congress who were leading the effort to restructure labor law in the southern states with Reconstruction measures. In congressional debates over the federal Eight Hour Act, its supporters drew connections between the plight of the former slaves and northern free workers, who all sought more control and autonomy in their working lives.

According to historian David Montgomery, labor's "struggle for shorter hours, in other words, was seen as a fight for the liberty of the worker." Philadelphia Trade Association President Jonathan Fincher's *Trade Review* masthead proclaimed, "Eight Hours: A Legal Day's Work for Freemen." Labor reformers proposed the eight-hour legislation "to draw a clear delineation between that part of the workman's day which might be purchased for wages and that which remained inalienably his own."[44] Ashley and his radical allies responded favorably to the call.

---

[41] Cong. Globe, 39th Cong., 2nd Sess. 1571–1572.
[42] Cong. Globe, 39th Cong., 2nd Sess., H. 346; Steinfield, *Invention of Free Labor*, 184.
[43] Montgomery, *Beyond Equality*, 97.   [44] Montgomery, *Beyond Equality*, 238–239.

In the spring of 1866, in the midst of congressional debates over the 1866 Civil Rights Act, the Freedman's Bureau Act, and the Fourteenth Amendment, Representative Ebon Ingersoll proposed a bill that would have established an eight-hour working day in the District of Columbia. Ingersoll argued that "it is one of the paramount duties of all legislative bodies to lighten as much as possible the burdens upon the laboring classes and promote the general welfare." The House voted in favor of Ingersoll's resolution on April 23, 1866, but that bill did not progress in the Senate. A year later, Ashley friend and ally George Julian introduced a bill that would establish an eight-hour workday for all federal employees. In the House, the bill passed on an easy vote of 78–23, with little debate. James Ashley voted in favor of the measure.[45] The bill was referred to the Senate, which engaged in a robust debate over the measure. During the Senate debate, the bill's supporters evoked the Free Soil ideology of the antislavery movement, emphasizing the value and dignity of labor. They cited the sacrifices of the workers in the Union Army to justify measures to improve their lot. Said Senator Henry Wilson, "In this matter of manual labor I look only to the rights and interests of labor. In this country and this age, as in other countries and in other ages, capital needs no champion; it will take care of itself, and will secure, if not the lion's share, at least its full share of profits in all departments of history."[46] A majority of his Senate colleagues agreed, and approved the measure.

The Eight Hour Act tested Republicans' ideology of freedom of contract. Opponents of the bill argued that it was a paternalistic measure that intruded on the workers' liberty of contract. Conservative Republican Senator William Pitt Fessenden of Maine argued that the bill "works against the industrious, against the enterprising, against those who want to better their condition by work." Fessenden concluded, "I am opposed utterly to the idea of regulating hours of labor by law." Maine Senator Lot Morrill concurred that "it is a degradation of the working men of our country to deprive them of the privilege of making contracts to work for just whatever sum and for whatever time they please." Morrill continued,

---

[45] 39th Cong., 1st Sess. 1969 (1866) (referral to committee of Rogers resolution); 39th Cong., 1st Sess., 2118 (April 23, 1866) (vote on Ingersoll resolution); 40th Cong., 1st Sess., 105, 425 (1867).

[46] Referred to Senate, 40th Cong., 2nd Sess., 346 (Jan. 7, 1868). For example, California Senator John Conness declared, "I am one of those who believe that toil is reputable; that it is enabling, that it lends true courage. I believe that the toilers, after all, are the men upon whom every society that is well ordered has to rely." Cong. Globe, 40th Cong, 1st Sess., 412 (1867); Cong. Globe, 40th Cong., 2nd Sess., 3426 (1868).

"I believe in leaving the people of this country at perfect liberty to make any contracts they please." Connecticut Senator Orris Ferry agreed, saying that if he was a day laborer, "I never would consent that the Government under which I live should interfere either with my rates of wages or with my hours of labor."[47] However, these opponents were outvoted by those, like Ashley, who argued that freedom of contract entailed more than an abstract right to noninterference. Here, Congress rejected a formalist right to contract and adopted substantive protections for workers exercising that right.

The 1868 Eight Hour Act is absent from most accounts of the Reconstruction Era. It led a short life. The Johnson administration attempted to undercut the statute by cutting the pay of some federal employees, and the Grant administration was ambivalent about the measure. The law was never repealed but it was subverted by appropriations bills and court rulings. By 1880, the Chairman of the House Committee on Education and Labor called the act a "dead letter."[48] However, the 1868 Eight Hour Act has a symbolic significance well beyond its practical effect. Along with the 1867 Anti-Peonage Act, the Eight Hour Act reveals that Republicans in the Reconstruction Era were willing to interfere with the formal right to contract to protect workers from undue exploitation. With the 1868 Eight Hour Act, the Reconstruction Congress again broadly defined the meaning of "undue coercion" prohibited by the positive right to free labor.

These congressional measures call into question the extent to which a formalist ideology of freedom of contract dominated the Reconstruction Congress. According to Amy Dru Stanley, proponents of freedom of contract "idealized ownership of self and voluntary change between individuals who were formally equal and free." Stanley points out that the 1866 Civil Rights Act enforced freedom of contract, as "the equal right of contract was the nub of the legislation." Scholar Ken Kersch argues that freed slaves embraced an ideology of individualism, which

---

[47] 40th Cong., 1st Sess., 413 (1867) (Fessenden); 40th Cong., 2nd Sess., 3428 (1868) (Fessenden); 40th Cong., 2nd Sess., 3426 (1868) (Morrill); 40th Cong., 2nd Sess., 3428 (1868) (Ferry).

[48] The notable exception is David Montgomery's book, *Beyond Equality: Labor and the Radical Republicans 1862–1872*, an in-depth analysis of the relationship between the radical Republicans and the labor movement during the Reconstruction Era. Montgomery, *Beyond Equality*, 318, 320–322. The Supreme Court gutted the statute, interpreting it as not applying to employment of government contractors. *United States v. Driscoll*, 96 U.S. 421 (1877).

flowed naturally from the "individualist-oriented free labor ideology" of the antislavery cause.[49] However, Kersch oversimplifies the role that freedom of contract played in both the antislavery movement and during the Reconstruction Era.

It is indisputable that freedom of contract was a necessary precondition of free labor. However, an overly formalist freedom of contract could undermine substantive measures to ensure that freed slaves could bargain on equal terms with their employers. As Donald Nieman has shown, the ideology of freedom of contract adversely affected Freedman's Bureau officials as they implemented a free labor system in the South. Some officials investigated labor contracts to ensure that they were fair, but too many officials simply imposed contracts on freed slaves regardless of their terms.[50] Thus officials on the front lines struggled with a substantive versus formalist vision of freedom of contract. In Congress, members engaged in the same debate. To James Ashley, and what he fondly referred to as the "old antislavery guard," abolishing slavery and establishing freedom of contract was not the end of their efforts. Freedom of contract was a means to the end of achieving equal citizenship and fundamental rights for freed slaves and establishing a positive right to free labor for all workers. Establishing those rights required substantive steps to ensure that those workers would not be unduly coerced or exploited by their employers, and that they would not be subjected to racial subordination.

The 1866 Civil Rights Act enabled the government to intervene to bar race discrimination in contract relations. The Anti-Peonage Act prohibited workers from voluntarily signing exploitative contracts, and the Eight Hour Act reduced the authority of employers to impose contacts on workers that forced them to work longer hours than they desired. These measures reveal that members of the Reconstruction Congress were willing to intervene in the market to enforce a substantive vision of freedom of contract that empowered workers and leveled the playing field.

Ashley supported and voted in favor of all of the measures protecting a positive right to free labor, and they reflected positions that he had long expressed. However, in 1867 and 1868, Ashley was no longer actively participating in congressional debates. He had become embroiled in the

[49] Stanley, *Bondage to Contract*, x, 56; Ken I. Kersch, *Constructing Civil Liberties: Discontinuities in the Development of American Constitutional Law* (New York: Cambridge University Press, 2004) 22, 188–191.
[50] Nieman, *To Set the Law in Motion*, 162.

attempt to impeach President Andrew Johnson. Ashley was one of the first members of Congress to call for Johnson's impeachment, and he led the first impeachment effort in the House. Like his allies in Congress, Ashley had initially been willing to work with Johnson after Lincoln's assassination. However, Ashley's optimism faded as early as May 1865, when Johnson issued a proclamation granting amnesty to all rebels who took an oath of allegiance. During Ashley's trip to the western territories, he became increasingly upset at Johnson's leniency toward the former Confederate officers. By December 1865, Ashley was convinced that Johnson should be impeached.[51]

In the spring of 1866, Johnson simply refused to execute every Reconstruction effort, including the Confiscation Act, and he vetoed the 1866 Civil Rights Act and the Freedman's Bureau Amendment. According to Michael Les Benedict, "By May 1866, Johnson's interference on behalf of the South had become so blatant that many Republicans had feared the President might attempt a coup d'etat." When Congress adjourned on July 28, 1866, the president and Congress had reached an open state of hostility. Ashley spent the rest of the year preparing a case against the president. President Johnson channeled funds to Ashley's opponent in the 1866 congressional election, adding to Ashley's hostility. On January 27, 1867, "in a voice quivering with nervous excitement," Ashley called on Congress to investigate Johnson to determine whether he had committed impeachable offenses. The proposal passed 108–38, and Ashley began to work on his case. "Ashley was a zealot" in this effort, and gained the nickname the "Great Impeacher."[52]

In a March 1867 speech urging impeachment of the president, Ashley argued that Johnson's attempt to implement his own Reconstruction policy in 1865 unconstitutionally usurped the powers of Congress. He explained, "The duty of the President is to execute, not to make laws." Ashley continued, "He has corruptly used the appointing, pardoning, and veto powers, he has corruptly disposed of public property of the United States, corruptly interfered with elections." Ashley claimed that Johnson's nonenforcement of Reconstruction measures was also an impeachable offense. The president should "give loyal men at least the same protection

---

[51] Horowitz, *Great Impeacher*, 11–113, 115; Leonard L. Richards, *Who Freed the Slaves? The Fight over the Thirteenth Amendment* (Chicago: University of Chicago Press, 2015), 255, 239.

[52] Benedict, *Compromise*, 248, 250–251; Horowitz, *Great Impeacher*, 121–125; Richards, *Who Freed the Slaves?*, 241.

he has given rebels." However, Ashley failed to convince his colleagues and they rejected his articles of impeachment.[53]

Some historians later said Ashley was motivated by the bizarre belief that Johnson had plotted to assassinate Lincoln. Ashley never directly accused Johnson of this, but he did imply it, saying "I am confident . . . that a widespread conspiracy, representing the pro-slavery rebel faction in the nation, was organized for the purpose of assassinating Mr. Lincoln, and all know of its success." Ashley was ridiculed for these accusations, but nevertheless, his "desire to impeach Johnson became a consuming passion." This made Ashley a "persona non grata" to many Republicans, who mounted a second attempt to impeach the president but excluded Ashley from the proceedings. This second time the House voted to impeach, but the Senate fell one vote short of conviction.[54] Ashley's "brilliant political career was severely damaged," and he was devastated by Congress's failure to impeach. Ashley believed that "the failure of impeachment was a defeat for democratic constitutional government" and feared that other presidents would abuse power as Johnson had. By the November 1867 election, the tide had turned against Ashley and his radical allies. *The Toledo Blade* and other papers throughout the country printed editorials saying the country could no longer endure the impeachment effort.[55]

Although opposition to Johnson was strong, many of Ashley's colleagues thought that he had gone too far in his accusations against Johnson. In May 1868, Ashley introduced a new constitutional amendment that would have abolished the office of vice president and the Electoral College, and provided for direct election of the president. Introducing the amendment, Ashley argued that the Electoral College was antagonistic to principles of democratic government, and called the remedy of impeachment "but a scarecrow."[56] However, Ashley's effort to impeach had reduced his political clout, and his pleas fell on deaf ears.

---

[53] Horowitz, *Great Impeacher*, 125–126; Impeachment of the President: Remarks by Hon. James M. Ashley of Ohio, in the House of Representatives, March 7, 1867, *Souvenir*, 436, 437, 442, 444.

[54] Horowitz, *Great Impeacher*, 124–126, 154; Speech of Hon. James M. Ashley of Ohio, Delivered in the House of Representatives, May 29, 1868 – "Amend the Constitution – Abolishment of the Office of Vice-President – Neither Caucuses, Conventions, Electoral Colleges, nor the House of Representatives to Intervene between the People and Their Choice of a President," *Souvenir*, 465.

[55] Horowitz, *Great Impeacher*, 142–143, 154.

[56] Speech of Hon. James M. Ashley of Ohio, Delivered in the House of Representatives, May 29, 1868 – "Amend the Constitution – Abolishment of the Office of Vice-President –

At the 1868 Ohio Republican convention, Ashley was nominated as a congressional candidate for the last time. Accepting the nomination, Ashley celebrated the accomplishments of the Reconstruction Congress. Ashley declared that the Thirteenth and Fourteenth Amendments were "worth the struggle of a century. By them liberty and justice are established throughout all the borders of the republic. All men are thus made equal before the law, and cannot be denied, in any State, the equal protection of the law." However, he failed to overcome the damage to his reputation and he lost the election. According to his biographer, by 1868 Ashley's "stands on Black suffrage, women's rights, his opposition to Pendleton's inflationary greenback plan, and his long-standing mistrust of special privilege branded him as radical, and a man of the past. With these views, he seemed too much of a political maverick for the conservative businessmen of the areas, who were looking for a new type of leader." Despite all his mistakes, though, Ashley lost by only 912 out of 30,000 votes. One of Ashley's last acts in Congress was his vote in favor of the Fifteenth Amendment.[57]

The failed impeachment effort also harmed radical Republicans as a whole. They had suffered severe losses in the 1867 congressional election. In March 1868, ultra-radical Thaddeus Stevens, a great friend and ally of James Ashley, died. Choked with emotion, Ashley spoke about his friend in a congressional memorial service, saying that "the nation has lost one of her most distinguished sons ... another of the uncompromising heroes of our anti-slavery revolution." Ashley recalled, "When I first entered this House, ten years ago, Mr. Stevens was one of the first to take me by the hand and welcome me. From that day until the day of his death he was my friend, and often my advisor and counselor." He continued, "[T]hrough some of the most eventful years in our history I have been intimately associated with him on this floor. During all that time, which included the darkest hours in the nation's life – hours which tested the constancy and courage of men – he bore himself with such unquestioned fidelity to the cause of human freedom, as to command even the respect of political opponents and the cordial endorsement of all liberty-loving men." Stevens's death was symbolic of the demise of radical dominance in

---

Neither Caucuses, Conventions, Electoral Colleges, nor the House of Representatives to Intervene between the People and Their Choice of a President," *Souvenir*, 475, 495.
[57] Hon. James M. Ashley Unanimously Re-Nominated for Congress by the Republican Congressional Convention of the Tenth District at Napoleon, August 19, 1868, *Souvenir*, 505, 513; Horowitz, *Great Impeacher*, 156–157.

Congress. The radicals had lost the impeachment battle, and lost power in the Republican Party. Ashley had lost one of his dear friends, and he would soon lose his seat in Congress. "A new economic era was beginning. The day of the antislavery radicals was passing."[58] Ashley was about to leave Congress with an uncertain future ahead of him.

[58] Horowitz, *Great Impeacher*, 140, 155; Benedict, *Compromise*, 257; Address of Hon. James M. Ashley of Ohio, Delivered in the US House of Representatives, December 17, 1868, on the Death of Hon. Thaddeus Stevens of Pennsylvania, *Souvenir*, 640, 641, 643.

8

After Congress

The "Old Antislavery Guard" and the Northern Worker

After Ashley lost his congressional election, he went to New York to join General Ulysses S. Grant's presidential campaign. Ashley celebrated Grant's victory, but faced a future without a job. He took advantage of the expertise that he had gained in his years as Chair of Committee on the Territories and asked his friends for help. A letter signed by 98 members of the House and a note signed by 15 senators asked for Ashley to be appointed governor of Montana Territory. On April 25, 1869, Grant nominated Ashley for the position. There was a bitter debate over his nomination, but the Senate approved it by one vote. Ashley wrote a joyful letter to his friend Charles Sumner in which he said he hoped to form a Republican Party in Montana and "perpetuat[e] the names of the Old Anti-Slavery Guard."[1] Once in Montana, however, Ashley faced a hostile audience. He was removed from his position and consigned to private life. As part of the antislavery guard, Ashley had been a leader in a successful movement that was remarkably united during the early days of Reconstruction. Now, however, the movement was splintering over issues that had been central to Ashley's ideology, including the rights of freed blacks and northern workers. In the 1870s, Republicans began to back away from their commitment to racial equality, eventually abandoning southern blacks to the racist "Redeemer" movement. The Republican Party also backed away from protecting workers' rights as it evolved into the party of big business. Ashley was forced to adapt to these changes and

[1] Robert F. Horowitz, *The Great Impeacher: A Political Biography of James M. Ashley* (New York: Brooklyn College Press 1979), 156, 158 (1978); Letter from James Ashley to Charles Sumner, Charles Sumner Papers, Houghton Library at Harvard University.

refine his approach to racial equality and the rights of workers. While in Congress, Ashley almost always adopted the most radical position on every issue. After he left, it became harder to categorize Ashley's views. He was mostly on his own as he sought to hew to the principles of the "old antislavery guard" while navigating the changing dynamics of race and class in the northern industrializing economy.

For the rest of his life, Ashley sought to apply the principles of the "old antislavery guard" to northern workers, including substantive steps to ensure that those workers would not be unduly coerced or exploited by their employers. Both former slaves in the South and industrial workers in the North sought more autonomy in their working lives. As governor of Montana, Ashley spoke out against what he viewed as the vestiges of slavery: apprenticeship and the Chinese "coolie" system. Ashley put himself forward as a populist champion of the working class. He advocated universal public education and supported suffrage rights. In later years, Ashley became increasingly concerned with the plight of northern industrial workers. As the owner of a small railroad, Ashley advocated the workers' right to organize and workers' ownership of the means of production. Ashley repeatedly explained that he supported northern workers for the same reasons that he had opposed slavery. Thus he sought to connect the ideology of the "old antislavery guard" to protecting workers' rights in the industrial economy.

As he left Congress in 1869, Ashley's Republican Party was changing. During the Civil War, Republicans held themselves out as the party of the people, promoting free labor and education for all. However, after the war a financial divide developed between the workers and the manufacturers that had profited from the war, and eventually Republicans were forced to take sides. After 1868, Ashley's views were no longer those of the Republican Party leadership. Moderates such as William Pitt Fessenden and Roscoe Conkling came to predominate. By then, the Republican Party was already shifting toward an antilabor and pro-corporate stance. Many Republicans concluded that the politics of Reconstruction hurt business.[2] According to historian Heather Cox

[2] Heather Fox Richardson, *The Death of Reconstruction: Race, Labor and Politics in the Civil War North, 1865–1901* (Cambridge, MA: Harvard University Press, 2001), 25, 44, 74 (2014). ("[N]o matter how fervently Republicans talked about equality, as early as 1864 it was apparent that their economic policies were creating a class of extremely wealthy men, a discrepancy between ideology and reality that would not bode well for the future"); Eric Foner, *Politics and Ideology in the Age of the Civil War* (New York: Oxford University Press, 1980), 125.

Richardson, "The tension between Republicans who supported the right of every man to have a say in his government and those who worried about radicalism created an interparty rift that would, within a decade, make Republicans the party of big business." The rise of the labor movement after the war exacerbated tensions within the party over economic issues. "[I]n the end, Reconstruction came full circle. It began with southerners trying to adjust to the northern system of free labor. It ended with northerners having to accept the reality of conflict between capital and labor – a reality that southerners, white and black alike, had understood all along." Along with his close allies, Sumner and Wade, Ashley sided with labor in their disputes with capital.[3] This position put Ashley increasingly at odds with the Republican Party as it evolved into a pro-business party.

The "old antislavery guard" had advocated the doctrine of free labor. During Reconstruction, they enforced free labor in the South but largely avoided the question of how it would apply in the North. After the war, advocates for labor also had to adjust to the postwar industrial economy. In the wake of the Civil War, the industrialization of the workplace and transition to wage work resulted in the revival of the antebellum "wage slavery" critique. Many northern workers demanded more than merely the right to sell their labor. They also wanted state measures that would empower them, including labor republicanism and industrial unions. Prior to the war, labor and antislavery advocates had decried wage slavery. After the war, they had to confront the fact that "Chattel slaves in the south and independent commodity producers in the north had been transformed into a class of hirelings." For the first time, wage earners outnumbered the self-employed. "The peculiar issue of the wage earner ... created an agonizing dilemma for radicals," who had idealized the self-made man. It raised the question of whether a wage-earning employee could be truly free notwithstanding his dependence on his employer. This was a real dilemma for Republicans, who had never reached a consensus about the meaning of "free labor."[4] Free labor could mean nothing more than the right to negotiate a contract with one's

---

[3] Foner, *Politics and Ideology*, 50, 73–74, 127.

[4] Amy Dru Stanley, *From Bondage to Contract: Wage Labor, Marriage, and the Market in the Age of Slave Emancipation* (New York: Cambridge University Press, 1998), 4; David Montgomery, *Beyond Equality: Labor and the Radical Republicans 1862–1872* (Urbana and Chicago: University of Illinois Press, 1967), 260; Adam Tuchinsky, *Horace Greeley's New York Tribune: Civil War Era Socialism and the Crisis of Free Labor* (Ithaca: Cornell University Press, 2009), 240.

employer. It could also mean the emancipation from wage labor, but that was increasingly unrealistic in the industrializing economy. Free labor could also mean labor-oriented reforms, including unions, cooperative organizations, or state intervention in the economy and market relationships.[5] Ashley chose the third, broader meaning of free labor and applied it to the northern worker.

The "old antislavery guard" had also advanced the equality rights of freed slaves. After Ashley left Congress, his congressional colleagues initially continued these efforts. Responding to reports of Ku Klux Klan violence, Congress enacted the 1870 and 1871 Enforcement Acts, which made all of the Reconstruction measures enforceable against state actors and private conspiracies. However, Reconstruction was entering its waning years. Southern resistance continued, as did rampant violence throughout the South. In many places, planters banded together. In others, planters engaged in random acts of violence. Mob violence reigned and riots erupted in cities such as Norfolk, Memphis, and New Orleans. Much of the violence was directed at freed slaves exercising their civil and political rights, but the violent tactics also sought to maintain black workers in their subservient and easily exploitable state. The hopes of black men and women in the rural South were crushed by the triumph of Democratic "Redeemers."[6] Redeemers formed paramilitary organizations to restore hierarchies of race, gender, class, and property. The Ku Klux Klan targeted not only black politicians, but also black and white women who exhibited independence, acting as a labor organization for whites and to discipline black workers. The southern "Redeemers" did not immediately disenfranchise black voters or impose legal segregation, "[b]ut in the realm of labor relations, there was no delay." During the 1870s, Redeemer legislators enacted a series of measures "for the protection of cotton planters," including criminal punishments against laborers violating contracts, and increasing rights of landlords. As a result, southern black workers were driven from the political arena and subject to the unrestrained exploitation of contract labor.[7]

---

[5] Tuchinsky, *Horace Greeley*, 240.

[6] See Xi Wang, "The Making of Federal Enforcement Laws, 1870–1872," *Chicago Kent Law Review* 70 (1995): 1013, 1020; Donald G. Nieman, *To Set the Law in Motion: The Freedman's Bureau and the Legal Rights of Blacks* (Millwood, NY: KTO Press, 1979), 122–124; David Montgomery, *Citizen Worker: The Experience of Workers in the United States with Democracy and the Free Market during the Nineteenth Century* (New York: Cambridge University Press, 1993), 126.

[7] Montgomery, *Citizen Worker*, 127–129; Foner, *Politics and Ideology*, 123.

Racial prejudice in the North was also a barrier to radical measures. "That there was a growing weariness with the struggle about racial equality was a commonly heard complaint – a trend of public opinion which had serious implications for Reconstruction, the success of universal suffrage, and a group whose principle article of faith was the elevation of the Negro."[8] In Montana, Ashley advocated equal protection for Chinese "coolies," but also used racially charged language to oppose immigration into the state. Eventually, Ashley was forced to acknowledge that the end of slavery had not brought about racial equality. After he left Congress, he had little influence on the plight of freed slaves in the South. However, he continued to argue that he favored racial justice even as he turned his focus toward economic issues. In the last years of his life, Ashley did not engage in efforts to further racial justice as he advocated for the rights of northern workers. Nonetheless, the Afro-American League organized a tribute to him in 1893, evidence that African Americans still considered him a friend and ally.

Ashley arrived in Montana in late July 1869. He traveled around the state and promised to bring a railroad to the territory within three years. Speaking to the Montana legislature that December, Ashley presented himself as a champion of workers' rights and an opponent of "special interest" legislation. Said Ashley, "The first and highest duty of the legislature is to protect the laboring man from the grasping avarice of capital. I have looked in vain for any general or specific act of the Legislative Assembly ... to secure the benefit of association or organization of any class of laboring men ... If labor cannot be helped by legislation, it has, at least, the right to demand that it shall not be taxed for the benefit of a favored few." Ashley condemned the importation of "laborers who are apprenticed for a term of years, no matter from what country they may come." But Ashley saved his strongest words to condemn the Chinese "coolie" system. Ashley had criticized the system as early as 1856, and he supported congressional bill to ban the "coolie" trade in 1862.[9] Now that he was in the West he had to directly confront

---

[8] Hans L. Trefousse, *The Radical Republicans: Lincoln's Vanguard for Racial Justice* (New York: Alfred A. Knopf, 1968), 373.

[9] December 1869 speech to Montana legislature – Message of Governor Ashley, House Journal, 6th Session, 1869–1870, Charles S. Ashley, Governor Ashley's Biography and Messages, in *Contributions to the Historical Society of Montana* (Helena, MT: Rocky Mountain Publishing, 1907), 210 (hereafter referred to as "Speech to Montana legislature"), 252, 271; Cong. Globe, 37th Cong., 2nd Sess. (Feb. 19, 1862).

the system, and the powerful economic interests that supported it, for the first time. That political pressure did not deter Ashley from condemning the practice at length in his first public speech.

Said Ashley, "The history of the importation of Chinese coolies into the colonies of Great Britain, France, and Spain, and into the United States, under the pretext of necessity for cheap labor, is a history of enormities and crimes only equaled in treachery and atrocity by the horrors of the slave trade." Ashley compared the coolie trade system with the slave trade, explaining, "On the shore of China these cheap laborers are induced by false promises to sign contracts, the contents of which they do not understand, after which they are persuaded on shipboard by their captors," put onto vessels "packed with its cargo of human chattels," and subjected to a "passage at sea which rivals in brutality the enormities practiced in the palmiest days of the slave trade." Chinese "merchants" then make "contracts for the labor of their slaves." Ashley concluded, "The importation of Chinese coolies into the United States today, is in violation of the spirit; if not the letter of our law."[10]

Supporters of the "coolie" trade argued that it was necessary to provide a source of cheap labor. Ashley acknowledged, "This is the kind of labor which the selfishness and cupidity of capital are seeking to introduce into this country, especially into southern states, under the pretext that 'the great want of America is cheap labor.'" However, Ashley disagreed that the lack of cheap labor was a problem, either in Montana or in the United States in general. Said Ashley, "It should be our purpose rather to aid the working men of Montana and America to escape the consequences of a competition with such laborers as Chinese coolies; a competition which can only be disastrous to them, and advantageous to capitalists and monopolists." Here, Ashley sided with the interests of labor over capital, arguing that depressing impact of "coolie" labor on wages was another reason to oppose it. Ashley explained, "the importation of cheap laborers from China, or any other country whose male adult population can be apprenticed for a term of years and treated as slaves will, beyond question, reduce the price of labor in this country." Ashley pointed out that newly freed slaves in the South had a similar concern, because the "competition" with cheap immigrant labor "will be felt more immediately and severely by the black men of the south, in the cultivation of rice, sugar and cotton."[11] Here Ashley claimed that

[10] Ashley, "Speech to Montana legislature," 271.   [11] Ibid., 272–273.

southern free slaves had a commonality of interest with northern workers – they all wanted to be paid better wages for their labor.

Ashley's speech contained some racially exclusionary language. Ashley said that he believed in "the adaptability and non-adaptability of climate to races, and that in our own country, as well as among the civilized nations of Europe, there are those better adapted to the climate, production and wants of Montana." He claimed that "Montana is far better adapted to the hardy races of men and women from Great Britain and Northern Europe than to any race from a tropical climate, whether white or black." Even more problematic, Ashley said that he was "opposed to the importation of laborers from any of the barbarous or semi-civilized races of men."[12] Here, Ashley seems to advocate the type of racially exclusionary policies that some northern states had adopted prior to the war, practices that he had always condemned in the past. It is possible that Ashley was pandering here to the sentiments of the former Confederates in the Montana state legislature. At any rate, Ashley's stance on race issues in this speech was at best ambiguous. On the other hand, Ashley's racist statements immediately preceded Ashley's condemnation of the "coolie" labor system, where he pointed out that the Chinese laborers were particularly vulnerable to exploitation.[13] As he had with the institution of slavery, Ashley pointed out that race discrimination against "coolies" furthered their economic subordination.

In other parts of his speech Ashley used more egalitarian language. Ashley insisted that "the citizens of China, who are now in the country, and all who may hereafter come, have the same rights secured to them which we demand for our own citizens while residing in China, in the pursuit of lawful employment." Ashley also insisted that every state and territory had a duty to protect those rights. He called for the abolition of the tax on Chinese laundries, "because the law operates unequally and unjustly, and is a violation of every democratic principle." Ashley reiterated, "Equal and exact justice, no less than good faith on our part, requires that all subjects of China residing in our territory, should be taxed as our own citizens are taxed – no more, no less. Any attempt to evade this just requirement, by 'unfriendly legislation,' is inconsistent with the dignity and the character of the American Government." Ashley

---

[12] Ibid., 269–271.

[13] Ibid., 271 ("I do not propose to cooperate in any scheme organized to bring such laborers into Montana, or into any part of this country").

also praised the newly enacted Fifteenth Amendment to the federal Constitution, which prohibits the denial of suffrage based on race, and recommended that the Montana Territory adopt a similar provision for its constitution.[14] These statements all suggest that, as governor of Montana, Ashley had not entirely abandoned his longtime commitment to racial equality in civil and political rights.

Finally, Ashley returned to his populist roots and called for a broad right to public education "to preserve the inestimable blessings of civil and religious liberty, and to teach, practically, the equality of all men before the law." Ashley had always argued that a free labor republic would provide free and universal public education. As governor, he tried to implement that vision. Ashley declared, "Universal education is the evangel of peace, order, and law in a republic. It is the best weapon and defense which civilized society can have." He explained, "I maintain ... that the crowning glory of our school system is the fact that children of the rich and poor sit side by side in all our public schools, and that the child of the poor man is at the head of the class oftener than the child of the rich man." In public school, "they learn with every lesson to respect intellectual and moral worth rather than riches and position, and thus at the very foundation of our political structure, the youth of our land are taught that the American Government recognizes neither class nor caste."[15] Thus, in his last political office, Ashley championed participatory democracy to achieve economic equality and empowerment for the lower classes.

Ashley's son Charles Sumner Ashley later claimed that Ashley had a good sense of humor that "was an offset and humanizing counterprise to the constitutional radicalism which formed the other side of his character." According to the younger Ashley, "[I]t was the former quality that won him friends all his life and the latter that aroused hostility and opposition, even among those divided from him by a comparatively narrow degree." Governor James Ashley's speech to the Montana legislature certainly revealed his "constitutional radicalism," and it made him some enemies. Some of his critics accused him of turning his back on black rights with his speech encouraging European immigration to Montana. More important to his political future, Ashley's remarks

[14] Ibid., 274. The US Supreme Court later struck down a similar tax in *Yick Wo v. Hopkins*, 118 U.S. 356 (1886).
[15] Ashley, "Speech to Montana legislature," 274–276.

criticizing special interest legislation went against the new trend in the Republican Party and offended powerful interests in the Ohio Republican Party.[16]

By far the most controversial part of Ashley's speech was his critique of the "coolie" labor system. Ashley claimed that his position was common because "the practical men of the two great political parties have pronounced against the introduction of coolie labor, or apprenticed labor, or any labor which can be secured by force or fraud. There is a wide distinction between voluntary and involuntary immigration." Indeed, other Republicans did share Ashley's view. In 1869, based on Charles Sumner's motion, Congress had strengthened the ban against the "coolie" trade, extending provisions of the act to Japanese and other Asian "coolies." In an attempt to stop Democrats from introducing "coolie" labor in the South, Republican Senator William Stewart of Nevada introduced a bill to amend the 1866 Civil Rights Act to extend its coverage to "all persons," including Asian immigrants. Stewart's bill was adopted with minor changes as Section 16 of the Civil Rights Act of 1870.[17] However, in the Montana territory, Ashley's criticism of the "coolie" system went over like a lead balloon.

Many of the original settlers of Montana were from the South or were Confederate sympathizers from border states such as Missouri. They had no interest in racial equality and lacked any sympathy for the Chinese "coolies." Democrats dominated Montana politics, including the state legislature. Moreover, "coolies" were deemed necessary to build the railroads that Ashley had promised. Ashley's relationship with the legislature degenerated into mutual hostility. He fought with the legislature over appointments and vetoed their legislation. Within weeks of his speech President Grant removed Ashley from office and appointed a political opponent from the Sherman group in Ohio to replace him. Ashley was shocked, and wrote to his friends for help. Charles Sumner

---

[16] Charles Ashley, "Governor Ashley's Biography," 212; Ashley, "Speech to Montana legislature," 160.

[17] Ashley, "Speech to Montana legislature," 273; Cong. Globe, 40th Cong., 3rd Sess. (Feb. 9, 1869). Sumner wrote that "it is abhorrent to the spirit of modern international law and policy ... to permit the establishment in its place of a mode of enslaving men different from the former in little else than employment of fraud rather than force to make its victims captive." Charles Sumner, Denunciation of the Coolie Trade, Sen. Res. (Jan. 16, 1867), cited in Charles J. McLain, "The Chinese Struggle for Civil Rights in Nineteenth Century America: The First Phase, 1850–1870," *California Law Review* 72 (1984): 529, 566; Civil Rights Act of 1870, ch. 114, §16, 16 Stat. 140, 144 (1869–1871).

tried to help by talking to President Grant, who refused to listen. On July 13, 1870, the Senate approved Ashley's successor and Ashley and his family returned to Ohio.[18] It was the end of Ashley's career in political office.

As Reconstruction was declining, and feeling abandoned by his party, James Ashley returned to private life. Once he no longer held political office, Ashley had more time to devote to his family and attend to the needs of his children. After all his travel, he was ready to settle down with his family. Ashley had a very close relationship with his wife, who shared his political beliefs.[19] His son, Charles, later recalled the warm relationship between his parents: "Sometimes Mrs. Ashley would be at work getting dinner and the husband would come out to the kitchen and read aloud some magazine article about evolution or woman suffrage or education while the kettle boiled and the wife went to and fro with her homely tasks." Charles observed, "It is in such place and ways ... which, when seen even by a child as the writer then was is at once known as the real thing and which one loves to look back upon, as upon the oasis in the desert of life." Ashley sent all four of his children to college, including his daughter, Mary, which was quite unusual at the time. In 1871, Ashley went on a speaking tour, and moved to Antioch, Ohio, so his children could attend Antioch College. In 1876, as President Rutherford B. Hayes ordered the northern troops to leave the south and thus ended Reconstruction, Ashley moved to Ann Arbor, Michigan, so his oldest son James could attend law school.[20]

Although he no longer held office, Ashley continued to be involved in politics. Disillusioned and alienated from President Grant, Ashley split from the Republican Party and endorsed his opponent, Horace Greeley, in the 1872 presidential election. In the early 1870s, Republicans had split into two factions, liberals and "stalwarts." The stalwarts were led by President Ulysses S. Grant, who promised to enforce Reconstruction measures but led an administration mired in corruption. The Liberal Republicans were a group of reformers, journalists, and disaffected Republicans who joined together to combat the corrupt and patronage-ridden

[18] Horowitz, *Great Impeacher*, 159, 162–163.
[19] Charles Ashley, "Governor Ashley's Biography," 216 ("Gov. Ashley was fortunate in having a wife in complete sympathy with his general ideas, and able to assist him greatly by independent and capable action when necessary").
[20] Ibid.; Horowitz, *Great Impeacher*, 163–164; 166.

Grant administration.[21] The Liberal Republicans represented a conservative backlash against Reconstruction by the war-weary North. Liberals shied away from class politics and saw democratic majorities as a threat to property interests. They nominated Horace Greeley, and the Democratic Party followed suit.[22]

Horace Greeley was an unlikely representative for the Liberal Republicans. Greeley had deep roots in the reform movement, but also had a history of disagreeing with the positions held by the Liberals. In 1868, Greeley had put himself forward as spokesperson of the radicals and declared himself dedicated to equality of human rights. As editor of the *New York Tribune*, Greeley had supported Chase's presidential candidacy in 1868 and staunchly advocated "impartial suffrage." Moreover, the Liberals' commitment to individualism was "profoundly alien to nearly everything which Greeley had ever stood."[23] As a socialist, Greeley had argued that "industrialization had rendered individuals interdependent" and saw inequality as the product of unfair consolidation of power. Nonetheless, in 1872, Greeley ran on an anti-Reconstruction, antiregulation platform and courted Democrats with racist attacks on freed slaves. On the campaign trail, Greeley called freedmen unproductive workers who were looting the Reconstruction government. Greeley's new motto was "Let us clasp our hands across the bloody chasm" and stop the conflict over Reconstruction.[24]

Given Greeley's positions on the issues in 1872, it is difficult to understand why Ashley supported his candidacy. Even more surprising was the fact that Sumner, Schurz, Sumner, Trumbull, and Julian joined Ashley and endorsed Greeley. The radicals were split over Greeley's candidacy. Benjamin Butler despised Greeley. Gerrit Smith and Frederick Douglass agreed and wrote letters to their supporters, urging them to vote for Grant, because they believed that Grant was more likely to continue an aggressive Reconstruction policy.[25] So why did Ashley and

---

[21] Montgomery, *Beyond Equality*, 384; Heather Fox Richardson, *The Death of Reconstruction: Race, Labor and Politics in the Civil War North, 1865–1901* (Cambridge, MA: Harvard University Press, 2001), 101; Tuchinsky, *Horace Greeley*, 212.

[22] Tuchinsky, *Horace Greeley*, 212–213, 222.

[23] Horace Greeley, *Reflections of a Busy Life* (1868), 508, cited in Montgomery, *Beyond Equality*, 387; Tuchinsky, *Horace Greeley*, 122, 221, 228.

[24] Richardson, *Death of Reconstruction*, 102; Tuchinsky, *Horace Greeley*, 221, 232.

[25] Tuchinsky, *Horace Greeley*, 220 ("It has always been one of the mysteries of 1872 that so many of the most aggressive advocates of comprehensive citizenship for the freedmen – George Julian, Lyman Trumbull and Charles Sumner – ended up joining a movement

his friends choose Greeley? One reason for their decision could be the new elitist tendencies of the Republican Party. Despite their flaws, Liberal Republicans "continued to argue that the role of government was to advance the interests of average Americans, even if it meant sharing the power with reform Democrats." In addition, Ashley had long been a fan of Horace Greeley, who was active in the antislavery and labor movements in the antebellum era. Perhaps Ashley thought Greeley's campaign rhetoric was mere rhetoric and he would return to his former positions once elected. Ashley tried to convince himself that despite Greeley's campaign rhetoric, he would still support black rights. Regardless, the one issue that united the radicals who chose Greeley was their opposition to President Grant. Like Ashley, they were "'on the outs' with the partisans who inherited the Republican Party after the War," and they put their principles aside to join the movement against their enemy.[26]

In his speech supporting Greeley, Ashley accused President Grant of corruption and surrounding himself with "unworthy and objectionable men, who both openly and secretly made war upon Sumner and Chase, Greeley and Trumbull, Schurz and Julian, and nearly all the old antislavery guard." Ashley claimed to have been friends with Greeley since he was twenty years old, and called Greeley his "steadfast friend." Saying that he had never failed to denounce measures "which I regarded as dangerous to the country, or unjust to the black man," Ashley asked rhetorically, "Has [Greeley] not always been on the side of the poor man, and on the side of the oppressed, trying to lift them up to better possibilities?"[27] Thus, Ashley championed Greeley's support for workers' rights while downplaying his questionable stance on racial equality. However, Ashley's endorsement of Greeley lacked his usual enthusiasm. Indeed, Ashley's support of Greeley came with a cost. Greeley suffered a humiliating defeat and died just a few weeks later. Ashley was now alienated from the Republican Party. In 1874, Ashley sought the Democratic Party

ostensibly devoted to the opposite"), 213 (Benjamin Butler), 232 (Smith and Douglass); Horowitz, *Great Impeacher*, 165.

[26] Heather Cox Richardson, "Legacies of Lincoln Symposium, Abraham Lincoln and the Politics of Principle," *Marquette Law Review* (2010): 1383, 1397; Tuchinsky, *Horace Greeley*, 215; Horowitz, *Great Impeacher*, 165.

[27] Hon. James M. Ashley on Greeley and Grant, the Greeley Campaign of 1872, Benjamin Arnett, ed., *Duplicate Copy of the Souvenir from the Afro-American League of Tennessee to Hon. James M. Ashley of Ohio* 3 (Philadelphia: Publishing House of the AME Church, 1894) (hereafter referred to as *Souvenir*), 560, 564, 566, 575.

nomination for Congress, but he came only in second place.[28] It seemed that Ashley's political career was over.

In 1876, Ashley embarked on another speaking tour in which he invoked the "old antislavery guard" to support his evolving position on the rights of workers. In his speech, Ashley claimed a continued alliance with Sumner, Chase, and Greeley, but added that "our greatest achievement in political reform during the century just closed." Reconstruction was over. Charles Sumner had died suddenly in 1874. In 1876, Republican President Rutherford B. Hayes entered into a compromise to withdraw troops, leaving southern black workers to the Ku Klux Klan, the convict leasing system, and second-class citizenship. Ashley directed his speech at the situation in the North. He said, "We have not yet all learned that a "privileged class," created or maintained by act of government, IS A THREEFOLD WRONG, IN THAT IT ENDANGERS THE STABILITY OF THE STATE, VIOLATES THE DEMOCRATIC IDEA, AND ENCROACHES UPON THE RIGHTS OF LABOR." Ashley accused government officials of using "class" legislation to maintain monopolies, and administering the municipal, state, and national governments "of the entire Union ... specially in the interests of corporations, 'rings,' political partisans and personal favorites." Ashley argued that government corruption was "seriously endangering our country as never before." He warned of the "dangerous tendency" of public men to "favor capital and pervert the national government from the purpose of its founders, into a government representing an aristocracy of wealth."[29] Before the war, Ashley condemned the slaveholding aristocracy and accused it of corrupting democracy. Now, Ashley accused some of his former allies of creating another corrupt aristocracy. As an antidote to this accumulation of power, Ashley advocated collective action by workers and labor republicanism.

According to William Forbath, "from the Reconstruction era until the 1890s the mainstream of American trade unionists and labor reformers believed that industrial wage labor and corporate ownership of the tools of industry was incompatible with a republican Constitution." As in the

---

[28] Horowitz, *Great Impeacher*, 166 (noting that a reporter for *The Toledo Blade* who covered the speech commented that "the most uncomfortable man within the city limits last night was Jas. M. Ashley," *Toledo Blade*, June 29, 1872). Les Benedict, "James M. Ashley, Toledo Politics and the Thirteenth Amendment," *University of Toledo Law Review* 38 (2007): 815, 836; Tuchinsky, *Horace Greeley*, 235.

[29] Richardson, *Death of Reconstruction*, 141; James Ashley, Centennial Oration, Wood County Centennial Celebration, July 4, 1876, *Souvenir*, 578, 584, 587–590.

South, northern workers linked economic empowerment to their rights of citizenship. Leaders of the movement argued that being forced to sell one's labor was inconsistent with the worker's status as a citizen. These labor leaders argued that the "dependence of permanent wage-laborers [was] incompatible with republican freedom." Writing on behalf of the International Labor Union, George McNeil declared that "there is an inevitable and irresistible conflict between the wage-system of labor and the republican system of government."[30] McNeil argued that the lack of control over one's working life was inconsistent with the active participation in democratic life required of a citizen in a republic. The republican theory of labor is "a theory of not just personal but structural domination." Groups such as the Knights of Labor called for "republicanization of industry," including workers' cooperative ownership of factories, mines, and railroads. They advocated a cooperative system, which "included the use of public power to regulate employment, through maximum hours laws, nationalized transportation and communication, and redistribut[ion of] land, credit, and property to support the creation of cooperatively owned and run stores and industries." Starting with the critique of "wage slavery," labor activists developed a republican argument for the transformation of industrial relations.[31]

In his 1876 speech, Ashley invoked the language of labor republicans. Labor activists such as Ira Steward argued that wage workers also had an ownership interest in their labor. As he had before the war, Steward stressed the commonality of interest between wage earners and former slaves, who all wanted more control over their labor and their working lives. Steward urged workers to use the state, "the omnipotent power of the people when acting in their *collective capacity*, which is legislating," to achieve reforms to improve their lives. Like Steward, Ashley stressed that commonality of interest as he explored measures to empower northern industrial workers. In 1876, Ashley observed a dangerous tendency for public men to "favor capital and pervert the national government from the purpose of its founders, into a government representing an aristocracy of wealth." Like Steward, Ashley urged workers to engage

---

[30] William E. Forbath, "The Ambiguities of Free Labor and the Law in the Guilded Age," *Wisconsin Law Review* 1985: 767, 768–769; Alex Gourevitch, "Labor Republicanism and the Transformation of Work," *Political Theory* 41 (May 2013): 591, 594; Declaration of the International Labor Union, 1873, in *The Labor Movement: The Problem of Today* , ed. G. McNeill (1886), 161, cited in Forbath, "Ambiguities," 768.
[31] Gourevitch, "Labor Republicanism," 597, 592, 594; Forbath, "Ambiguities," 808.

in political action. "Organization, free discussion, then intelligent action at the ballot-box, must be our weapons of protection and defense."[32]

Ashley also used his speech to put forth a postbellum theory of free labor. Ashley claimed to have given a lot of thought to "this industrial question … and watched with interest and sympathy every movement favorable to cooperation and the organization of labor, not only in this country, but in Europe." Ashley cited Germany as a country in which labor practices were more advanced than the United States. He continued, "As a necessity of self-preservation the laborers and toilers of all countries are considering and adopting methods of industrial organization, and co-operation. This is a healthy and encouraging sign." Ashley argued that labor unions, cooperative societies, "self-assurance associations," and patrons of husbandry and grange organizations "have each in them much to commend them to the hearty approval of all thoughtful men, who see and comprehend the formidable power which day by day and year by year, increases in strength, and on every hand imperils the rights and interests of labor." Ashley suggested political reforms that he said would enable this collective action, including direct election of the president, modifying the veto power, and reforming civil service.[33]

Ashley argued that his support of workers was the logical extension of his fight against slavery. In another speech at the time, Ashley explained, "Without a knowledge that other men in other lands had conceived substantially the same idea, I had, before attaining my majority, thought out for myself and affirmed, 'that labor was equitably entitled to a fair proportion of the wealth which it created.' Naturally enough, if this proposition be admitted, it follows of necessity, that the laborer must first own himself before he can own and hold any part of the property which his toil has produced." Here, Ashley explained that ending slavery, however important, was only the first step to improving the rights of workers. In a letter written late in his life, Ashley claimed that "for many years I have favored the organization and co-operation of all kinds and conditions of working men." He explained, "In all my speeches, beginning with

---

[32] Montgomery, *Beyond Equality*, 256, 252 (citing Letter of Ira Steward, *Daily Evening Voice*, Jan. 17, 1867: "Just as the motive for 'making a man a slave, was to get his labor, or its results, for nothing,' so the 'motive for employing wage labor, is to secure *some* of its results for nothing; and, in point of fact, larger fortunes are made out of the profits of wage-labor, than out of the products of slavery'"); James Ashley, Centennial Oration, Wood County Centennial Celebration, July 4, 1876, *Souvenir*, 578, 590–591.

[33] Ashley, Centennial Oration, Wood County Centennial Celebration, July 4, 1876, *Souvenir*, 578, 589.

our early anti-slavery struggle, you will find that I uniformly made my appeals for the rights of all labor, black and white, and demanded for each an equitable share in the property which his toil created."[34] As he had during the antebellum era, and throughout the Civil War, Ashley connected the plight of workers throughout the country.

Notwithstanding his continuing interest in politics, Ashley was broke, and he needed to make a living for his family. In July 1877 Ashley purchased the Ann Arbor–Toledo railroad with his two older sons, James and Henry. According to his friend and banker, John J. Baker, Ashley "never seemed to care for the money making end of it so much as he did for the achievement itself. He wanted to put the railroad through and have it as a monument." However, the railroad was successful, and the Ashleys expanded it. By 1887 they had extended the line to Frankfort, Michigan, and then to Wisconsin. As an employer and owner of a railroad, Ashley's interests sometimes conflicted with those of his workers. Ashley favored collective organizations that would cooperate with management and opposed the strikes that plagued the railroad industry. Within these parameters, Ashley adopted measures to advance the interests of his own employees. In 1887 Ashley introduced profit sharing to his workforce. In a circular addressed to the stockholders of his company, Ashley explained that "The direct allotment to the laborer, of a share in the profits produced by his labor, is a method older than the 'wage system,' and one for which we have the approving judgment of many of the ablest thinkers, both in this country and in Europe." He also announced a plan to establish a fund for accident and life insurance for employees.[35]

At the end of his life, Ashley continued to speak about the plight of industrial workers. In an 1891 speech before the Train Dispatcher's Convention in Toledo, Ohio, Ashley spoke in favor of a national federation of railroad workers. He pointed out that "all men who have given

---

[34] Maumee Valley Pioneer Association Celebration, Address of Governor Ashley to the Men and Women who came early to this part of Ohio, Liberty Center, Ohio, Aug. 19, *Souvenir*, 685, 686; Letter from Ashley to Benjamin Arnett, December 19, 1892, *Souvenir*, 598–599.

[35] Horowitz, *Great Impeacher*, 166–167; Charles Ashley, "Governor Ashley's Biography," Appendix A, "A Few Recollections of Governor Ashley by John J. Baker, President of the Toledo Savings Bank"; Ashley, Cooperation and Profit Sharing! Copy of Circular Addressed to the Stockholders of the Toledo, Ann Arbor and North Michigan Railway Company, *Souvenir*, 661, 664. In this circular, Ashley also proposed an increase in wages for employees who have been with the company for two five-year periods. Ibid.

the subject any reflection know that organized capital, with steam and electricity, has so changed the commercial and business forces of the world that today five men, by using this new power, can do the work which thirty or forty years ago required one hundred men," Ashley urged workers to organize "for the purpose of securing the rights and bettering the condition of all workers." Ashley argued that profit sharing was preferable to other forms of labor organizations. He predicted, "I believe that co-operation and profit-sharing will ultimately prove to be the most practical, and by far the best solution of the labor problem ... The idea has, within a few years, commended itself to the considerate judgment of many of the ablest men in Europe and in this country." Ashley continued, "When laboring men shall have been properly educated, co-operation and profit-sharing will, in my opinion, as certainly take the place of the present wage system as the wage system succeeded slavery and serfdom." Ashley told the railroad workers that "Intelligent men comprehend that the first duty of all railroad men, employer and employed, is to stand together. The interest of one is beyond question the interest of all." Ashley hoped that workers could "ultimately to obtain a business co-partnership with capital ... on a basis just and equitable to both capital and labor."[36] Thus, Ashley articulated the goals of the labor republicans, including profit sharing and cooperative ownership of the means of production.

As owner of a railroad, Ashley walked a fine line on issues of workers' rights. He hoped to foster cooperation between workers and employers at least in part to avoid the wave of strikes that had affected his industry. Ashley pointed out that strikes cause the delay and suspension of business, and sometimes the destruction of railroad property, and denounced as "parasites" the labor organizers who were encouraging workers to strike. He insisted, "The accumulated property of the world belongs, not wholly to its individual owners, but in part to the citizens of the world. He who wantonly or deliberately destroys the property which legally belongs to him, because his own labor, or the labor of his ancestors had produced it, is guilty of an offense punishable by the laws of all civilized states."[37] Thus, Ashley was wary of union organizers who might encourage workers to strike and disrupt his business.

---

[36] The Federation of Railroad Workers and all Wage Workers – Gov. Ashley's Address, June 10th, 1891, to the International Train Dispatcher's Convention, on Co-operation and Strikes, *Souvenir*, 667, 669–670, 672.
[37] Ibid., 669.

Ashley argued that any organization of workers should function democratically, with each worker having a vote. He insisted that a two-thirds vote should be required to make any decision, including whether to strike. This was a tactic often adopted by opponents of organized labor. It must be noted that some members of the Knights of Labor, such as Terrence Powderly, also opposed strikes. Ashley did not believe that a worker should be compelled to join a union as a prerequisite to employment.[38] He explained, "I favor a cooperation that shall not be secret and oath-bound, or be dominated by one or more selfish leaders, but an organization that shall be open and manly, and just enough to recognize the brotherhood of the human race." Again, here Ashley's support for labor organizations was equivocal. Labor unions supported "closed shop" contracts that required all workers to be members. By contrast, Ashley insisted that a worker should not be compelled to join a union as a prerequisite to employment.[39] Thus, holding himself out as the friend of the worker, Ashley urged railroad workers to adhere to practices that were less confrontational toward management than the more radical industrial unions.

What is truly notable is the extent to which Ashley, an old time antislavery activist, was still deeply engaged in the debate over workers' rights decades after he entered the fray in his 1856 Montpelier speech. In this speech, given only a few years before the end of his life, Ashley again connected his fight against slavery with his support for worker's rights throughout the country. Ashley explained, "The opinions which I hold touching organizations of working-men and the relations of capital and labor, are the logical outgrowth of my early fight against the right of capital to legal ownership in man." The connection was due to the fact that "[a]n intelligent discussion of slave ownership involved of necessity the question of the proper relation between labor and capital." To Ashley, his life had followed a logical trajectory. "Naturally enough, he who denied the right of slave barons to the ownership of their laborers and chattels, would deny the right of capital to enslave labor by any law or custom, which the hatred of race and spirit of caste, or the avarice or selfishness of unscrupulous men might invent."[40] By the 1890s, Ashley was clearly in the minority. Most of the "old antislavery guard" had

---

[38] Ibid., 672; Horowitz, *Great Impeacher*, 168.

[39] Letter from Ashley to Benjamin Arnett, December 22, 1892, *Souvenir*, 598, 599; Horowitz, *Great Impeacher*, 168.

[40] Closing Portion of Stump Speech Delivered in the Grove near Montpelier, Williams County, Ohio, September, 1856, by James M. Ashley, *Souvenir*, 601, 667.

already died, and the Republican Party that he helped to create had become the instrument of the big capital that Ashley now decried. Yet in these speeches late in his life, Ashley suggests what a positive right to free labor might look like in the industrial economy. Workers would have control over their lives, by organizing into groups that advocated for their interests, and, when possible, would own the means of production. Workers' organizations would be the best means to ensure that they were not unduly coerced and that they were paid fair wages.

In 1890 James Ashley turned the railroad over to his son and ran for Congress one last time, this time returning to the Republican Party. In his campaign, he advocated direct election of the president and US senators, abolition of the office of vice president, and phasing out nominating conventions in favor of direct primaries. He also supported tariffs. Ashley used his campaign to promote his ideas on industrial organization and profit sharing, and "pledged to work for the laboring man in Congress."[41] In his speech accepting the nomination, Ashley said, "I sincerely believe there are formidable forces at work, which, if unchecked, must drift the nation and party into conditions of peril and disaster." Having just returned from a trip to Europe, Ashley remarked, "The crumbling castles and prisons, and monasteries, all told of a despotism and grandeur, built on the unrequited toil and suffering and sorrow of the million, to gratify the pride and selfishness, the vanity and ambition of the few." According to Ashley, the people of Europe were living under a "government of force," contrasted with the "government of consent" in the United States. As a result, unlike the downtrodden Europeans, Americans have "an elastic step and stately tread ... the natural outgrowth of personal liberty and personal independence." Ashley clearly enjoyed his return to the political realm. However, he lost by a narrow margin when the former owner of *The Toledo Commercial*, Clark Waggoner, published and circulated pamphlets against him.[42]

---

[41] Horowitz, *Great Impeacher*, 168. Ashley tried to start a campaign to amend the Constitution consistent with these proposals when he was still in Congress, in 1868. See Speech of Hon. James M. Ashley of Ohio, Delivered in the House of Representatives, May 29, 1868 – "Amend the Constitution – Abolishment of the Office of Vice-President – Neither Caucuses, Conventions, Electoral Colleges, nor the House of Representatives to Intervene between the People and their Choice of a President," *Souvenir*, 459. The Ashley family lost control of the railroad in 1893 due to a panic of 1893 and ensuing strike. Horowitz, *Great Impeacher*, 167–168.

[42] Extracts from Governor Ashley's First Address in the Congressional Campaign of 1890; *Souvenir*, 675, 676, 678–679; Horowitz, *Great Impeacher*, 168.

After his last failed campaign, Ashley retired from public life. He spent his time traveling, fishing, and swimming, activities that he truly loved. His son Charles recalled that his father "was an exceedingly good and patient fisherman, and all his life was willing to go to great fatigue and endure a broiling sun and much discomfort to entice the shy inhabitants of river and lake. So too he was fond of all manner of sports, and was probably the best swimmer ever known by the writer." Ashley also worked on writing his memoir, which was never completed. Ashley took sick on a fishing expedition in Michigan and died of a heart attack in 1896.[43] Three years before Ashley died, he was honored at the Columbia Exposition by the Afro-American League of Tennessee. Led by Benjamin Arnett, the league compiled an impressive collection of speeches that Ashley had given throughout his career. Those speeches, and the draft memoir, are the only papers of Ashley's that remain. His personal papers were destroyed while Ashley was alive. It is not known whether Ashley destroyed his papers purposefully or whether it was an accident. Ashley had always been a controversial character, and perhaps he wanted to control how historians viewed his legacy. Unfortunately, the lack of historical evidence has limited the ability of historians to learn about Ashley, and he has been largely overlooked.[44] This unfortunate omission has skewed our understanding of the Reconstruction Era.

Ashley was a leading member of Congress during the Civil War and during the crucial period of early Reconstruction. Without Ashley, the history of radical Reconstruction is truly incomplete. As Frederick Douglass noted, Ashley was "so to speak, ever far out on the skirmish line, in the most exposed position."[45] At the height of his career, Ashley convinced many of his colleagues to follow him out on the "skirmish line." Ashley's Thirteenth Amendment was a truly radical measure, intended to transform our Constitution into a document that promised freedom and equality to people within its jurisdiction. Moreover, Ashley's later life provides a guide for understanding how the Thirteenth Amendment transformed not only the lives of freed slaves, but also workers' rights throughout the country.

---

43 Charles Ashley, "Governor Ashley's Biography," 212. According to Charles, his father used to love to swim in Coney Island, New York, where he would "swim far out beyond the limits and lie floating quietly for long periods." Ibid., 213. See Horowitz, *Great Impeacher*, 168. Ashley also suffered from late-onset diabetes. Ibid.
44 See Benedict, "Toledo Politics," 815.
45 Frederick Douglass, Introduction, *Souvenir*, 3.

Ashley and his allies left an impressive legacy for the future. "To Negroes they bequeathed a promise of equality, enshrined in the organic law of the land." To the working classes, "they bestowed the idea of popular use of governmental machinery to promote the common good, and a conception of that good as something nobler than a larger gross national product."[46] In the labor movement, many workers agreed with Ashley that they were continuing the fight against slavery. Labor republicanism sought to fight "wage slavery" by asserting workers' control over the means of production. Labor union organizers argued that collective action was necessary to prevent workers from being enslaved, and claimed that laws that limited their right to organize treated them as slaves and violated the Thirteenth Amendment. James Ashley represents a link between these late nineteenth-century movements and their antebellum predecessors. As such, Ashley legitimizes the claim of the labor leaders and the workers that they were continuing a longstanding fight to improve workers' rights. In the battle to achieve a positive right to free labor, abolishing slavery was a necessary and groundbreaking accomplishment, but it was not the end of the struggle.

[46] Montgomery, *Beyond Equality*, 447.

Epilogue

Economic inequality in the United States has reached the crisis stage. Without active enforcement of a positive right to free labor, low wage and middle-class workers have suffered setbacks in the past forty years. Real wages have declined since the 1970s for all workers. The gap between wages earned by women and men remains today about the same as it was in the 1970s. On average, people of color earn significantly less than white people, and women of color remain at the bottom of real wages, income, and assets.[1] Labor union membership is down from the high point of almost 40 percent in the 1950s to below 10 percent of the workforce.[2] Low wage workers often work at jobs where they are subjected to rigid, inflexible, and unpredictable work schedules, depriving them of autonomy and control over their lives.[3] Low wages also harm our economy, because workers cannot afford to purchase consumer goods. In the "Uber" economy of independent contractors, even middle-class and upper-middle-class workers have less job security, and fear for their future. The existing paradigms of our civil rights and labor law have been inadequate to address these shared concerns. What we

---

[1] See Carmen DeNavas-Walt, Bernadette D. Proctor, and Jessica C. Smith, "Income, Poverty and Health Insurance Coverage in the United States: 2010," *United States Department of Commerce* 12 (2011), www.census.gov?prod/2011 pubs/p60-239.pdf.

[2] Sophia Z. Lee, *The Workplace Constitution: From the New Deal to the New Right* (New York: Cambridge University Press, 2014), 257.

[3] See Liz Waterson and Jennifer Swanberg, "Flexible Workplace Solutions for Low-Wage Hourly Workers: A Framework for a National Conversation," *American University Labor and Employment Law Forum* 3 (2013): 380, 384.

can learn from Ashley's life and politics is that, to address the economic inequality that threatens to cripple our democracy today, workers must organize across class and racial lines to revitalize a positive right to free labor.

The story of James Ashley reveals the importance of political action to constitutional change. Ashley developed his theories as a political organizer, influenced by other antislavery and pro-labor activists who engaged in constitutional politics. The Thirteenth Amendment came into being during the Civil War, the most violent conflict in our nation's history, and enforcing its promise has always been a struggle. Constitutional politics brought about the Thirteenth Amendment, and it has been enforced primarily not by courts but through sustained political action.[4] Coalition building has also been necessary to enforce the Thirteenth Amendment's dual promise of racial equality and workers' empowerment. In the twentieth century, advocates for racial equality and workers' rights engaged in constitutional politics to enforce the promise of the Thirteenth Amendment. Advocates for a positive right to free labor have continually faced retrenchment and resistance, but when they succeeded, they established a paradigm for equality rights in the twenty-first century.

In the late nineteenth century, the promise of Reconstruction waned and Jim Crow laws dominated the southern states. Tragically, the convict leasing system evolved into inhuman employment practices akin to chattel slavery. Racist southern Jim Crow laws not only treated blacks as second-class citizens lacking basic human rights, but also enabled the exploitation of low wage black labor.[5] If you were black and lived in the South in the early twentieth century, you could be forgiven for denying that the Thirteenth Amendment even existed. In the North, African Americans suffered from race discrimination that excluded them from many employment opportunities and consigned them to segregated neighborhoods. Northern blacks who transgressed racial boundaries also faced violence and intimidation. The extent of the racialized violence throughout the country is

---

[4] Rebecca E. Zietlow, "The Political Thirteenth Amendment," *Maryland Law Review* 71 (2011): 283.

[5] See Douglas A. Blackmon, *Slavery by Another Name: The Re-Enslavement of Black Americans from the Civil War to World War II* (New York: Anchor Books, 2009), 155, 246, 324–331, 7 ("By 1900, the South's judicial system had been wholly reconfigured to make one of its primary purposes the coercion of African Americans to comply with the social customs and labor demands of whites").

evident in the fact that the primary goal of the US civil rights movement in the early twentieth century was federal antilynching legislation.[6]

Even as Jim Crow thrived in the South, leaders of the labor movement developed a theory of constitutional rights for working people. They claimed that the Thirteenth Amendment protected their right to organize into unions and to strike, because working without those rights was tantamount to slavery.[7] On the ground, workers fought for these rights by engaging in collective action and political activism. Lacking legal training, most workers in the early twentieth century did not invoke the Thirteenth Amendment per se. However, they used images of slavery and freedom to advocate for better wages and working conditions, and the right to organize into unions.[8] As members of Congress debated the National Labor Relations Act in Washington, supporters of the act referred to those workers and invoked the Reconstruction Era's free labor ideology as they enacted measures to enable workers to advocate more effectively for a positive right to free labor.[9]

Meanwhile, black workers in the South voiced their own complaints about their working conditions and lack of autonomy. They wrote letters to the federal government asking for help to combat the "slavery," "peonage," and "involuntary servitude" that characterized their lives.[10] The black workers who had petitioned the federal government were largely excluded from the New Deal Congress's implementation of

---

[6] Risa L. Goluboff, *The Lost Promise of Civil Rights* (Cambridge, MA: Harvard University Press, 2007); Martha Biondi, *To Stand and Fight: The Struggle for Civil Rights in Postwar New York City* (Cambridge, MA: Harvard University Press 2003); see Kevin Boyle, *Arc of Justice: A Saga of Race, Civil Rights and Murder in the Jazz Age* (New York: H. Holt, 2004) (describing racial violence confronted by blacks who attempted to move into white neighborhoods in Detroit during the early nineteenth century); Biondi, *To Stand and to Fight*, 60–66 (describing northern violence against returning African American GIs in the North), 42 (describing Congressman Adam Clayton Powell's legislative agenda in 1946).

[7] James Gray Pope, "Labor's Constitution of Freedom," *Yale Law Journal* 106 (1997): 941.

[8] James Gray Pope and Rebecca E. Zietlow, "The Auto-Lite Strike and the Fight against 'Wage Slavery,'" *University of Toledo Review* 38 (2007): 839, reprinted in Kenneth M. Casebeer, ed., *American Labor Struggles and Law Histories* (Durham, NC: Carolina Academic Press, 2011). Many of those workers also demanded equal pay for equal work; an end to job discrimination based on age, race, or sex; and that job decisions be made based on seniority rather than favoritism. Lizabeth Cohen, *Making a New Deal: Industrial Workers in Chicago, 1919–1939* (New York: Cambridge University Press, 1990), 252, 315.

[9] Hearing before the Senate Committee on Education and Labor, 73rd Cong., 2nd Sess., on S. 2926 (April 2, 1935); see Rebecca E. Zietlow, *Enforcing Equality: Congress, the Constitution, and the Protection of Individual Rights* (New York: NYU Press, 2006), 75–77.

[10] Goluboff, *Lost Promise*, 51, 60, 69, 51–52, 56, 106 ("Although race runs through these complaints, the central goal of these letters was simply work").

Ashley's legacy due to compromises with southern segregationists.[11] Outside Congress, however, both political actors and courts made significant contributions to achieving racial equality for workers in the New Deal era. Unions were far from immune from race discrimination, but black labor leaders such as A. Philip Randolph played a crucial role in the early civil rights movement.[12] Responding to this movement, lawyers in the Civil Rights Section of the Department of Justice under Presidents Franklin Roosevelt and Harry Truman sought to fill in the gaps left by the New Deal measures protecting workers, and establish a positive right to free labor as a matter of federal civil rights law.[13]

In 1938, Roosevelt's solicitor general Robert Jackson said that "the liberal movement of the present is concerning itself more with economic rights and privileges than with political rights and privileges." In the 1944 case of *Pollock v. Williams*, interpreting the Anti-Peonage Act, then Justice Robert Jackson articulated a test for determining whether an employment practice violated the prohibition against involuntary servitude. According to Justice Jackson, "[W]hen the master can compel and the laborer cannot escape the obligation to go on, there is no power below to redress and no incentive above to relieve a harsh overlordship or unwholesome conditions of work."[14] Jackson's *Pollock* decision establishes a broad legal standard for the positive right to free labor, but the standard requires activists and lawyers to enforce it.

After the early 1950s, the Civil Rights Section stopped focusing on the rights of workers and instead shifted its focus to enforcing the Equal Protection clause against state-mandated racial discrimination. However, the union movement continued to strengthen and advocate for economic rights for workers. During the 1950s, 40 percent of the US labor force belonged to unions, including one and half million black workers. While some unions discriminated against black workers, others provided a vehicle for economic empowerment and against racial discrimination. A. Philip Randolph and his allies worked within the labor movement to advance the cause of civil rights. They formed coalitions with their union brothers and sisters and helped to bring about the Second Reconstruction in the 1960s.[15]

[11] Zietlow, *Enforcing Equality*, 94–95.
[12] Goluboff, *Lost Promise*, 97; Biondi, *To Stand and Fight*, 4, 17, 22.
[13] Lee, *Workplace Constitution*, 21; Goluboff, *Lost Promise*, 4, 6.
[14] Goluboff, *Lost Promise*, 18, 27; *Pollock v. Williams*, 322 U.S. 4 (1944).
[15] Goluboff, *Lost Promise*, 258, 219; William P. Jones, *The March on Washington: Jobs, Freedom, and the Forgotten History of Civil Rights* (New York: W. W. Norton, 2013),

Almost a century after the Thirteenth Amendment became law, a group of labor leaders and civil rights advocates met to organize the March for Jobs and Freedom in Washington. Led by noted labor leader and civil rights activist A. Philip Randolph, the march originated in a proposal from the Negro American Labor Council (NALC), an organization of black trade unionists. The organizers of the march sought to "ensure that Americans of all races had access to quality education, affordable housing, and jobs that paid a living wage."[16] At the March, Reverend Martin Luther King, Jr., charged that "the Negro lives on a lonely island of poverty in the midst of a vast ocean of material prosperity." Here, this iconic civil rights leader also drew connections between racial and economic subordination. In 1968, King initiated his Poor People's Campaign, a coalition effort with the National Welfare Rights Organization and the American Friends Service Committee. The Poor People's Campaign demanded economic and human rights for people regardless of their race.[17]

These are just some examples of political movements following the path of James Ashley and his allies to enforce racial and economic rights. Since the mid-1960s, however, advocates for racial equality and worker's rights rarely invoke the Thirteenth Amendment. Like Ashley, the amendment itself has been largely forgotten. At the same time, workers of all races have confronted declines in their standard of living and working conditions. These losses are due in part to a concerted campaign of conservative constitutional advocacy, the "right to work" movement.[18] These conservative activists also engaged in constitutional politics and invoked the image of slavery to oppose labor unions. Another tactic of the conservative "right to work" movement exploited racial tensions to split alliances between labor and the civil rights movement.[19]

---

124. For an excellent analysis of the complex relationship between organized labor and the civil rights movement, see Lee, *Workplace Constitution*.

[16] Jones, *March on Washington*, ix, xvii.

[17] David J. Garrow, *Bearing the Cross: Martin Luther King, Jr. and the Southern Christian Leadership Conference* (New York: Vintage Books 1988). King planned the campaign in conjunction with his Southern Christian Leadership Council, the National Welfare Rights Organization, and the American Friends Service Committee. Gordon Keith Mantler, *Power to the Poor: Black-Brown Coalition and the Fight for Economic Justice* (Chapel Hill: University of North Carolina Press, 2013), 102–106.

[18] Lee, *Workplace Constitution*, 59, 71, 73.

[19] Ibid., 177. For example, from 1965 to 1971, leading Senators Everett Dirksen and Pete Dominici repeatedly introduced legislation that they called a "laboring man's bill of rights," which included both right to work and antidiscrimination measures. Ibid., 241.

Disputes over racially discriminatory unions and affirmative action measures exacerbated tensions in the 1970s. At the same time, resisting unions has become a mainstream business position. The election of Ronald Reagan as president in 1980 was a victory for the New Right, a coalition of Goldwater Republicans and next-generation conservatives who strongly supported the right to work. When President Reagan fired the striking air traffic control workers, it was an important symbolic milestone in the downturn of workers' rights. Since then, the power of unions has declined, as have real wages for middle-class and lower income workers.

To combat this decline, workers must use the precedent that James Ashley and his Reconstruction allies established and return to the integrated vision of economic rights and racial justice that animated their mid-twentieth-century predecessors. Their positive right to free labor includes the right to work free of undue coercion, for a living wage, and without discrimination based on immutable characteristics. An effective movement for workers' rights must confront racism head on and acknowledge racism's destructive impact on communities of color. It is also essential to acknowledge the very real class-based concerns of the white working class, concerns that they share with workers of all races. History reveals that workers' movements are most effective when they confront both racial and economic subordination. During the middle of the twentieth century, labor leaders and civil rights leaders again formed coalitions to further workers' rights and racial equality.[20] These historical examples suggest some organizing principles for a twenty-first-century movement for workers' rights. The following considers what concrete measures advocates might want to pursue.

What would a positive right to free labor look like in the twenty-first century? First, there would be no slavery or involuntary servitude. While the United States ended slavery 150 years ago, there are still vestiges of slavery in this country, including the mistreatment of migrant farm workers and sweat shops full of vulnerable illegal immigrants. With the Thirteenth Amendment–based 2000 Anti-Trafficking Act, members of Congress sought to bring the global fight against slavery and peonage into the twenty-first century economy. That act outlaws the use of psychological as well as physical coercion to confine workers in workplaces

[20] Biondi, *To Stand and Fight*.

where they are poorly treated and underpaid.[21] However, legislation alone is ineffective without aggressive enforcement. Currently, our economy depends on the labor of over 11 million undocumented immigrants. Although these workers are not slaves, they work for low wages under difficult conditions. Undocumented workers are vulnerable to being deported if they assert their rights in any way.[22] Moreover, in our global economy, slavery all over the world affects workers in the United States.[23] Products manufactured by slave labor can be sold more cheaply than those made by relatively well-paid American workers, threatening the jobs of workers in the United States and depressing their wages. The first step to establish a positive right to free labor is to confront these vestiges of slavery.

In addition, a positive right to free labor should guarantee the right to work free of undue coercion that is short of outright slavery and involuntary servitude. The 2000 Anti-Trafficking Act takes a step in this direction by outlawing psychological coercion, but that act does not define the outer limits of undue coercion. For example, on-demand scheduling of low wage workers requires them to be on call at all hours in case they might be required to come in to work. Once they arrive at work, they are in peril of being sent home without warning if their employer deems it unnecessary for them to be there.[24] Arguably, these scheduling practices are unduly coercive and tantamount to involuntary servitude. In the 1930s, Auto-Lite workers in Toledo, Ohio, fighting for the right to form unions argued that similar employer practices made them feel like slaves.[25] The recently adopted Seattle Secure Scheduling Ordinance is an important measure enforcing that right.[26] In another context, it might be

[21] Trafficking Victims Protection Act of 2000, Pub. L. No. 106–386, §102(b)(22), 114, Stat. 1464, 1468. See Rebecca E. Zietlow, "Free at Last! Anti-Subordination and the Thirteenth Amendment," *Boston University Law Review* 90 (2010): 255, 306.
[22] See Maria Ontiveros, "Immigrant Workers' Rights in a Post-Hoffman World: Organizing around the 13th Amendment," *Georgetown Immigration Law Journal* 18 (2004): 651.
[23] Marley Weiss, "Human Trafficking and Forced Labor: A Primer," *ABA Journal on Labor and Employment Law* 31 (2015): 1.
[24] Waterson and Swanberg, "Flexible Workplace Solutions."
[25] Pope and Zietlow, "Auto-Lite Workers." The Autolite workers' proposed remedy was the right to organize into a union and bargain collectively, to enhance their power to combat this treatment. Ibid.
[26] The groundbreaking Seattle Secure Scheduling Ordinance provides, inter alia, that employees have a right to request to schedule preferences, and requires employers to post employees' work schedules fourteen days in advance. SMC 14.22 (effective July 1, 2017).

unduly coercive for employers of white-collar workers to expect those workers to be on call at all times, answering email and phone messages, with work taking over their personal lives. Seeking control over one's working life was a central concern of the nineteenth-century labor movement, and measures empowering workers to assert that control promote a key component of the positive right to free labor.

Second, a positive right to free labor requires that workers be paid a fair wage for their work. In the nineteenth century, many workers argued that they were being subjected to wage slavery when they did not own the means of production. In the twenty-first century, workers are accustomed to working for wages and the concept of wage slavery would likely seem foreign to them. Nonetheless, real wages have declined in this country since the mid-1970s, making it harder for low-wage workers to afford the basic necessities of life. The gap between rich and poor in the United States has been increasing dramatically and the federal minimum wage lags well behind inflation.[27] Moreover, the failure to pay for the basic necessities in life contributed to feelings of despair in the white working class, leading to drug abuse and even suicide.[28] Clearly, there is a crying need to enforce this second prong of a positive right to free labor. In the early twenty-first century, the movement for an increase in the minimum wage has gained momentum, with states and localities filling the gap left by congressional inaction. The right to a living wage is a crucial component of the positive right to free labor.

Third, a positive right to free labor would include a robust right to be free of discrimination based on immutable characteristics. As early as the *Slaughter House Cases*, the Supreme Court recognized Congress's authority to combat the badges and incidents of slavery with measures enforcing the Thirteenth Amendment.[29] Racial subordination was a central component of the system of chattel slavery in the South, and race discrimination has facilitated the exploitation of black workers throughout our

---

[27] Josh Bivens, Elise Gould and Lawrence Mishel, "Wage Stagnation in Nine Charts," *Economic Policy Institute* (January 6, 2015), www.epi.org/publication/charting-wage-stagnation/.

[28] See Jessica Body, "The Forces Driving Middle-Aged White People's 'Deaths of Despair,'" NPR, March 23, 2017, www.npr.org/sections/health-shots/2017/03/23/521083335/the-forces-driving-middle-aged-white-peoples-deaths-of-despair; Anne Case and Sir Angus Deaton, "Mortality and Morbidity in the 21st Century," www.brookings.edu/bpea-articles/mortality-and-morbidity-in-the-21st-century/.

[29] *Slaughter House Cases*, 83 U.S. 36 (1873).

nation's history. In the Jim Crow South, a racially discriminatory criminal justice system endangered the lives of black men and women and fed the convict leasing system that was one step short of out-and-out chattel slavery.[30] Race discrimination in our criminal justice system continues to this day. Despite civil rights legislation, including the 1866 Civil Rights Act, the 1964 Civil Rights Act, and federal executive measures combatting discrimination, the badges and incidents of slavery still plague our society and hamper the economic opportunities of black workers. It is crucial to recognize that race discrimination against people of color harms all low wage white workers. For centuries, employers have used race discrimination to divide workers from each other and impede the development of class solidarity among workers.[31] Therefore, a positive right to free labor for all workers requires combatting discrimination based on race and other immutable characteristics.

Finally, a positive right to fair labor cannot be achieved without an effective safety net for those workers who fall through the cracks and are unable to find gainful employment. Workers need a safety net so they are not forced to work in jobs that are unduly coercive for subpar wages.[32] During the New Deal, Congress established a safety net with the Social Security Act, Unemployment Insurance, and the Aid for Families with Dependent Children (AFDC) program.[33] In 1996, Congress ended the entitlement to welfare benefits for working-age people raising children and replacing the AFDC program with a short-term Temporary Assistance for Needy Families (TANF) program.[34] The lack of a guaranteed income makes these low wage workers even more vulnerable to exploitation and forces them to work for subpar wages because they have no

---

[30] Douglas A. Blackmon, *Slavery by Another Name: The Re-Enslavement of Black Americans from the Civil War to World War II* (New York: Anchor Books, 2009); Michelle Alexander, *The New Jim Crow: Mass Incarceration in the Age of Colorblindness* (New York: New Press, 2010).

[31] See James Gray Pope, "Why Is There No Socialism in the United States? Law and the Racial Divide in the American Working Class, 1676–1974," *Texas Law Review* 94 (2016): 1555.

[32] *See* Sheila R. Zedlewski, "Work Activity and Obstacles to Work among TANF Recipients," The Urban Institute (1999), www.urban.org/url.cfm?ID=309091.

[33] Social Security Act of 1935, 42 U.S.C. §§401–406. Under AFDC, all persons who were eligible were entitled to benefits.

[34] Personal Responsibility and Work Opportunity Reconciliation Act of 1996, Pub. L. No. 104–193, 110 Stat. 2105 (1996) (codified at 42 U.S.C. §§601–619 (2006)). Under TANF, there is no entitlement to benefits, and recipients are subject to a five-year lifetime limit. See ibid., §403.

other option for survival.[35] An effective safety net is a crucial prerequisite to an effective positive right to free labor.

These measures are only preliminary suggestions of how to enforce a positive right to free labor in the twenty-first century. James Ashley's story illustrates the importance of political mobilization to achieving these and other reforms. Today, the positive right to free labor is not being enforced, and workers' complaints now are remarkably similar to those of workers from the nineteenth century. However, Ashley's legacy provides a window to consider measures to revive his vision and improve the lives of workers of all races.[36] Supporters of a positive right to free labor need to articulate a compelling vision and engage in hardscrabble politics to enforce that vision. James Ashley did just that, at a crucial moment in this country's constitutional development. Ashley's example of political engagement and struggle to achieve justice and equality may be his most important legacy.

[35] Avis Jones-Deweever, Janice Peterson, and Xue Song, *Before and after Welfare Reform: The Work and Well-Being of Low-Income Single Parent Families* (Washington, DC: Institute for Women's Policy Research, 2003), 33–34 (describing the impact of TANF reforms on single-mother low-income households).
[36] For a more in-depth discussion of how a positive right to free labor might be enforced in the twenty-first century, see Rebecca E. Zietlow, "A Positive Right to Free Labor," *Seattle University Law Review* 39 (2016): 859.

Bibliography

ARCHIVES

Abraham Lincoln Papers at the Library of Congress
Charles Sumner Papers, Houghton Library, Harvard University
John M. Morgan papers relating to James M. Ashley, University of Toledo libraries, Ward M. Canaday Center Manuscript Collection ("Morgan Papers")
Proceedings of the Anti-Slavery Convention, held at Putnam, on the twenty-first, twenty-second, and twenty-third of April, 1835 (Beaumont and Wallace, Printers)
Salmon P. Chase, An Argument for the Defendant, Submitted to the Supreme Court of the United States, as the December Term, 1846: In the Case of Wharton Jones vs. John Vanzandt (1847)
Salmon P. Chase Papers, Manuscript Division, Library of Congress, Washington, DC

ARTICLES

Aynes, Richard L. "On Misreading John Bingham and the Fourteenth Amendment," *Yale Law Journal* 103 (1993): 57.
Barnett, Randy E. "Whence Comes Section One? The Abolitionist Origins of the Fourteenth Amendment," *Journal of Legal Analysis* 3 (2011): 165.
Benedict, Les. "James M. Ashley, Toledo Politics and the Thirteenth Amendment," *University of Toledo Law Review* 38 (2007): 815.
Birney, James G. "Can Congress, under the Constitution, Abolish Slavery in the States?," *The Albany Patriot*, May 12, 19, 20, 22, 1847.
The Philanthropist, January 13, 1837.
Bivens, Josh, Elise Gould, and Lawrence Mishel. "Wage Stagnation in Nine Charts," *Economic Policy Institute* (January 6, 2015), www.epi.org/publica tion/charting-wage-stagnation/.

Body, Jessica. "The Forces Driving Middle-Aged White People's 'Deaths of Despair,'" NPR, March 23, 2017, www.npr.org/sections/health-shots/2017/03/23/521083335/the-forces-driving-middle-aged-white-peoples-deaths-of-despair.

Case, Anne, and Sir Angus Deaton. "Mortality and Morbidity in the 21st Century," www.brookings.edu/bpea-articles/mortality-and-morbidity-in-the-21st-century/.

Curtis, Michael Kent. "John A. Bingham and the Story of American Liberty: The Lost Cause Meets the 'Lost Clause,'" *Akron Law Review* 36 (2003): 617.

DeNavas-Walt, Carmen, Bernadette D. Proctor, and Jessica C. Smith. "Income, Poverty and Health Insurance Coverage in the United States: 2010," *United States Department of Commerce* 12 (2011), www.census.gov?prod/2011 pubs/p60-239.pdf.

Douglass, Frederick. "A Change of Opinion Announced," *The North Star*, May 15, 1851, reprinted in *The Liberator*, May 23, 1851.

"Comments on Gerrit Smith's Address," *The North Star*, March 30, 1849.

Forbath, William E. "The Ambiguities of Free Labor and the Law in the Gilded Age," *Wisconsin Law Review* 1985: 767.

Fox, James W. Jr. "Publics, Meanings and the Privileges of Citizenship," *Constitutional Commentary* 30 (2015): 567.

Garrison, William Lloyd. "The Constitution: A Covenant with Death and an Agreement with Hell," *Liberator* 12 (1842).

Gourevitch, Alex. "Labor Republicanism and the Transformation of Work," *Political Theory* 41 (May 2013): 591.

Graber, Mark. "The Second Freedman's Bureau Bill's Constitution," *Texas Law Review* 94 (2016): 1361.

"Subtraction by Addition? The Thirteenth and Fourteenth Amendments," *Columbia Law Review* 112 (2012): 1501.

Klarman, Michael J. "Rethinking the Civil Rights and Civil Liberties Revolutions," *Virginia Law Review* 82 (1996): 1.

Lofton, William H. "Appeal of the Abolitionists to the Northern Working Classes," *The Journal of Negro History* 33, no. 3 (July 1948): 249.

McLain, Charles J. "The Chinese Struggle for Civil Rights in Nineteenth Century America: The First Phase, 1850–1870," *California Law Review* 72 (1984): 529.

McPherson, James M. "America's Greatest Movement," *New York Review of Books*, October 27, 2016.

Morgan, Denise C., and Rebecca E. Zietlow. "The New Parity Debate: Congress and Rights of Belonging," *Cincinnati Law Review* 73 (2005): 1347.

Nice, Julie A. "Whither the Canaries? On the Exclusion of Poor People from Equal Constitutional Protection," *Drake Law Review* 60 (2012): 1023.

Ontiveros, Maria. "Immigrant Workers' Rights in a Post-Hoffman World: Organizing around the 13th Amendment," *Georgetown Immigration Law Journal* 18 (2004): 651.

"Is Modern Day Slavery a Private Act or a Public System of Oppression?" *Seattle University Law Review* 39 (2016): 665.

Pinckney, Darryll. "Kerry James Marshall: Mastry," *New York Review of Books*, January 2, 2017.

Pope, James Gray. "Contract, Race, and Freedom of Labor in the Constitutional Law of 'Involuntary Servitude,'" *Yale Law Journal* 119 (2010): 1474.

"Labor's Constitution of Freedom," *Yale Law Journal* 106 (1997): 941.

"Why Is There No Socialism in the United States? Law and the Racial Divide in the American Working Class, 1676–1974," *Texas Law Review* 94 (2016): 1555.

Pope, James Gray, and Rebecca E. Zietlow. "The Auto-Lite Strike and the Fight against 'Wage Slavery,'" *University of Toledo Review* 38 (2007): 839. Reprinted in Kenneth M. Casebeer, ed., *American Labor Struggles and Law Histories* (Durham, NC: Carolina Academic Press, 2011).

Post, Robert C., and Reva B. Siegel. "Legislative Constitutionalism and Section Five Power: Policentric Interpretations of the Family and Medical Leave Act," *Yale Law Journal* 112 (2003): 1943.

Richardson, Heather Cox. "Legacies of Lincoln Symposium, Abraham Lincoln and the Politics of Principle," *Marquette Law Review* (2010): 1383.

Soifer, Aviam. "Federal Protection, Paternalism, and the Virtually Forgotten Prohibition of Voluntary Peonage," *Columbia Law Review* 112 (2012): 1607.

tenBroek, Jacobus. "Thirteenth Amendment to the Constitution of the United States: Consummation to Abolition and Key to the Fourteenth Amendment," *California Law Review* 39 (1951): 171.

VanderVelde, Lea S. "Henry Wilson, Cobbler of the Frayed Constitution, Strategist of the Thirteenth Amendment," *Georgetown Journal of Law and Politics* 15 (2017): 173.

"The Labor Vision of the Thirteenth Amendment," *University of Pennsylvania Law Review* 138 (1989): 437.

"The Thirteenth Amendment of Our Aspirations," *University of Toledo Law Review* 38(2007): 855.

Wang, Xi. "The Making of Federal Enforcement Laws, 1870–1872," *Chicago Kent Law Review* 70 (1995): 1013.

Waterson, Liz, and Jennifer Swanberg. "Flexible Workplace Solutions for Low-Wage Hourly Workers: A Framework for a National Conversation," *American University Labor and Employment Law Forum* 3 (2013): 380.

Weiss, Marley. "Human Trafficking and Forced Labor: A Primer," *ABA Journal on Labor and Employment Law* 31 (2015): 1.

Weld, Theodore Dwight. "The Power of Congress over the District of Columbia," *The Antislavery Examiner No. 6*. Reprinted from the *New York Evening Post*, with additions by the author, published by the *American Antislavery Society* (New York, 1838).

Zedlewski, Sheila R. "Work Activity and Obstacles to Work among TANF Recipients," *The Urban Institute* (1999), www.urban.org/url.cfm?ID=309091.

Zietlow, Rebecca E. "Free at Last! Anti-Subordination and the Thirteenth Amendment," *Boston University Law Review* 90 (2010): 255.

"The Political Thirteenth Amendment," *Maryland Law Review* 71 (2011): 283.

"A Positive Right to Free Labor," *Seattle University Law Review* 39 (2016): 859.

"The Rights of Citizenship: Two Framers, Two Amendments," *University of Pennsylvania Journal of Constitutional Law* 11 (2009): 1269.

BOOKS

Aarim-Heriot, Najia. *Chinese Immigrants, African Americans, and Racial Anxiety in the United States* (Urbana: University of Illinois Press, 2003).

Alexander, Michelle. *The New Jim Crow: Mass Incarceration in the Age of Colorblindness* (New York: New Press, 2010).

Arnett, Benjamin, ed. *Duplicate Copy of the Souvenir from the Afro-American League of Tennessee to Hon. James M. Ashley of Ohio* (Philadelphia: Publishing House of the AME Church, 1894).

Ashley, Charles S. "Governor Ashley's Biography and Messages," in *Contributions to the Historical Society of Montana* (Helena, MT: Rocky Mountain Publishing, 1907).

Baer, Judith A. *Equality under the Constitution: Reclaiming the Fourteenth Amendment* (Ithaca: Cornell University Press, 1983).

Baruch, Mildred C., and Ellen J. Beckman. *Civil War Union Monuments* (Washington, DC: Daughters of Union Veterans of the Civil War, 1978).

Beatty, Paul. *The Sell Out* (New York: Farrar, Strauss and Giroux, 2015).

Benedict, Michael Les. *A Compromise of Principle* (New York: W. W. Norton, 1974).

Biondi, Martha. *To Stand and Fight: The Struggle for Civil Rights in Postwar New York City* (Cambridge: Harvard University Press, 2003)

Blackmon, Douglas A. *Slavery by Another Name: The Re-Enslavement of Black Americans from the Civil War to World War II* (New York: Anchor Books, 2009).

Bowers, Claude G. *The Tragic Era: The Revolution after Lincoln* (1929).

Boyle, Kevin. *Arc of Justice: A Saga of Race, Civil Rights and Murder in the Jazz Age* (New York: H. Holt, 2004).

Brandwein, Pamela. *Reconstructing Reconstruction: The Supreme Court and the Production of Historical Truth* (Durham: Duke University Press, 1999).

Coates, Ta-Nehisi. *Between the World and Me* (New York: Spiegel & Grau, 2015).

Cohen, Lizabeth. *Making a New Deal: Industrial Workers in Chicago, 1919–1939* (New York: Cambridge University Press, 1990).

Curtis, Michael Kent. *No State Shall Abridge: The Fourteenth Amendment and the Bill of Rights* (Durham: Duke University Press, 1986).

Deyrup, Marta Mestrovic, and Maura Grace Harrington. *The Irish-American Experience in New Jersey and Metropolitan New York: Cultural Identity, Hybridity, and Commemoration* (Lanham: Lexington Books, 2014).

Douglass, Frederick. *Two Speeches* (New York, 1857).

Efford, Alison Clark. *German Immigrants, Race, and Citizenship in the Civil War Era* (New York: Cambridge University Press, 2013).

Evans, Sara M. *Born for Liberty: A History of Women in American* (New York: Free Press, 1989).

Finkelman, Paul. *Slavery and the Founders: Race and Liberty in the Age of Jefferson* (Armonk, NY: M. E. Sharp, 1996).

Finkelman, Paul, Gary W. Gallagher, and Margaret E. Wagner. *The Library of Congress Civil War Desk Reference* (New York: Simon and Schuster, 2002).

Fladeland, Betty. *James Gillespie Birney, Slaveholder to Abolitionist* (Ithaca: Cornell University Press, 1955).

Foner, Eric. *Free Soil, Free Labor, Free Men: The Ideology of the Republican Party before the Civil War* (New York: Oxford University Press, 1995).

Politics and Ideology in the Age of the Civil War (New York: Oxford University Press, 1980).

Reconstruction: American's Unfinished Revolution, 1863–1877 (New York: Harper Collins, 1988).

Foner, Philip Sheldon. *History of the Labor Movement of the United States* (New York: International Publishers, 1947).

Foner, Philip S., and Herbert Shapiro, eds. *Northern Labor and Antislavery: A Documentary History* (Westport, CT: Greenwood Press, 1994).

Foner, Philip S., and George E. Walker, eds. *Proceedings of the Black State Conventions, 1840–1865* (Philadelphia: Temple University Press, 1980).

Garrow, David J. *Bearing the Cross: Martin Luther King, Jr. and the Southern Christian Leadership Conference* (New York: Vintage Books, 1988).

George, Harold A. *Civil War Monuments of Ohio* (Mansfield, OH: Book Masters, 2006).

Goluboff, Risa L. *The Lost Promise of Civil Rights* (Cambridge, MA: Harvard University Press, 2007).

Goodell, William. *Views of American Constitutional Law, in Its Bearing upon American Slavery* (Utica, NY: Jackson & Chaplain, 1844).

Grubb, Farley. *German Immigration and Servitude in America, 1709–1920* (New York: Routledge, 2013).

Horowitz, Robert F. *The Great Impeacher: A Political Biography of James M. Ashley* (New York: Brooklyn College Press, 1979).

Jones, William P. *The March on Washington: Jobs, Freedom, and the Forgotten History of Civil Rights* (New York: W. W. Norton, 2013).

Jones-Deweever, Avis, Janice Peterson, and Xue Song, *Before and after Welfare Reform: The Work and Well-Being of Low-Income Single Parent Families* (Washington, DC: Institute for Women's Policy Research, 2003).

Kersch, Ken I. *Constructing Civil Liberties: Discontinuities in the Development of American Constitutional Law* (New York: Cambridge University Press, 2004).

Kramer, Larry D. *The People Themselves: Popular Constitutionalism and Judicial Review* (New York: Oxford University Press, 2004).

Lee, Sophia Z. *The Workplace Constitution: From the New Deal to the New Right* (New York: Cambridge University Press, 2014).

LeMay, Michael C. *Transforming America: Perspectives on U.S. Immigration* (Santa Barbara: Praeger, 2013).

Magliocca, Gerard. *American Founding Son: John Bingham and the Invention of the Fourteenth Amendment* (New York: NYU Press, 2013).

Mantler, Gordon Keith. *Power to the Poor: Black-Brown Coalition and the Fight for Economic Justice* (Chapel Hill: University of North Carolina Press, 2013).

Matthews, Jean W. *Women's Struggle for Equality: The First Phase, 1828–1876* (Chicago: Ivan V. Dee, 1997).

Montgomery, David. *Beyond Equality: Labor and the Radical Republicans 1862–1872* (Urbana and Chicago: University of Illinois Press, 1967).

    Citizen Worker: The Experience of Workers in the United States with Democracy and the Free Market during the Nineteenth Century (New York: Cambridge University Press, 1993).

Nieman, Donald G. *To Set the Law in Motion: The Freedman's Bureau and the Legal Rights of Blacks* (Millwood, NY: KTO Press, 1979).

Oakes, James. *Freedom National: The Destruction of Slavery in the United States, 1861–1865* (New York: W. W. Norton, 2013).

Paine, Byron. *Unconstitutionality of the Fugitive Slave Act: Argument of Byron Paine, Esq. and Opinion of Hon. A. D. Smith, Associate Justice of the Supreme Court of the State of Wisconsin* (Milwaukee: Free Democrat Office, 1854).

Phan, Hoang Gia. *Bonds of Citizenship: Law and the Labors of Emancipation* (New York: NYU Press, 2013).

Phillips, Wendell. *The Constitution: A Proslavery Compact, Or Selections from the Madison Papers* (New York: American Anti-Slavery Society, 1844).

    A Review of Lysander Spooner's Essay on the Unconstitutionality of Slavery (Boston: Andrew Prentiss, 1847).

Richards, Leonard L. *Who Freed the Slaves? The Fight over the Thirteenth Amendment* (Chicago: University of Chicago Press, 2015).

Richardson, Heather Fox. *The Death of Reconstruction: Race, Labor and Politics in the Civil War North, 1865–1901* (Cambridge, MA: Harvard University Press, 2001).

Richardson, James D., ed. *Messages and Papers of the Presidents of the United States, 1789–1897* (Washington, DC: Government Printing Office, 1896–99).

Rutherglen, George. *Civil Rights in the Shadow of Slavery: The Constitution, Common Law, and the Civil Rights Act of 1866* (New York: Oxford University Press, 2013).

Schultz, David A., ed. *Encyclopedia of the Supreme Court* (New York: Facts on File, 2005).

Sewell, Richard H. *Ballots for Freedom: Antislavery Politics in the United States 1837–1860* (New York: Oxford University Press, 1976).

Smith, Rogers. *Civic Ideals: Conflicting Visions of Citizenship in U.S. History* (New Haven: Yale University Press, 1997).

Sinha, Manisha. *The Slave's Cause: A History of Abolition* (New Haven: Yale University Press, 2016).

Spooner, Lysander. *The Unconstitutionality of Slavery* (Boston: B. Marsh, 1845).

Stanley, Amy Dru. *From Bondage to Contract: Wage Labor, Marriage, and the Market in the Age of Slave Emancipation* (New York: Cambridge University Press, 1998).

Stein, Gertrude. *Three Lives* (Boston: Bedford St. Martin's, 2000).

Steinfeld, Robert J. *The Invention of Free Labor: The Employment Relation in English and American Law and Culture, 1350–1870* (Chapel Hill: University of North Carolina Press, 1991).

Thatcher, Joseph. *The Library of Original Sources* (New York and Chicago: University Research Extension, 1907).

Tiffany, Joel. *A Treatise on the Unconstitutionality of Slavery, together with the Powers and Duties of the Federal Government in Relation to That Subject* (Cleveland: D. J. Calyerk, 1849).

Tomlins, Christopher L. *Law, Labor, and Ideology in the Early American Republic* (New York: Cambridge University Press, 1993).

Trefousse, Hans L. *The Radical Republicans: Lincoln's Vanguard for Racial Justice* (New York: Alfred A. Knopf, 1968).

Tsesis, Alexander. ed. *Promises of Liberty: The History and Contemporary Relevance of the Thirteenth Amendment* (New York: Columbia University Press, 2010).

The Thirteenth Amendment and American Freedom: A Legal History (New York: NYU Press, 2004).

Tuchinsky, Adam. *Horace Greeley's New York Tribune: Civil War Era Socialism and the Crisis of Free Labor* (Ithaca: Cornell University Press, 2009).

Vorenberg, Michael. *Final Freedom: The Civil War, the Abolition of Slavery, and the Thirteenth Amendment* (New York: Cambridge University Press, 2001).

Whitehead, Colson. *The Underground Railroad* (New York: Doubleday, 2016).

Wiecek, William M. *The Sources of Antislavery Constitutionalism in America, 1760–1848* (Ithaca: Cornell University Press, 1977).

Wilentz, Sean. *Chants Democratic: New York City and the Rise of the American Working Class, 1788–1850* (New York: Oxford University Press, 1984).

Zietlow, Rebecca E. *Enforcing Equality: Congress, the Constitution, and the Protection of Individual Rights* (New York: NYU Press, 2006).

STATUTES

A Bill to Designate the United States Courthouse located at 1716 Spielbusch Avenue in Toledo, Ohio as the "James M. Ashley and Thomas W. L. Ashley United States Courthouse"; H.R. 3712, P.L. 110–284 (July 23, 2008)

Anti-Peonage Act, March 2, 1867, ch. 187, 14 Stat. 546, now codified as amended at 18 U.S.C. §1581 et seq. and 42 U.S.C. §1994

Civil Rights Act of 1866, ch. 31, 14 Stat. 27 (codified at 42 U.S.C. §§1981–1983 (2000)

Civil Rights Act of 1870, ch. 114, §16, 16 Stat. 140, 144 (1869–1871)

The Freedmen's Bureau Act, 14 Stat. 174, 176–177 (1866)

Fugitive Slave Act of 1793, ch. 7, 1 Stat. 302 (repealed 1864)

Fugitive Slave Act of 1850, ch. 60, 9 Stat. 462 (repealed 1864)

Personal Responsibility and Work Opportunity Reconciliation Act of 1996, Pub. L. No. 104–193, 110 Stat. 2105 (1996) (codified at 42 U.S.C. §§601–619 (2006))

Seattle Secure Scheduling Ordinance, SMC 14.22 (effective July 1, 2017)

Social Security Act of 1935, 42 U.S.C. §§401–406
Trafficking Victims Protection Act of 2000, Pub. L. No. 106–386, §102(b)(22), 114, Stat. 1464

CONSTITUTIONAL PROVISIONS

U.S. Const. art. I, §2, cl. 3
U.S. Const. art. I, §9, cl. 1
U.S. Const. art. IV, §2, cl. 3
U.S. Const, art. IV, §4
U.S. Const. amend. XIII
U.S. Const. amend. XIV

COURT CASES

Barron v. Mayor and City Council of Baltimore, 32 U.S. (7 Pet.) 243 (1833)
Brown v. Board of Education, 347 U.S. 483 (1954)
Dandridge v. Williams, 397 U.S. 471 (1970)
Dred Scott v. Sanford, 60 U.S. (19 How.) 393 (1857)
Jones v. Alfred Mayer Co., 392 U.S. 409 (1968)
Parents Involved in Community Schools v. Seattle District No. 1, 551 U.S. 701 (2007)
Pollock v. Williams, 322 U.S. 4 (1944)
Prigg v. Pennsylvania, 41 U.S. 539 (1842)
Robertson v. Baldwin, 165 U.S. 275 (1897)
Slaughter House Cases, 83 U.S. 36 (1873)
United States v. Driscoll, 96 U.S. 421 (1877)
Yick Wo v. Hopkins, 118 U.S. 356 (1886)

Index

racial subordination, 2, 12–13, 77, 152
racism, 4–5, 77, 93, 114, 183
Radical Republicans, 15, 17, 49, 53, 72,
    90–91, 93, 102–104, 130, 133, 141,
    145, 151, 159, 161, 194–195
radicals, 53, 59, 66, 72, 75, 90, 120, 127,
    129–130, 144–146, 156, 159, 167
railroad, 11, 122, 158, 161, 172–175
Randolph, A. Philip, 8, 181
Reagan, Ronald, 183
Reconstruction, xii, 1–3, 6–7, 9–16, 18–19,
    23–24, 28, 32, 40, 44, 53, 67–68, 70,
    78, 80, 82, 84–85, 90, 100–101,
    105–106, 109, 111–113, 115–116,
    119, 122, 128–131, 133, 138,
    140–142, 144–149, 151–153, 155,
    157–158, 160–161, 166–167, 169,
    176, 179–181, 183, 192–194
  territorial theory of Reconstruction, 70,
    89, 95, 98–100, 111–112, 128, 145
Reconstruction Act, 10, 100, 109, 111, 145
Reconstruction Amendments, 12, 18
Reconstruction Congress, xii, 1–2, 9, 15,
    18, 24, 28, 32, 40, 70, 78, 80, 100,
    106, 129–130, 138, 144, 147–149,
    151–152, 155
Reconstruction Era, xii, 3, 6–7, 10–11, 13,
    16, 18–19, 45, 80, 101, 111, 131,
    143–144, 151–152, 176, 180
Redeemers, 160
Republican Party, 1–2, 6, 10, 15, 22–23, 27,
    30, 35–36, 43, 45, 51, 54, 56, 66, 68,
    70, 72, 75, 80, 83–84, 86–87,
    89–91, 95, 101, 103, 109, 125, 139,
    156–158, 165–166, 168, 175, 193
  platform, 23, 41–42, 61, 65, 75, 85, 89,
    167
republicanism, 60, 66, 177
Rhode Island Anti-Slavery Society, 58
right to vote, 8, 13, 25, 84, 111, 113, 126,
    134, 141–142, 144
"right to work" movement, 182
rights of belonging, 4
Rogers, Nathaniel P., 58, 122, 142, 150,
    194
Ryckman, L. W., 59

Saulsbury, Willard, 115, 138
Scofield, Glenni, 125
Seattle Secure Scheduling Ordinance,
    184

Second Confiscation Act, 99
Second Freedman's Bureau Act, 131–132
segregation, 5, 119, 160
serfdom, 8, 50–51, 60, 134, 173
Seward, William, 72, 91, 122, 129–130
Shannon, Thomas, 67, 116
sharecropping, 3
Shellabarger, Samuel, 106
Sherman, John, 128, 138
Sherman, William Tecumseh, 118
slave barons, 18, 77, 96, 174
Slave Power, 72, 83, 114
slaveholding elites, 93
Smith, Gerrit, 23, 37, 41, 75, 141, 167,
    190
Speed, James, 147
Spooner, Lysander, xii, 23, 31, 34–35, 38,
    194
Stanton, Elizabeth Cady, 143
state sovereignty, 89, 98, 124, 139
Stevens, Thaddeus, 26, 65, 88, 91, 98, 101,
    126, 144–145, 155–156
Steward, Ira, 56, 59, 94, 170
Stewart, Alvan, 23, 33, 39, 59, 75, 165
Stewart, William, 165
Stowe, Harriet Beecher, 25
suffrage, 2, 13, 21, 85, 113, 116, 120,
    126–128, 130, 134, 141, 143–144,
    147, 155, 158, 164, 166–167
  black, 128
  universal, 13, 71, 85, 131, 142, 161
  women's, 2, 13, 85, 141, 143
Sumner, Charles, 16, 50, 86, 91, 95,
    100–101, 105, 110, 112, 114,
    118–119, 122, 128–129, 144, 157,
    159, 165, 167–169, 189

Taney, Roger, 40, 42, 105–106, 121
Temporary Assistance for Needy Families,
    186
tenBroek, Jacobus, 135
textualist, 38, 42
Thayer, Martin, 137
Thirteenth Amendment, xi, 1–2, 4, 6–7, 10,
    12, 14–16, 24, 33, 45, 51, 56–57, 69,
    71, 73, 80, 86–87, 90–91, 94, 99,
    102, 104, 107–111, 113–117, 119,
    121–122, 125, 127, 129–130, 132,
    135, 137–140, 143, 147–149, 153,
    169, 176–177, 179, 182–183, 185,
    189, 191, 194–195

CPSIA information can be obtained
at www.ICGtesting.com
Printed in the USA
LVHW091054250619
622286LV00002B/240/P